THE ISLANDS AND THE SEA

THE ISLANDS AND THE SEA

Five Centuries of Nature Writing from the Caribbean

Edited by
JOHN A. MURRAY

New York   Oxford
OXFORD UNIVERSITY PRESS
1991

To Bill Sisler
who made this book possible

Oxford University Press

Oxford   New York   Toronto
Delhi   Bombay   Calcutta   Madras   Karachi
Petaling Jaya   Singapore   Hong Kong   Tokyo
Nairobi   Dar es Salaam   Cape Town
Melbourne   Auckland

and associated companies in
Berlin   Ibadan

Copyright © 1991 by Oxford University Press, Inc.

Published by Oxford University Press, Inc.
200 Madison Avenue, New York, New York 10016

Library of Congress Cataloging-in-Publication Data
The Islands and the sea :
five centuries of nature writing from the Caribbean /
edited by John A. Murray.
p. cm. ISBN 0–19–506677–4
1. Natural history—Caribbean Area. 2. Nature stories.
I. Murray, John A., 1954——.
QH109.A1I83 1991 508.729—dc20 90–22372

The following page is regarded as
an extension of the copyright page.

9 8 7 6 5 4 3 2 1
Printed in the United States of America
on acid-free paper

Preface

Like many people, I first saw the Caribbean from the air. Flying south from Texas en route to Cozumel, we crossed the Gulf of Mexico, where heavy oil tankers steamed north with Venezuelan crude and Galveston shrimpers pulled their finally woven seines through the dull green waters. Gradually the quality of the water began to change—to absorb some of the blueness of the sky—and the mood on board the plane began to lighten. Soon, we passed over the shallows of the Campeche bank and the low flat northern coast of the Yucatan. The interior was a wild country, with few roads and towns, and to the south an unbroken tract of closed canopy forest stretched away toward Belize, a wilderness into which Yellowstone and Yosemite, if put together, would disappear. Here the familiar animals of the temperate latitudes—cougars, white-tailed deer, diamond-backed rattlesnakes, turkeys, opossums—lived side by side with tropical species—jaguars, brocket deer, bushmasters, resplendent quetzals, howler monkeys. These triple-leveled jungles, topped with ten-story tall mahoganies, have functioned as the green lungs of the Earth since before the Pleistocene, absorbing the carbon dioxide and releasing the oxygen on which all life depends. At the time of my visit, these fragile woodlands had yet to experience the massive destruction that would begin in the 1980s. Midway across the peninsula, the captain pointed out the ruins of Chichen-Itza, where the Mayans built a flourishing metropolis while Europe languished in the dark ages. The enormous El Castillo Pyramid, with one step for every day of the year, was conspicuously prominent, and brought to mind the ancient ziggurats of Ur. Not visible was the sacred cenote, a deep limestone sinkhole into which sacrificial victims, weighted down with gold, were thrown to Chac-Mool, the rain god. Like other civilizations, the Mesoamericans turned to desperate measures as they exhausted the resources on which their culture was dependent.

Shortly thereafter, everyone on the wide-bodied jet scrambled for the windows as the Caribbean coast came into view. Directly below, the second longest barrier reef in the world cut sharply through the water just parallel to the shore. Here, warmed by the sun and nourished by the oxygen-rich waters, lived some of the most specialized animals on earth, species as diverse as the red-backed cleaning shrimp, which from its cleaning station on the reef removes parasites from the open mouths of host fish; and the queen parrotfish, which eats coral with its beaklike teeth and is one of the major converters of hard coral into smooth white beach sand. Beyond the outer coral heads, the water deepened into the dark Phoenician purple of the Caribbean Sea. By contrast with the reef, the open sea was a biological desert, with none of the extensive plant life necessary to sustain a large animal population. Unlike the Gulf of Mexico, there was little ship traffic here, and one could easily imagine the light rigs of buccaneer Henry Morgan darting out from the manatee lagoons to intercept the slow convoys of Spanish transports carrying silver pieces of eight back to the Old World. The pilot pointed out Cancun to the north, where the Mexican government was then constructing an international resort to help make the interest payments on its international debt. This enormous resort complex—literally hewn from the wilderness—was later devastated by Hurricane Gilbert in 1988. Beyond Cancun was Isla Mujeres, where Jacques Cousteau discovered the "Cave of the Sleeping Sharks." At the furthest distance, our attention was drawn to Cabo San Antonio on the rocky Cuban coast. Over that hazy eastern horizon were the rest of the Antilles, an aggregate of islands extending in a wide arc all the way to the coast of South America.

Soon Cozumel, a coralline island shaped like a green obsidian arrowhead, appeared ahead. The Mayans once paddled their mahogany sea canoes here to worship Ix Chel, their version of Diana, the Greek moon goddess. The masonry shrine to Ix Chel was desecrated in 1517 by Cortés, who erected a wooden cross in its place and admonished the inhabitants to convert. As we turned and descended on final approach, the whole island, surrounded by the Palancar reef, came clearly into view: mosquito-filled mangrove swamps, former sea turtle nesting beaches, and cultivated groves of coconut palms. The inland forest—composed of short, thin-trunked acacias and wild palms with a thick brush understory—was florally less diverse than forests on the mainland. Similarly, Cozumel had fewer, less-specialized animal species with broader niches than the mainland, a result of the fact that animals have few opportunities to colonize islands. A green iguana on Cozumel, for example, might occupy a niche that on the Yucatan peninsula would be shared by several small mammals, ground birds, and other reptiles. Because they have so few species, islands are more vulnerable to disruption from alien predators (dogs, cats, mongooses) and habitat loss (tourist development). When the cabin doors were finally cracked open a strange wonderful air filled our lungs, humid and hot, but redolent with the welcome fresh scent of the sea and the sweet fragrance of blossoming flowers. As we walked across the concrete runway to the terminal, a flock of roseatte flamingoes fluttered overhead, as they have since before our species crossed the Bering Land Bridge, as they will when the mundane artifacts of our resort culture are displayed in museums beside the rusting Spanish muskets and the jade Mayan death masks.

For the purposes of this collection, the Caribbean will be considered to be those islands and mainland littorals where the major Western Atlantic coral species are found, as well as those adjoining regions having significant intercourse with the Caribbean proper. Such a definition includes not only the islands of the Greater and Lesser Antilles—traditionally the heart of the Caribbean—but also Bermuda (north latitude 32°), Florida south of the St. John's River, the Central American coast from Isla Mujeres to Panama, and the northern coast of South America from Columbia to the Guyana coast, including the drainage of the Orinoco River. Only one selection—the Barry Lopez account of the burning of the Aztec aviary in the Mexican highlands— takes place outside this region, and is presented here because the essay speaks eloquently to the prevailing theme of the sixteenth century, and because both Cortés in Mexico, and Pizarro in the Andes, launched their invasions from islands in the Caribbean.

   The Islands and the Sea offers readers the first comprehensive anthology of nature writing in the Caribbean from 1492 to the present. Many of these selections—particularly those written prior to 1918—have never been made widely available to a general audience. Most of the genres common to nonfiction nature writing are found in this collection: the official expedition narrative, the individual adventure narrative, the essay, the scientific mono-graph, the personal journal and memoir, and the extended letter. The genres of poetry and of fiction, which include some of the finest writing about nature in Caribbean literature, are also represented here. Lovers of nature will I hope find much in *The Islands and the Sea* to edify and delight them; the legendary beauty and natural history of the West Indies and their environs have inspired some of the most distinctive nature writing in the Americas. Every effort has been made—in offering a larger number of shorter selections—to feature the works of both well-known and lesser known authors, and to include alterna-tive views of nature from women and from authors not of European descent.

   As more and more wild regions of the Earth become *de facto* islands, encircled by an ever-rising flood of humanity, an increasing amount of attention has been directed toward the history, both natural and human, of the oceanic islands and archipelagoes. Indeed, the future of wilderness—whether in Barbados, Botswana, or Belgium—is very much a scenario of isolated tracts no longer in communication with the larger continuums that once genetically sustained them. The Caribbean, in this context, provides a timely focus, for the region offers a well-documented history of human occupation as well as some of the most fascinating plants and animals in nature. It is, finally, fitting and appropriate, as we pass the 500th anniversary of Columbus' discovery of the New World, that we reacquaint ourselves with the events that have transpired in the Caribbean, and reflect upon the larger issues of nature and culture raised by the historical and literary record. With the help of these diverse writers, let us now roam through space and time across the length and breadth of the Caribbean, from the far-famed coral reefs of Virgin Islands National Park on St. John to the cool green woods atop Mont Pelée on Martinique.

Fairbanks   J. A. M.
November 1990

Acknowledgments

I would like to thank the following individuals and organizations for their generous assistance in the preparation of this book: Cesar Rodriguez, Curator, Latin American Collection, Yale University; Allan B. Goodrich, Supervisory Archivist, Ernest Hemingway Collection, John Fitzgerald Kennedy Library; Ruth Norris, Director, Nongovernmental Services, The Nature Conservancy; Victoria Lukach, United States Virgin Islands Division of Tourism; Chuck Weikert, Chief of Interpretation, Virgin Islands National Park; Biscayne National Park; Everglades National Park; Caribbean Conservation Association; Island Resources Foundation; Ron Dathorne, Professor of English, University of Kentucky, Lexington and Executive Director, Association for Caribbean Studies. I must particularly express my gratitude to the Inter-Library Loan Department of Rasmusson Library at the University of Alaska, Fairbanks, for promptly securing many rare works of literature and history from distant collections around the country. I would like to thank the English Department at the University of Alaska, Fairbanks for continued good cheer, as well as the Dean of the College of Liberal Arts, Anne D. Shinkwin, and the Chancellor, Patrick J. O'Rourke. I'm grateful to the many authors and publishers who have been wonderfully helpful; no anthology can be successfully undertaken without such eager assistance, and I thank them all for their enthusiasm and cooperation. I would like to thank my wife and son for their constant love and support, and my parents for innumerable acts of kindness and words of encouragement.

Contents

Guide to the Maps

1. Christopher Columbus
2. Hernando Cortés
3. Gonzalo de Oviedo
4. Ferdinando de Soto
5. Bartholomew de las Casas
6. Pietro Martire D'Anghiera
7. René Laudonniere
8. John Hawkins
9. Joseph Acosta
10. Walter Raleigh
11. George, the Earl of Cumberland
12. William Strachey
13. The Bermuda Assembly
14. Richard Norwood
15. William Dampier
16. Lionel Wafer
17. Hans Sloane
18. Daniel Defoe
19. Mark Catesby
20. Griffith Hughes
21. Janet Schaw
22. William Bartram
23. Alexander von Humboldt
24. George Pinkard
25. Joseph Sturge and Thomas Harvey
26. Charles Darwin
27. John L. Stephens
28. Harriet Beecher Stowe
29. John Murray
30. Lafcadio Hearn
31. George Kennan
32. Frederick Upham Adams
33. Elsie Clews Parsons
34. William Beebe
35. Ernest Hemingway
36. Marjory Stoneman Douglas
37. Rachel Carson
38. V. S. Naipaul
39. Paul Brooks
40. Archie Carr
41. Derek Walcott
42. Edward O. Wilson
43. Roger Caras
44. Barry Lopez
45. Daryl C. Dance
46. Jamaica Kincaid
47. David Rains Wallace
48. John A. Murray

**These Maps have numbers on them corresponding to the authors repre-
sented in the anthology, so that the reader can geographically locate each
selection.**

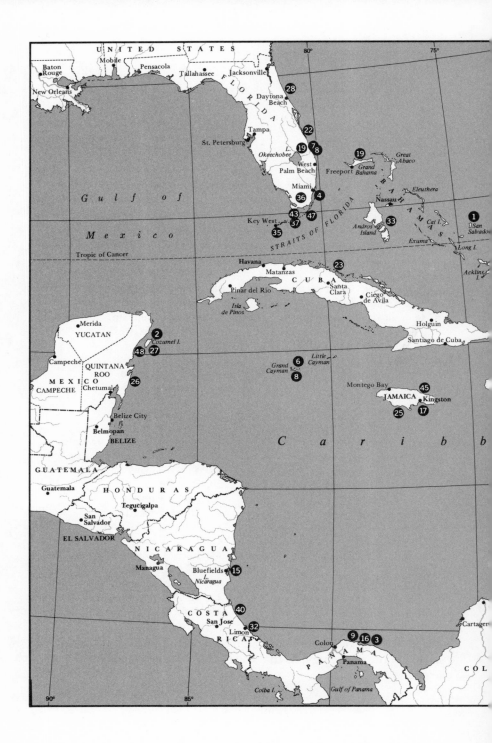

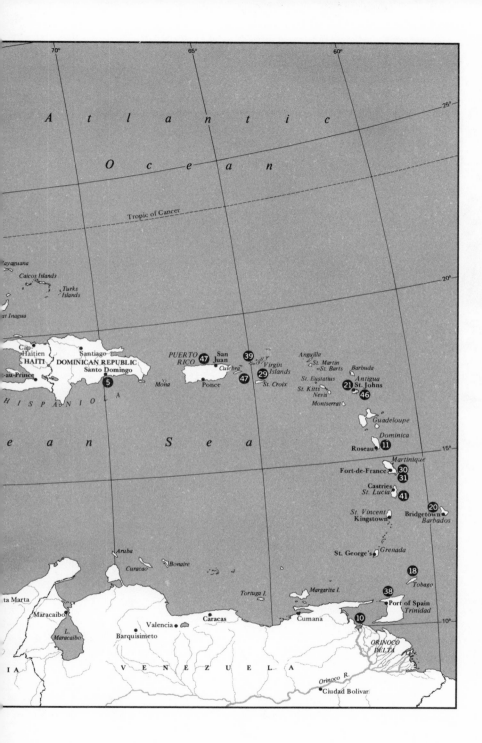

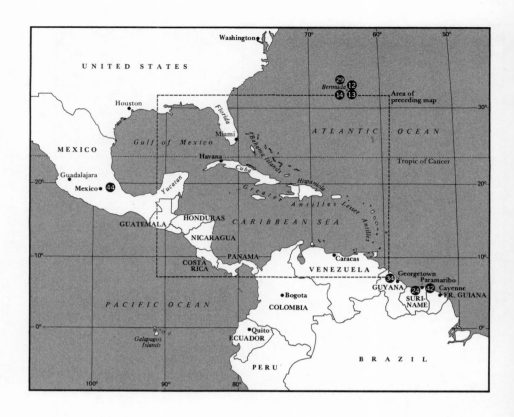

THE ISLANDS AND THE SEA

Two hours after midnight land appeared, at a distance of about two leagues from them. They took in all sail, remaining with the mainsail . . . waiting for day, a Friday, on which they reached a small island of the Lucayos [San Salvador or Watling's Island in the Bahamas at latitude 24° North and longitude 74° 30° West], which is called in the language of the Indians "Guanahani." Immediately they saw naked people, and the admiral went ashore in the armed boat. . . . When they had landed, they saw very green trees and much water and fruit of various kinds. The admiral . . . took possession of the island . . . for the King and Queen. . . . Afterwards, [the people] swam to the boats, and brought us parrots and cotton thread in balls, and spears and many other things, and we exchanged for them other things. . . . In fact, they took all and gave all, such as they had, with good will. . . . They should be good servants and of quick intelligence . . . and I believe that they would easily be made Christians.

Christopher Columbus
Friday, October 12, 1492

Introduction

Since the Discovery nature has figured centrally in the writings of those who have visited or lived in the Caribbean. These tropical islands and littorals, with their coral reefs, coconut palms, and climax rain forests, have inspired the human imagination to produce everything from comprehensive expedition narratives to Nobel-prize-winning novels.[1] The Caribbean merits such praise. Here are animals as varied as the frigate bird, that soars above Barbuda on wings eight feet wide, the green turtle, that somehow returns across thousands of miles of open sea to nest on its Costa Rican natal beach, and the Florida panther, which may soon join the 87 other vertebrate species that have been exterminated in the region within historic time.[2] Other animals are less familiar: the rare Caribbean monk seal, the once-ubiquitous agouti, and the little known Haitian Solenodon (a shrew-like insectivore). The trees of the Caribbean are among the most beautiful on Earth. Columbus was the first European to take note of them: "[There are] trees of a thousand kinds and tall, and they seem to touch the sky. And I am told that they never lose their foliage. . . . There are six or eight kinds of palm, which are a wonder to behold on account of their beautiful variety . . . [and] there are marvelous pine groves."[3] Even the common names of the trees are lovely: the spreading ceiba, the royal palm, the *lignum vitae,* the Spanish cedar, and the Caribbean pine. From the standpoint of geography, cartographers have long noted the many distinctive features of the region on their maps: the world's most northerly coral reef in Bermuda; the prodigious Gulf Stream, first studied by Benjamin Franklin,[4] that warms Great Britain with waters born in the Bahamas; the longest barrier reef in the hemisphere (Yucatan-Belize); one of the deepest submarine trenches known to science (29,500′); and several of the finest natural harbors ever formed in Havana, Cuba; Kingston, Jamaica; and San Juan, Puerto Rico.

The Caribbean is also—despite popular myths of gentle trade winds, rhythmic Reggae songs, and sun-washed beaches—the frequent scene of some of nature's most impressive displays of destructive power. On May 8, 1902, Mont Pelée erupted with the force of an atomic bomb; of the 30,000 inhabitants of St. Pierre, only one person—an African-American prisoner in the city jail—survived the superheated shock wave and the subsequent barrage of lava and pumice. George Kennan, a member of the U. S. relief expedition, wrote that the man, Auguste Ciparis, was "more frightfully burned . . . than any man I had ever seen."[5] Kennan's description of the obliterated city of St. Pierre, formerly known as the "Paris of the Antilles," is reminiscent of John Hersey's later account of Hiroshima:

> The first impression that it [St. Pierre] made upon me . . . was one of loneliness, stillness, grayness, and almost unimaginable desolation. There was . . . no sign whatever of recent life. . . . It was almost impossible to realize, or even to believe, that, within a month, this had been a bright, gay, beautiful city of thirty thousand inhabitants.[6]

Hurricanes—severe tropical cyclones unique to the West Indies—strike regularly every year in the late summer and early fall. On September 2, 1935, a 17-foot tidal surge generated by the Matecumbe hurricane drowned hundreds of people in the Florida Keys. Ernest Hemingway, a resident of Key West, traveled to the scene and reported that:

> . . . nothing could give [you] an idea of the destruction. Between 700 and 1000 dead. . . . The foliage absolutely stripped as though by a fire for thirty miles and the land looking like the abandoned bed of a river. Not a building of any sort standing. . . . Saw more dead than I'd seen in one place since the lower Piave [World War I] in June of 1918.[7]

Elsewhere, events ranging in magnitude from earthquakes—a 1907 earthquake leveled parts of Kingston, Jamaica—to shark attacks—the 1750 selection by Griffith Hughes relates a particularly gruesome incident—have periodically served to remind a forgetful humanity of the ultimate authority of nature.

Above all, writers have been impressed with the natural beauty of the Caribbean—the lowland rain forests of William Dampier's Mosquito Coast, the wild subtropical hammocks of Marjory Douglas' Everglades, the green-mantled Pitons of Derek Walcott's St. Lucia, the rugged Cockpit Country of Edward Brathwaite's Jamaica, and the luminous beaches and coral lagoons of Jamaica Kincaid's Antigua. Joseph Acosta, a sixteenth-century Jesuit priest, described the New World as a kind of Renaissance Utopia. "Men should find in these Lands," Acosta wrote in 1588, "that which other Poets sing of the Elisean fields [the 'land of the blessed' in Greek Mythology] . . . or that which Plato reports or feignes of his Atlantike Iland [the myth of Atlantis]."[8] Sir Walter Raleigh, riding the salt tide up the Orinoco River a few years later, stated that "On both sides of this river, we passed the most beautiful countrey that ever mine eyes behld."[9] A century later, American colonialist William Bartram was struck by the magnificence of south Florida: "What a beautiful retreat is here! blessed unviolated spot of the earth, rising from the limpid waters of the lake [with] fragrant groves and blooming lawns. . . . A fascinating atmosphere surrounds this blissful garden."[10] Writing in 1902, Lafcadio Hearn, a peripatetic Paul Theroux of his day, called the West Indies "an enormous silent poem of color and light"[11] and suggested that while "in the great centres of civilization we admire and study only the results of mind, here [in the Lesser Antilles] one views only the works of nature . . . as in the legendary frostless morning of creation."[12] Even V. S. Naipaul, the contemporary novelist who has often been critical of the Caribbean in his writing, has praised the natural beauty of his native Trinidad:

> It seemed to me [on Trinidad] that I was seeing the landscape for the first time. . . . I was taken by the common coconut tree, the cliche of the Caribbean. I discovered, what every child in Trinidad knows, that . . . the branches are like the spokes of a perfectly circular wheel. . . . I saw that even sugar cane can be beautiful . . . [and that] the cocoa woods were . . . like the woods of fairy tales, dark and shadowed and cool.[13]

Culturally, the Caribbean is one of the most complex regions on Earth, and the state of human culture here, as everywhere, is inextricably intertwined with the fate of wild nature. One need only look at two of the several dozen major islands to appreciate the unique heterogeneity of these diverse societies. On Martinique, for example, the original inhabitants were Arawaks, who, shortly after the first European contact, were replaced by Caribs.[14] There followed large influxes from France, Africa, India, as well as immigrants from French colonies in North Africa and Asia. Curacao, on the other hand, which was also first inhabited by the Arawaks, was then settled by the Spanish, who were replaced by the Dutch, with brief incursions by the British and French.[15] Curacao was also a major center for the slave trade prior to emancipation. A large number of Jewish settlers arrived in the eighteenth century from Europe—particularly Portugal—and in 1732 established the first synagogue in the Western Hemisphere in Willemstad. On both Martinique and Curacao, a century of international tourism has further diversified the populations, as travelers have become residents. These two islands illustrate the difficulty of generalizing about the human condition in the Caribbean, but, nevertheless, a few broad statements that apply more or less universally to human culture and its relationship to nature in this region can be made. First, the Amerindians of the Caribbean are now essentially a vanished people—even the 3750-acre Carib Indian Reservation on Dominica has very few true Caribs among its inhabitants—while the Amerindians of the mainland coasts—such as the Maya of the Yucatan, the Cuna of Panama, and the Arawak of Surinam—in some cases still endure. All that essentially remains of the original inhabitants of the Caribbean islands are a few place names (Cuba, Haiti), a scattering of rock drawings, and a handful of sonorous, albeit Anglicized words (hurricane, barbecue, cannibal, hammock, canoe). Second, the pernicious effects of the slave-based plantation system continue to be seen in many Caribbean societies today, as evidenced by high infant mortality rates, high birth rates, high

population densities, low literacy rates, and low per capita incomes. Many of
these people have no property and little if any political power, and are trapped
in the most serious form of poverty. Economic injustice and environmental
injustice, in these cases, go hand in hand. Third, the intense monoculture
agriculture of the colonial and post-colonial periods (sugar cane, bananas,
cotton, pineapple, tobacco) has in some cases had a devastating effect on the
tropical environment. Although tropical nature is relatively resilient, soils can
be quickly exhausted and erosion—because of the heavy rainfall—can proceed
with surprising alacrity. Agricultural practices in the West Indies have often
led to deforestation, erosive destruction of watersheds, siltation of coral reefs,
elimination of indigenous species, and the introduction of alien species. There
can be no real solution for the environmental problems in the region—which
many of the twentieth-century nature writers in this anthology address—
without a comprehensive look at social and economic changes, as well.

Prevailing viewpoints with respect to nature have changed significantly
over the past 500 years, and the readings gathered here chart the journey of the
collective Caribbean mind from the twilight of the European feudal age to the
dawn of the third millenium. In that period, the homocentrism of the Age of
Conquest—grounded in a literal reading of the Old Testament—has been
largely replaced by the biocentric outlook of the current Age of Conscience,
which is based on the discoveries of science vis-à-vis the ultimate unity of life
and which is, ironically, similar in many respects to the *weltanschauung* of the
original Amerindians. The conquistadores, in their clinking suits of armor and
pointed steel helmets, conquered a supernatural Caribbean inhabited by
devils, angels, mermaids, leviathans, and Mandevillean monsters. El Dorado
was on the Orinoco River north of the "Land of the Amazons," and the
Fountain of Youth was located somewhere in the unicorn-infested swamps of
south Florida. These ambitious captains reflexively appropriated New World
lands and killed and enslaved non-Christians in the belief that the decrees of
dominion over nature in Genesis 1:28 provided a legitimate moral authority
for such actions:

> And God blessed them, and God said unto them, Be fruitful and multiply,
> and replenish the earth, and subdue it: and have dominion over the fish of the
> sea, and over the fowl of the air, and over every living thing that moveth upon
> the earth.

To them nature writing—if they knew it at all—was a species of prose writing
related to medieval herbals and bestiaries, a genre once practiced in antiquity
by Aristotle and Pliny the Elder, and now the idle stuff of eccentric wandering
Jesuit priests and leech-carrying apothecaries. Science, as we know it, had not
been born—or, more properly, reborn—yet, and the long shadows of the
Feudal Age still darkened the corridors of rational inquiry.

By contrast, nature writing at the current time is a major literary form
widely taught in colleges and universities and practiced by some of the most
distinguished authors of the age, as evidenced here with selections written by

authors of the stature of Rachel Carson, Archie Carr, Roger Caras, Barry Lopez, and David Rains Wallace. Modern science, revivified by the same spirit of Renaissance skepticism that launched Columbus on his first voyage, has begun to provide a firm empirical basis for the belief that all life is interdependent and that every life form has value. Nature writers play an intrinsic role in disseminating these historic findings to the masses, by translating the specialized discourse of scientists into a form palatable to the general reading public. Three authors from each of the three sections of this book—Joseph Acosta, Griffith Hughes, and Edward O. Wilson—illustrate the degree to which the relationship between human culture and nature has changed since the Discovery, as well as the extent to which the natural history essay as a literary form has evolved during the same period.

Joseph Acosta's 1590 *Historia Natural y Moral de las Indies* is most significant in this context for what it so brilliantly anticipates, namely the radical shift from the supernatural point of view that shaped thinking in the Middle Ages to the scientific perspective that defines the world view of the modern era. Although Acosta's world view—he was a Jesuit priest who traveled in the Caribbean for 15 years—was strongly grounded in Christianity, he also possessed an independent spirit and a questioning mind. In his book, Acosta frankly wrestled with one of the most puzzling mysteries of the age: Given the fact, according to the Old Testament, that every animal on Earth had been represented on Noah's ark, how could the animals of the New World (armadillos, nutria, ocelots) be so strikingly different from the animals of the Old World? "It were a matter," Acosta wrote, "difficult, to shew, and prove, what beginning many and sundrie sorts of beasts had, which are found at the [West] Indies, of whose kindes we have non in this Continent [Europe]."[16] Although much of Acosta's writing was influenced by the Christian Middle Ages—his quotations from Virgil and the Bible in the midst of a serious scientific treatise and his similar interpolation of personal anecdotes and hearsay—we nevertheless see in his questioning of the authority of the Bible, and in his quest to rationally organize and analyze, the birth of the modern mind and of the contemporary naturalist. Acosta boldly cracked open the door to free and open discussion on issues of natural history, and in so doing became part of the increasingly larger effort to replace superstition and mythology with a secular order based on empirical fact and scientific method.

By the time of Gilbert Hughes' *The Natural History of Barbados* (London, 1750), the scientific essay had been formalized by Robert Boyle and a transnational culture of science had begun to flourish as a result of the formation of the Royal Society in England, chartered by Charles II in 1662, as well as similar bodies in France and Russia. Gilbert Hughes, a Fellow of the Royal Society and Rector of St. Lucy's Parish on Barbados, attempted in *The Natural History of Barbados* not only to provide a rigorous account of the fauna and flora of Barbados, but also to express his observations in a genuine literary style. Had Hughes organized his book differently—it is structured somewhat like a herbal or bestiary—it would probably be *The Natural History of Barbados* and not Gilbert White's *The Natural History and Antiquities of*

Selborne (London, 1789) that would be referred to as the first nature book in English. Hughes' book was widely read and discussed in England—its subscriber's included Samuel Johnson and other luminaries—and probably influenced White and others writing about nature. The Preface to *The Natural History of Barbados* is an extraordinary piece of writing for the mid-eighteenth century, and is one of the earliest attempts—after John Evelyn's *Silva: or, a Discourse of Forest-Trees* (1664)—to deal significantly with the historic relationship between nature and culture. Hughes even offers some advice about nature writing:

> . . . [Just] as, in traveling over [the country], we must climb high rocky Hills, and pass through dreary Desarts, as well as open Lawns, and flowry Meads; so the Reader must not always expect to be entertained with beautiful Images, and a Loftiness of Style. In Variety of Subjects, this must alter with the Nature of the Things to be described.[17]

Above all, Hughes sets the tone for future nature writers by emphasizing the need for complete fidelity to the truth: "This I can with Truth say, that I have not represented one single Fact, which I did not either see myself, or had from Persons of known Veracity."[18] His meticulous observation of and experimentation with a sea anemone—Hughes called it the "animal-flower"[19]—also anticipates the importance of firsthand field study for future writers of the natural history essay, many of whom, if not professional scientists, have been self-educated to the extent of being reliable sources of factual information. Such has been the case in American literature, for example, with nature writers like Henry David Thoreau, who compiled an important study on the dispersal of forest seeds, and John Muir, who established himself as an expert on glaciers.

Edward O. Wilson, a professor of science at Harvard University and the winner of the Pulitzer prize in general nonfiction, is one of the most influential natural history writers of our time. Not only does his writing have a firm basis in fact—an unassailable standard of truth that was only nascent in the writings of Acosta and Hughes—but it also possesses a literary quality that earlier works lacked. Wilson, of course, has an advantage in that he is writing in a literary form that now has several centuries of tradition behind it, and that has become established and institutionalized as a genre. Acosta wrote before Montaigne invented the essay, and Hughes wrote before Darwin discovered the mechanism of natural selection and evolution and Watson elucidated the genetic code. Wilson's writing is most important here, though, and is most characteristic of nature writing in our time, for its strong political content. Neither Acosta or Hughes displayed any interest in the moral implications of scientific knowledge; in the twentieth century, on the other hand, the findings of science have often influenced literature and public policy. Only in the writings of de las Casas can a precursor be found for Wilson's direct attack, in his collection of nature essays entitled *Biophilia* (Cambridge: Harvard University Press, 1984), on the government of the Caribbean country in which he conducted his biological research:

In 1980 all this bright picture was darkened by the advent of Barbarism. The democratically elected government of Henk Arron was overthrown by Revolutionary Leader Desi Bouterse, a military physical-education instructor with scant education . . . [who] began to court Fidel Castro and the Soviet Union . . . [and who] without warning, ordered the arrest and execution of fifteen of the country's leading citizens, including lawyers, journalists, and union leaders . . . As I write, it is a Surinam of silence and fear.[20]

Wilson's writing is also typically modern in the sympathy it expresses for animals as brethren on the planet instead of being lesser creatures in the order of creation, as they were to the Jesuit priest Joseph Acosta, or soulless machines in the clockworks of the cosmos, as they were to a Deist like Griffith Hughes. Wilson writes that he "felt uneasy—perhaps the word is embarrassed—in the presence of a captive [peccary]" and that the peccary was "a powerful presence . . . now a mute speaker trapped inside the unnatural clearing, like a messenger to me from an unexplored world."[21]

Although a taxonomy of selections based strictly on theme would be reductive, there are several recurring themes in Caribbean nature literature that may be helpful in considering these works: the quest for discovery, the quest for conquest, and the quest for liberation. For travelers past and present, the Caribbean has meant the recovery of innocence, the child-like wonder of finding new lands, new people, new plants, new animals, and, less benignly, new wealth. Discovery pervades the earliest writings of the Age of Conquest, from Columbus' description of the Bahamas on his first voyage to George, the Earl of Cumberland's account of Dominica. In a sense, Ferdinando de Soto's Fountain of Youth was very real, for the miracles of nature in the New World restored the boy or girl in everyone who encountered them, and made the world seem fresh and bright and new again. This spirit of Discovery endures in modern times; arriving at the Mayan ruins of Tulum in 1842, pioneer archaeologist John "Indiana Jones" Stephens could hardly conceal his excitement:

> We had undertaken our long journey to this place in utter uncertainty . . . but already we felt indemnified for all our journey. We were amid the wildest scenery we had yet found in Yucatan; and, besides the deep and exciting interest of the ruins themselves, we had around us what we wanted at all the other places, the magnificence of nature. Clearing away the platform in front, we looked over an immense forest; walking around the moulding of the wall, we looked out upon the boundless [Caribbean] ocean, and deep in the clear water at the foot of the cliff we saw gliding quietly by a great fish 8 or 10 feet long.[22]

Stephens, like so many before and since, discovered what the French philosopher Rousseau would say is lost in civilization—the essential union with all that is good and pure in wild nature.

Conversely, that part of us that Rousseau saw as derived from our social relationships—the need to control people and land—provides the basis for another distinctive theme in Caribbean nature writing: the quest for conquest.

Although this theme remains evident in current culture and literature, it is *most* prevalent in the writings from the "Age of Conquest." Columbus, it will be recalled, was motivated not by selfless altruism but by the worldly desire for fame and gold in his voyages; he regularly captured and enslaved Amerindians and seized lands for the Spanish crown that had long been inhabited by other human beings. The exploits of Cortés are well known—every schoolchild reads William H. Prescott's famous *The Conquest of Mexico* (New York, 1843)—and Cortés's acquisitive approach to the New World is evident here in the account of his landing on the island of Cozumel, which is located off the Yucatan Peninsula. Although Cortés is represented by Diaz as having expressed dismay at the looting of the Mayan village, he later tears apart a Mayan religious shrine and orders his carpenters to install a wooden cross. The persistence of this theme of conquest in later periods is perhaps best evident in Frederick Upham Adams' notorious *The Conquest of the Tropics, the Story of the Creative Enterprises Conducted by the United Fruit Company* (New York: Doubleday, Page and Company, 1914), which describes the destruction of vast regions of pristine tropical nature in order to facilitate the monoculture cultivation of bananas for consumption in North America. Adams writes cheerfully of "The Conquest of the Tropics":

> Everywhere the observor sees the manifestations of a carefully designed machine calculated to yield the greatest possible result from a given application of endeavor. Here is an industrial army engaged in a constant battle with the forces of tropical nature. There is no telling when nature may strike an unexpected blow. . . . Sixty thousand trained men are working in the American tropics under the command of the skilled generals of the United Fruit Company . . . to me this mastery of time and space and flood and sea has all the spell of the romantic, and the subject should command the genius and melody of a poet rather than the halting comments of a worker in prose.[23]

For Adams, and for the colonialism his writing extols and embodies, tropical nature—meaning both the plants and the animals *and* the human beings who had been born and lived there—was an adversary of western civilization that needed to be mastered at whatever cost.

The theme of liberation involves not only the uplifting experience of deliverance that attends any close contact with wild nature, but also the quest for political freedom that is evident—albeit in submerged form—in the writings of those who were enslaved or otherwise disenfranchised. In Daniel Defoe's *Robinson Crusoe* (London, 1719), a man is separated from the Old World culture in which he had been raised and forced, as a castaway, to come to terms with nature as it is found on a wild Caribbean island. The result is, surprisingly for readers of the early eighteenth century, not an impoverishment of the spirit and of life, but rather an enrichment and revivification of both. Crusoe discovers what European civilization, old and worn out and in need of rejuvenation, had forgotten—that nature represented not the curse of humankind but rather its salvation. An alternative variation to this theme of liberation is sometimes apparent in Caribbean folklore, where the subversive theme of political liberation can be found in seemingly innocent stories derived from the natural world. This is evident, for example, in Anne Wolfe's 1918 story "The Escape," which, on one level, relates the escape of a sea turtle from captivity, and, on another, expresses the longing of those once enslaved to flee from the poverty that oppresses them on Andros Island in the Bahamas.

Some of the selections make for fairly depressing reading, but any consideration of the Caribbean that aspires to be truthful must be honest about the past, if only to insure that these events—and their lessons—are never forgotten. Bartholomew de las Casas comes to mind first, as he chronicles the atrocities committed in the Caribbean during the Conquest. We read here of "great slaughters and spoyles of people,"[24] of entire islands being enslaved to work in the gold mines, and of torture, murder, and rape conducted on the scale of a New World Holocaust. Scholars are in general agreement as to the veracity of las Casas' reporting. The conquerors, for example,

> . . . laid wagers with such as with one thrust of a sword would paunch or bowell a man in the middest. . . . They took the little soules by the heeles, ramping them from the mothers dugges, and crushed their heads against the cliffs. Others they cast into the Rivers laughing and mocking. . . . They taughte their Hounds, fierce dogs, to tear [the Amerindians] in peeces.[25]

Both the French explorer René Laudonniere and Sir Walter Raleigh noted in their chronicles how terrified the Caribs and Arawaks were of the conquistadores, and how relieved they were to learn their visitors were French or British. Laudonniere wrote of one encounter off Dominica:

> But the poore fellow became so astonied in beholding us, that he knew not which way to behave himselfe, because . . . he feared that he was fallen into the Spaniards hands, of whom he had bene taken once before, and which, as he shewed us, had cut of his stones [testicles].[26]

Sadly, the French and British, as well as the Dutch, would soon perpetrate their own truculence in the name of colonialism.

With respect to slavery, George Pinkard, a physician to a British expedition in the early nineteenth century, graphically described the inhumanity of the Dutch slave market and later wrote of the murder of a slave:

> . . . tying down first the man, he [the owner of the plantation] made the drivers flog the man with many hundred lashes, until, on releasing him from the ground, it was discovered that he was nearly exhausted: and in this state the inhuman monster struck him on the head, with the butt end of a large whip, and felled him again to the earth; when the poor negro, escaping at once from his slavery and his sufferings, expired at the murder.[27]

The wife was then tied down and similarly beaten. Pinkard—who supervised the woman's recovery—later noted that the funeral of her husband was attended "with all the mirthful ceremonies of African burial" for "[the slaves] all seemed to rejoice more in his escape from pain and misery, than they sorrowed for his loss."[28] Sir Hans Sloane observed in an earlier (1725) account that the African-Americans actually looked forward to death, believing that only then would they finally return home to Africa. Pinkard concluded: "[Slavery] is a violation of nature, in which humanity is outraged, and our species degraded!"[29]

Alexander von Humboldt, a kind of Carl Sagan of the Romantic Age, wrote of a group of sailors on his expedition who wantonly shot and dismembered nesting sea birds at Cay Bonito Cuba:

> Though we expostulated with them against this cruelty and useless torment-ing, they would not desist; these men, accustomed to long obediance in the solitude of the sea, take a singular pleasure in exercising a cruel *dominion* [emphasis added] over the animal creation. The ground was covered with wounded birds, struggling with dead, so that this retired spot, which before our arrival was the abode of peace, seemed now to exclaim, man has entered here.[30]

Similarly, Harriet Beecher Stowe, while on a pleasure cruise in south Florida, observed a group of men who were shooting animals just to watch them die:

> A parcel of hulking fellows sit on the deck of a boat, and pass through the sweetest paradise God ever made, without one idea of its loveliness. . . . All the way along is a constant fusillade upon every living thing that shows itself on the bank. Now a bird is hit, and hangs, head downward, with a broken wing; and a coarse laugh choruses the need . . . we once saw a harmless young alligator, whose dying struggles, as he threw out his poor little black paws piteously like human hands, seemed to be vastly diverting to these cultivated individuals. . . . Killing for killing's sake belongs not even to the tiger. The tiger kills for food; man, for amusement.[31]

In these lines of outrage are seen the roots of the modern animal rights movement, which, in recent years, has successfully lobbied for legislation protecting animals as diverse as the Mexican green turtle and the Caribbean manatee.

There is also humor in these pages. The humor comes in two forms—the unintentional and the intentional. Most of the passages in the former category are there because human knowledge about the natural world has increased to the extent that the apocryphal anecdotes and superstitious legends of earlier times now seem ridiculous and sometimes comical by comparison with what we currently know. Take, for example, Gonzalo de Oveido's firsthand account of a "great Water-monster, which at times lifted it selfe right up above the Water so farre that the head and both the armes might bee seene, which seemed higher then our Caravell and all her Masts."[32] This "stupendious Sea Mon-ster" had arms "five and twentie foot long" and a head "fourteene or fifteene foote high and much more in breadth; and the rest of the body larger."[33] The native residents of Hispaniola Oveido compared to the ancient "Philosophers of the Pythagoras Sect," who with their "divellish practises" and "secret Magicall Operations and Superstitions" have "familiaritie with Spirits, which they [allure] into their own bodies."[34] Elsewhere, Oviedo told of "Dragons" that inhabit "the Marishes and desarts of the firme Land" and of frogs so large their bones "appear to be the bones of Cats, or of some other beasts of the same bignesse."[35] Speaking of frogs, Joseph Acosta described rains that were full of frogs and fleas,[36] and, not to be outdone by the Spanish, Captain John Hawkins describes the unicorns of Florida ("Of those unicornes they have many") and serpents with three heads and four legs.[37] Captain René Laudonniere soberly reported that an old chief in south Florida was 250 years old.[38] In a similar hyperbolic vein, Sir Walter Raleigh wrote not only of Eldorado, where men covered themselves in gold dust, and the Land of the Amazons, where there were no men, but also described the country of the "Ewaipanoma," a people—anticipating and perhaps inspiring the later imaginary voyages of Jonathan Swift—who "have their eyes in their shoulders and their mouths in the middle of the breast."[39]

The intentional humor—that of men laughing at themselves and others and of playing practical jokes on one another—came later, after the dreadfully serious business of sailing to the New World had become safer and more predictable. We have, first of all, Lionel Wafer, a surgeon for a band of English buccanneer, who playfully described the monkeys of Darien:

> They are a very waggish kind of Monkey, and plaid a thousand antick Tricks as we march'd at any time through the Woods, skipping from Bough to Bough, with the young ones hanging at the old ones Back, making Faces at us, chattering, and if they had opportunity, pissing down purposely on our Heads.[40]

George Pinkard, in an hilarious story worthy of a Charlie Chaplin or a Monty Python sketch, related a joke played upon two sailors by a cook who told them to "fetch an [electric] eel, which was laying the tub in the yard, and give it [to him] to dress for dinner."[41] This eel shocked the first sailor severely: "Damme, Jack what a thump he fetched me with his tail."[42] His messmate "laughing at 'such a foolish notion'" tried to pick up the eel with the same results; they both finally left shaking their numb arms and swearing that "it was the devil in the tub in the shape of an eel."[43] In modern times, researcher Bernard Nietschmann describes the drudgery of chasing pigs from a Mosquito village outhouse with a club during the rainy season, and of trying to devise a "pig-proof privy" for himself, his wife, and son during their year-long stay.[44] On any frontier, laughter has made the hardship, travail, and loneliness easier to bear. The ability to laugh at oneself also reflects a balanced perspective that was lacking during the solemn, bloody Conquest.

With regards to alternative views of nature, it is important to remember that for at least 8000 years before the Discovery the Caribbean was inhabited by a variety of Amerindian people who successfully exploited the mainland and marine resources of the region. These diverse, locally specialized cultures produced a rich oral literature of songs, prayers, imaginative stories, speeches, and historical chronicles; in the case of the Maya there was also a written literature. Oral literatures are by definition more perishable than written ones, and unfortunately much of the cultural and oral traditions of the island Carib and Arawak, other than what was preserved by proto-ethnographers like de las Casas and Father Labat, has been tragically lost. The case of the Panamanian Cuna is a notable exception, for their culture has been well documented by explorers through historic time, as well as intensively studied in the twentieth century by European and American anthropologists. The Cuna, who were described as early as 1515, are of particular interest in the history of western civilization because their unique political system possibly influenced Jean-Jacques Rousseau's revolutionary essay *Discourse on the Origins and Foundations of Inequality Among Men* (Geneva, 1754) and because the Cuna have survived relatively intact—especially the Darien Cuna—into modern times. Both the San Blas (Caribbean) and Darien (Gap) Cuna are protected in Panama by substantial reserves; the 1-million-acre Darien National Park owes its existence in part to the fact that the Pan-American Road was never completed through the Darien Gap in order to prevent the spread of various South American cattle diseases into Central and North America.

Early explorers—as evidenced in the Lionel Wafer selection—were most impressed by the large gathering houses found in every Cuna village; these substantial structures are still used on a daily basis to resolve internal disputes, engage in ritual chanting, and discuss matters pertaining to the outer world. Rousseau would have been familiar with the Cuna from several sources— French buccaneers were living with and intermarrying with the Cuna (who fought beside them against the British and French in the early eighteenth century); Wafer's popular book was probably available to him; and there were several French exploration narratives describing the region, such as Raveneau de Lussan's *Journal de Voyage Fait a la Mer du Sud Avec les Flibustiers de L'Amerique* (Paris, 1705).[45] The Cuna were distinctive with respect to their democratic community meetings, and were favorably described by the British and French. There are several direct references to Caribbean Indians in Rousseau's seminal *Discourse on Inequality,* which influenced not only Thomas Jefferson in writing the "Declaration of Independence," but also helped form the philosophical basis for the French Revolution; notably, one of the first documents of the French Revolution was the "Declaration of the Rights of Man," which eventually led to the abolition of slavery in the French Caribbean colonies.

In the folk-stories from Andros Island in the Bahamas and from Jamaica, both from collections assembled in the twentieth century, we have a view of nature strikingly different from that represented by those writing in the European tradition. At the core of these stories is a rejection of the dualism and the anthropocentrism that characterize the Western European outlook. Much of the thinking is derived from West African traditions, which emphasize the ultimate unity of nature and the subordination of all living things—including humans—to the larger organic whole. The Andros stories are rich with African and European antecedents, and, not surprisingly, a common theme— as in the previously mentioned story of the escaping sea turtle—is the struggle for freedom. In the Jamaican stories we often meet the African duppy spirits which "are very different from the ghost spirits with whom most of us are familiar. Unlike the rather drab, colorless ghosts that float around in European lore, Jamaican duppies take on many interesting and different forms and personalities."[46] In the story included here, a man uses his dog—named Tiger—to ward off a duppy spirit. We see in these folk-stories a much closer relationship to nature than is evident in the writings derived from Western culture: process is emphasized over life itself, and death is seen not as the initiation of a series of punishments or rewards, but as a final reintegration with nature. Modern writers in the alternative tradition—Derek Walcott, E. K. Brathwaite, and Jamaica Kincaid—have been harshly critical of what the West has done to the Caribbean, and frequently express their views with what to outsiders is surprising frankness, as in the Jamaica Kincaid selection.

The writings of women in this anthology offer a perspective on nature often fundamentally different from that expressed in the writings of men. Although this is not as evident in the 1774 Janet Schaw selection—she was to a great extent bound by her ethnocentrism—certainly with Harriet Beecher Stowe we have seen in the earlier reference a very blunt denunciation of the world of men with respect to nature. Marjory Stoneman Douglas, a citizen activist and one of the founding spirits of Everglades National Park, has shown in her life and writing the power that one woman and her written words can have in moving public policy in the direction of conservation. Similarly, Rachel Carson, whose 1961 classic *Silent Spring* resulted in the pesticide DDT being banned from use in the United States (American companies still export the chemical for use where it remains legal), demonstrated the extraordinary influence that nature writing can have. Rachel Carson, like Marjory Stoneman Douglas, also recognized the importance of nature writing as an educational tool, and tried in a number of books, including the book excerpted here (*The Edge of the Sea*), to share her knowledge with the general public. Jamaica Kincaid takes us back full circle to the same Antigua Janet Schaw chronicled two centuries earlier, and offers the viewpoint of one born to the island; Salman Rushdie has called her bitter essay "A jeremiad of great clarity and a force that one might have called torrential were the language not so finely controlled."[47] In her writing, the outrage of centuries pours forth. Finally, in the Bahaman folk-story from Lizzie Richardson, we have what on the surface seems a very simple story—a woman falls in love with a fish, which is then killed by a man—but which, on another level, is an allegory of the primal union with nature that is severed by the male-dominated society in which women, and men, find themselves living apart from nature.

The ecofeminist reading—which stipulates that the subjugation of nature and women arises from the same source—is a particularly valuable one with respect to these Caribbean nature selections, and offers some helpful insights. Early on, for example, we have Sir Walter Raleigh writing enviously "of

Charles the 5. [King of Spain] who had the *maidenhead* [emphasis added] of Peru."⁴⁸ Nature in this reference is seen as a female—a virgin—whose hymen, or "maidenhead" is violated by the Spanish throne in order to acquire her treasures of gold and silver. American naturalist William Bartram, wandering through the swamps of south Florida, wrote of "How fantastical looks the libertine Clitoria, mantling the shrubs, on the vistas skirting the groves!"⁴⁹ Nature is again represented as a feminized seductress who is, in this instance, being inseminated with words. Daniel Defoe's Robinson Crusoe is ship- wrecked—isolated from the paternal order—and finds much happiness as he restores his harmonious childhood relationship with a nurturing "mother" earth. In earlier references we have seen the dismay of both Alexander von Humboldt and Harriet Beecher Stowe with the cruelties perpetrated on innocent nature by man. Frederick Upham Adams, in his history of the United Fruit Company, writes graphically of the violation of the tropics by the paternal "Machine":

> By the "Machine" I mean the aggregate result of the work of the thousands who had striven to attain mechanical efficiency, and who had wonderfully succeeded. . . . The Machine was the relentless incarnation of efficiency. It had no useless parts. It made no useless motions. It made no mistakes. The quantity and quality of its output was a known factor. It had been created to perform a mission. The machine was *a big thing* [emphasis added].⁵⁰

In these and other selections it is clear that the male desire to conquer a feminized nature is at the heart of the dualism that has traditionally divided Western Civilization from nature; this view has become increasingly chal- lenged in recent years—by writers like Roger Caras, Barry Lopez, and David Rains Wallace—who have attempted to reintegrate an alienated civilization with the nature that ultimately sustains it.

Those who read through these selections in chronological order will be treated to a self-guided tour of the English language and its literature since the Renaissance. In Sir Walter Raleigh's and Sir William Strachey's selections we find the language as it existed during the Elizabethan "Golden Age," a period when English had a vitality, elegance, and purity that some believe has not been surpassed since. Strachey's vivid account of being shipwrecked for nine months on Bermuda is of particular interest to scholars because the narrative very possibly inspired Shakespeare to write his last important play "The Tempest," a drama in which nature, as with the Strachey chronicle, is as much a character as the human participants. These are the richly descriptive lines that Shakespeare read in Strachey:

> Once [during what Strachey calls the "Tempest"], so huge a Sea brake upon the poope and quarter, upon us, as it covered our Shippe from stearne to stemme, like a garment or a vast cloude, it filled her brimme full . . . I thought her [the ship] alreadie in the bottome of the Sea; and I have heard [Sir George Summers] say, wading out of the floud thereof, all his ambition was

but to climbe up above hatches to dye in Aperto coelo, and in the company of his old friends.[51]

And these are the familiar lines from Shakespeare's "The Tempest":

> *Gonzalo:* Now would I give a thousand furlongs of sea for an acre of barren ground—long heath, brown furze, anything. The wills above be done, but I would fain die a dry death. (I, i, 60–63)

By the time of Daniel Defoe's *Robinson Crusoe* in 1719, the language had been "corrupted" by the rise of the prosperous middle class to the extent that Defoe's contemporary Jonathan Swift suggested the establishment of a National English Academy to standardize grammar and spelling. The publication of Dr. Johnson's monumental *Dictionary* in 1755 helped to normalize the rapidly evolving language. Of special note linguistically in Defoe's *Robinson Crusoe,* which takes place on an island near the mouth of the Orinoco River, is the *pidgin* English spoken by the Carib Indian Friday whom Crusoe befriends. Pidgin-is a makeshift language informally devised so that people of differing languages can communicate in some sort of limited, intermediary fashion; it possesses words and grammatical characteristics of both languages. Pidgin would later influence the development of Caribbean English, which we see here in the distinctive patois of the Jamaican and Bahaman folklore selections. E. K. Braithwaite has written of Caribben English that

> We [Jamaicans] are at the stage Chaucer was in his time [1340?–1400]. That's my assessment of it. Chaucer had just started to gel English, French, and Latin [English was not spoken in the English court from the Battle of Hastings to 1415]. We are doing the same thing with our Creole [Creole is a pidgin that has become the principal language of community] concepts, our standard English, our American, and our Modernism.[52]

Following the time of Defoe and Swift, the Romantic period revolutionized English literature and the English language by truly restoring the primacy of nature as a theme. Although the 1832 Parliamentary Reform Bill is often cited by scholars as signaling the demise of Romanticism, the spirit lingered on well into the nineteenth century and is evident here in the 1838 Jamaican selection by Joseph Sturge and Thomas Harvey. The authors describe a ride over the Portland Mountains, where they encounter "the wild domain of nature" complete with "a valley of immense depth," and a "vast forest," where "the multitude of mountain springs and rivers give ten-fold luxuriance to the productions of a fertile soil vivified by a tropical sun."[53] Much of their nature description—the two were abolitionists checking on the progress of reform in the colonies—follows the conventions of the Romantic era, but nevertheless is distinctive with respect to the Caribbean influence. Similarly, the purple prose of Lafcadio Hearn, writing in the Victorian Age—

that historical epoch characterized by material excess and universal
optimism—is uniquely West Indian in its imagery, themes, and even in its
cadence. Hearn gushes effusively about everything from sunsets to sugar cane.
The sunset "comes with a great burning yellow glow, gading up through the
faint greens to lose itself in violet light;—there is no gloaming."[54] The sea is
"black-blue" like the "color that bewitches in certain Celtic eyes."[55] The
sugar-cane fields shine "like a pooling of fluid bronze, as if the luminous
essence of the hill tints had been dripping down and clarifying there."[56] Hearn
takes all of the best qualities of eighteenth-century and early nineteenth-
century nature writing—the rediscovery of landscape, the glorification of the
commonplace, and the supernatural "strangeness" of wild beauty—and carries
them off into another realm. Like so many writers of his milieu, Hearn is best
tasted in small portions, or else one will become dizzy and then depressed from
the excess of sweeteners.

Just a few years later, by the time of William Beebe, the English language
went through another upheaval with the sudden rise of modern science and
technology, both of which also radically transformed humankind's relation
with nature. Beebe's lexicon is studded with dozens of new words and is
characterized by a more restrained prose that countered the purple prose
excesses of the age preceding, and by a sometimes dark realism that replaced
the unqualified optimism that had also predominated in the previous generation. His was a vastly different world from Hearn's, and is reflected here in new
words like "aeroplane" and "futurist":

> From an aeroplane, Barbados would appear like a circular expanse of
> patchwork, or a wild futurist painting set in deepest ultramarine; a maze of
> rectangles or squares of sugar-cane, with a scattering of sweet potatoes and sea
> island cotton.[57]

With each new war, revolution, and technological breakthrough in the
twentieth century, the English language has undergone another change. In
the hands of its best current practitioners—writers like Roger Caras, Barry
Lopez, Edward O. Wilson, David Rains Wallace, and others—the language
remains a powerful tool, capable of expressing a wide range of experiences with
nature. Few have mastered the language in this regard—its inherent strengths
and latent grace—so well as Edward O. Wilson:

> I walked into the forest. . . . I was a transient of no consequence in this
> familiar yet deeply alien world that I had come to love. The uncounted
> products of evolution were gathered there for purposes having nothing to do
> with me; their long Cenozoic history was enciphered into a genetic code I
> could not understand. The effect was strangely calming. . . . It seemed to
> me that something extraordinary in the forest was very close to where I stood,
> moving to the surface and discovery.[58]

Why is Caribbean-American nature writing important? There are at least
five reasons to consider the natural history writing of this region as having

literary significance. First, the Caribbean is a miniature of the world. What has happened in the Caribbean since the Discovery—habitat and species loss as a direct result of human population growth—has occurred all over the planet. To contemplate the fragment—whether a single coral reef or the enormity of Cuba—is to comprehend the whole. Second, because wild areas all over the world are becoming increasingly isolated as a result of human interference, the close examination of these oceanic islands has considerable relevance, particularly to those living at higher latitudes whose parks and preserves have become "habitat islands."[59] Third, insofar as nonfiction nature writing has emerged as one of the most important prose genres of the late twentieth century, any study of this genre—especially in the much-needed comparative context—is intrinsically useful, both to the understanding of literature and of human culture. Fourth, because the history of the Caribbean is inextricably connected with the history of Europe over the past 500 years—from the raids of Drake and Hawkins to the 1962 Cuban Missile Crisis—there can be no full accounting of Western Culture and its relationship to nature without a study of the Caribbean. Fifth, these writings are important in the final analysis simply for their own sake, as the highest expression of the residents of and travelers to this magnificent part of the world.

Many tides have risen and fallen since Columbus rolled out his maps with the charted oceans surrounded by sea monsters and whirling maelstroms and decided to pit fact against myth, and boldly strike out for the east by sailing west. Twenty-story manned spacecraft now drop their rocket boosters into the seas over which Columbus led his ragged fleet just twenty generations ago. Much has changed, but much remains the same. Human nature—with all of its capacity for kindness and cruelty—endures, and the seas and the islands—more threatened than ever—are still there. Mark Twain wrote of the Discovery that, "It was wonderful to find America, but it would have been more wonderful to miss it."[60] Considering the accounts of de las Casas, Pinkard, von Humboldt, Stowe, Lopez, and others, Mark Twain was right, but, whether we like it or not, we have inherited the Discovery and all that followed, and, as a result, both human culture and wild nature in the Caribbean are in need of attention. Perhaps most remarkable is the fact that enclaves of wildness can still be found throughout the Caribbean. In that there is promise for the future. Above all, we must remember the ancient Mayan proverb: "He who makes an enemy of the earth makes an enemy of his own body."[61] This collection is gathered together in the hope that not only will readers come to a greater appreciation of nature in Caribbean-American literature, but also that they will learn some of the environmental lessons evident in Caribbean history. Let us turn the page now, and begin anew, for the fogs of yesteryear are lifting, and the *Nina*, the *Pinta*, and the *Santa Maria* are pulling up into a fresh land breeze, and the heavy anchor chains are rumbling down through the rusty hawseholes, and over the side a landing craft—watched closely from the shore—is being lowered into the rising tide.

Notes

1. See, for example, Alexander von Humboldt, *A Personall Narrative of Travels to the Equinoctial Regions of America*. Trans. and ed. Thomasina Ross. 3 volumes. (London: Henry G. Bohn, 1862); and Ernest Hemingway, *The Old Man and the Sea* (New York: Charles Scribner's and Sons, 1952).

2. Frank H. Wadsworth, "Management of Mountain Habitat on a Densely Populated Tropical Island." *Second World Conference on National Parks* (Morges: IUCN, 1974), 187.

3. Christopher Columbus, *Select Letters of Columbus*. Trans. and ed. R. H. Major (London: Hakluyt Society, 1870), 6.

4. Ronald W. Clark, *Benjamin Franklin: A Biography* (New York: Random House, 1983), 206–207.

5. George Kennan, *The Tragedy of Pelée, a Narrative of Personal Experience and Observation in Martinique* (New York: The Outlook Company, 1902), 75.

6. Kennan, 188.

7. Ernest Hemingway, "To Maxwell Perkins," 7 September 1935, *Selected Letters 1917–1961*, Ed. Carlos Baker (New York: Charles Scribner's Sons, 1981), 421.

8. Joseph Acosta, "The Naturall and Morall Historie of the Indies." *Purchas His Pilgrimes*. Ed. Samuel Purchas. Vol. 15 (reprint ed., Glasgow: Maclehose, 1906), 12.

9. Walter Raleigh, "The Discoverie of the large, rich, and beautiful Empire of Guiana." *The Principal Navigations, Voyages, Traffiques, and Discoveries of the English Nation*. Ed. Richard Hakluyt. Vol. 10 (reprint ed., Glasgow: Maclehose, 1904), 404.

10. William Bartram. *Travels Through North and South Carolina, Georgia, East & West Florida*. Ed. Mark Van Doren (Philadelphia, 1791; reprint ed., New York, 1955), 143.

11. Lafcadio Hearn, *Two Years in the French West Indies* (New York: Harper and Brothers, 1902), 96.

12. Hearn, 63.

13. V. S. Naipaul, *The Middle Passage* (New York: Random House, 1981), 62.

14. Sidney W. Mintz, "The Caribbean as a Socio-cultural Area." *Peoples and Cultures of the Caribbean*. Ed. Michael Horowitz (New York: The Natural History Press, 1971), 32.

15. Mintz, 32.

16. Acosta, 132.

17. Griffith Hughes, *The Natural History of Barbados in Ten Books* (London, 1750), vi.

18. Hughes, vii.

19. Hughes, 293–298.

20. Edward O. Wilson, *Biophilia* (Cambridge: Harvard University Press, 1984), 143.

21. Wilson, 4–5.

22. John L. Stephens, *Incidents of Travel in Yucatan*. Vol. 2 (New York, 1843), 264.

23. Frederick Upham Adams, *Conquest of the Tropics, the Story of the Creative Enterprises Conducted by the United Fruit Company* (Garden City: Doubleday, 1914), 252.

24. Bartholomew de las Casas, "A briefe Narration of the destruction of the Indies by the Spaniards." *Purchas His Pilgrimes*. Ed. Samuel Purchas. Vol. 18 (reprint ed., Glasgow: Maclehose, 1906), 89.

25. de las Casas, 90.

26. René Laudonniere, "The Voiage of captaine René Laudonniere to Florida in 1564." *The Principal Navigations, Voyages, Traffiques, and Discoveries of the English Nation.* Ed. Richard Hakluyt. Vol. 9 (reprint ed., Glasgow: Maclehose, 1904), 3.

27. George Pinkard, *Notes on the West Indies.* Vol. 3 (London, 1806), 65.

28. Pinkard, 67.

29. Pinkard, 74.

30. Alexander von Humboldt, *The Island of Cuba* (New York, 1856), 375.

31. Harriet Beecher Stowe, *Magnolia Leaves* (New York, 1873), 259–261.

32. Gonzalo de Oviedo, "General and Natural History of the Indies." *Purchas His Pilgrimes.* Ed. Samuel Purchas. Vol. 15 (reprint ed. Glasgow: Maclehose, 1906), 252.

33. Oviedo, 253.

34. Oviedo, 158.

35. Oviedo, 165 (*Note: Bufo marinus,* the venomous cane toad, grows to the size of a salad plate, but not to the dimensions suggested here).

36. Acosta, 13.

37. John Hawkins, "The second voyage made by Sir John Hawkins knight." *The Principal Navigations, Voyages, Traffiques, and Discoveries of the English Nation.* Ed. Richard Hakluyt. Vol. 10 (reprint ed., Glasgow: Maclehose, 1904), 59.

38. Laudonniere, 10.

39. Raleigh, 406 (*Note:* see also p. 360 for a discussion of El Dorado and pps. 366–367 for a discussion of the Amazons).

40. Lionel Wafer, *A New Voyage and Description of the Isthmus of America.* Ed. L. E. Elliott Joyce (Oxford: Hakluyt Society, 1934), 66.

41. Pinkard, 37.

42. Pinkard, 37.

43. Pinkard, 38.

44. Bernard Nietschmann, *Caribbean Edge: The Coming of Modern Times to Isolated People and Wildlife* (New York: Bobbs-Merrill, 1979), 79.

45. See also Nils M. Holmer, ed., *Inatoipippiler, or the Adventures of Three Cuna Boys* (Goteborg: Etnografiska Museet, 1952), 9.

46. Daryl C. Dance, *Folklore from Contemporary Jamaicans* (Knoxville: The University of Tennessee Press, 1985), 35.

47. Rushdie's remarks are appended to Jamaica Kincaid, *A Small Place* (New York: Farrar Straus Giroux, 1988).

48. Raliegh, 346.

49. Bartram, 142.

50. Adams, 67.

51. William Strachey, "A true repertory of the wracke." *Purchas His Pilgrimes.* Ed. Samuel Purchas. Vol. 19 (reprint ed., Glasgow: Maclehose, 1906), 19.

52. E. K. Brathwaite, "English in the Caribbean." *English Literature.* Ed. Leslie A. Fiedler and Houstan A. Baker, Jr. (Baltimore: Johns Hopkins University Press, 1981), 112.

53. Joseph Sturge and Thomas Harvey, *The West Indies in 1837* (London: Hamilton, Adams, and Company, 1838), 86.

54. Hearn, 19.

55. Hearn, 20.

56. Hearn, 33.

57. William Beebe, *Jungle Peace* (New York: Henry Holt, 1918), 63.

58. Wilson, 7.

59. L. R. Heaney and B. D. Patterson, eds., *Island Biogeography of Mammals* (New York: Academic Press, 1986). See in particular the following articles: W. D. Newmark, "Species-area relationship and its determinants for mammals in western North American national parks"; T. E. Lawlor, "Comparative biogeography of mammals on islands"; and G. S. Morgan and C. A. Woods, "Extinction and the zoogeography of West Indian land mammals."

60. Lee Clark Mitchell, *Witnesses to a Vanishing America: The Nineteenth-Century Response* (Princeton: Princeton University Press, 1981), 253.

61. Dennis Tedlock, ed., *Popol Vuh: The Definitive Edition of the Mayan Book of the Dawn of Life and the Glories of Gods and King* (New York: Simon and Schuster, 1985), 14.

 **PART I**

1492–1599
PARADISE FOUND:
THE AGE OF
CONQUEST

Considering with my selfe, the pleasing temperature of many Countries at the [West] Indies, where they know not what Winter is, which by his cold doth freeze them, nor Summer which doth trouble them with heat, but that with a Mat they preserve themselves from the injuries of all weather, and where they scarce have any neede to change their garments throughout the yeere. I say, that often considering of this, I find that if men at this day would vanquish their passions, and free themselves from the snares of covetousnesse, leaving many fruitlesse and pernicious designes, without doubt they might live at the Indies very pleasant and happily: for that which other Poets sing of the Elisean fields & of the famous Tempe, or that which Plato reports or feignes of his Atlantike Iland; men should finde in these Lands, if with a generous spirit they would choose rather to command their silver and their desires, then to remayne to it slaves as they are.

Joseph Acosta
Historia Natural y Moral de las Indies
(1588)

8000 B.C. (or earlier), human cultures actively utilize the resources of Mesoamerica and the Caribbean littoral. 1000 B.C. (or earlier), Amerindian ancestors of Caribs and Arawaks disperse throughout the Caribbean. 400–900 A.D., the classic era of Mayan civilization. 900–1521, Toltec and Aztec cultures flourish in central highland Mexico. 900–1534, Incan culture flourishes in the northern Andes. 1000, Leif Erickson reaches North America. 1415, Portugal begins overseas expansion in Morroco. 1441, Portugese initiate slave trade in West Africa. 1453, Constantinople falls to the Ottoman Turks, closing East-West trade routes. 1454, Guttenberg publishes the first printed Bible. 1456, Cadamosto discovers Cape Verde Islands. 1485, Henry VII founds the Tudor Dynasty, ending the War of Roses. 1488, Dias rounds the Cape of Good Hope. 1492, Columbus discovers the Caribbean, and claims several islands for Spain. 1494, Columbus' second voyage. 1494, the Treaty of Todesillas partitions the New World between Spain and Portugal. 1496, Santo Domingo founded on Hispaniola (first European city). 1498, da Gama reaches India. 1498, Columbus' third voyage. 1500, Cabral claims Brazil for Portugal. 1502, Columbus' fourth and final voyage. 1503, Bermudez discovers Bermuda. 1506, first sugar mill on Hispaniola. 1507, Martin Waldseemuller's world map names the New World "America" for Italian navigator Amerigo Vespucci. 1510, Spanish authorize slavery in the Caribbean. 1513, de Leon discovers Florida. 1513, Balboa sights the Pacific Ocean from Panama. 1513, the Portugese reach China. 1521, Luther breaks with the Pope. 1521, Cortés defeats the Aztecs. 1522, Magellan's expedition circumnavigates the Earth. 1532, Pizarro conquers the Incas. 1534, Henry VIII forms the Anglican Church. 1535, the first university in the New World is convened in Santo Domingo. 1536, British and French privateers and buccaneers begin to attack Spanish cities and towns in the Caribbean. 1539, De Soto explores Florida. 1540, the Jesuit Order is formed. 1543, Copernicus proves the Earth orbits the sun. 1548, the Portugese reach Japan. 1549, Diego de Landa burns Mayan books and codices, and is recalled to Spain. 1588, Elizabeth I succeeds to the English throne. 1563, Hawkins brings slaves to the Caribbean. 1580, the

Spanish empire absorbs Portugal. 1580, Drake circumnavigates the world. 1580, Montaigne publishes *Essais*. 1586, Drake raids Santo Domingo and sacks Cartagena. 1588, English defeat Spanish Armada. 1589, Hakluyt publishes *The Principal Navigations*. 1595, Hawkins and Drake defeat the Spanish off Puerto Rico.

The First Letter of Columbus

CHRISTOPHER COLUMBUS
(circa 1493)

It was the failure of the Crusades—closing old East-West trade routes—and the liberating spirit of the Renaissance that made the European discovery of the Western Hemisphere inevitable. Although we now know that Scandinavian mariners reached Labrador by at least 1000 A.D., it was the Italian explorer Christopher Columbus (1451–1506) who first braved the long empty quarters of the Atlantic in search of a route to the Far East. The savants of the day estimated that the circumference of the Earth was around 20,000 miles. Combining this theory with the facts recorded in the journals and maps of Marco Polo, Columbus postulated that the Atlantic was no more than 2,400 miles wide (that is the approximate distance from the Canary Islands to the West Indies). On August 3, 1492, the Santa Maria, Pinta, *and* Nina *left Palos, Spain, and on October 11, 1492, land was sighted. No single person has ever made a greater geographic discovery.*

Columbus functioned not only as a pioneering explorer, but also as the first European naturalist of the New World, assiduously noting the fauna and flora of the Caribbean Islands, as well as the customs and life-styles of the native residents. His descriptions are often so exuberant as to be Edenic: "This island and all the others are very fertile to a limitless degree. In it there are many harbours on the coast of the sea, beyond comparison with others that I know in Christendom." He writes of "marvelous pine groves" and "very wide and fertile plains" and "honey" and "birds of many kinds and fruits in great diversity" and, less accurately, of "mines of metals." Nowhere is the ambivalence of the European psyche toward the New World more evident than in Columbus' description of the innocence and generosity of the natives, which is followed by a discussion of how they could be Christianized and converted into slaves.

From *Select Letters of Columbus,* edited by R. H. Major (London: Hakluyt Society, 1870).

SIR, As I know that you will be pleased at the great victory with which Our Lord has crowned my voyage, I write this to you, from which you will learn how in thirty-three days, I passed from the Canary Islands to the Indies with the fleet which the most illustrious king and queen, our sovereigns, gave to me. And there I found very many islands filled with people innumerable, and of them all I have taken possession for their highnesses, by proclamation made and with the royal standard unfurled, and no opposition was offered to me. To the first island which I found, I gave the name *San Salvador* [generally thought to be Watling Island in the Bahamas], in remembrance of the Divine Majesty, Who has marvelously bestowed all this; the Indians call it "Guanahani." To the second, I gave the name *Isla de Santa Maria de Conception;* to the third, *Fernandina;* to the fourth, *Isabella;* to the fifth, *Isla Juana,* and so to each one I gave a new name.

When I reached Juana, I followed its coast to the westward, and I found it to be so extensive that I thought that it must be the mainland, the province of Catayo. And since there were neither towns nor villages on the seashore, but only small hamlets, with the people of which I could not have speech, because they all fled immediately, I went forward on the same course, thinking that I should not fail to find great cities and towns. And, at the end of many leagues, seeing that there was no change and that the coast was bearing me northwards, which I wished to avoid, since winter was already beginning and I proposed to make from it to the south, and as moreover the wind was carrying me forward, I determined not to wait for a change in the weather and retraced my path as far as a certain harbour known to me. And from that point, I sent two men inland to learn if there were a king or great cities. They travelled three days journey and found an infinity of small hamlets and people without number, but nothing of importance. For this reason, they returned.

I understood sufficiently from other Indians, whom I had already taken, that this land was nothing but an island. And therefore I followed its coast eastwards for one hundred and seven leagues to the point where it ended. And from that cape, I saw another island, distant eighteen leagues from the former, to the east, to which I at once gave the name "Espanola." And I went there and followed its northern coast, as I had in the case of Juana, to the eastward for one hundred and eighty-eight great leagues in a straight line. This island and all the others are very fertile to a limitless degree, and this island is extremely so. In it there are many harbours on the coast of the sea, beyond comparison with others which I know in Christendom, and many rivers, good and large, which is marvelous. Its lands are high, and there are in it very many sierras and very lofty mountains, beyond comparison with the island of Teneriffe. All are most beautiful, of a thousand shapes, and all are accessible and filled with trees of a thousand kinds and tall, and they seem to touch the sky. And I am told that they never lose their foliage, as I can understand, for I saw them as green and as lovely as they are in Spain in May, and some of them were flowering, some bearing fruit, and some in another stage, according to their nature. And the nightingale was singing and other birds of a thousand kinds in the month of November there where I went. There are six or eight kinds of palm, which are a wonder to behold on account of their beautiful variety, but so are the other trees and fruits and plants. In it are marvelous pine groves, and there are very large tracts of cultivatable lands, and there is honey, and there are birds of many kinds and fruits in great diversity. In the interior are mines of metals, and the population is without number. Espanola is a marvel.

The sierras and mountains, the plains and arable lands and pastures, are so lovely and rich for planting and sowing, for breeding cattle of every kind, for building towns and villages. The harbours of the sea here are such as cannot be believed to exist unless they have been seen, and so with the rivers, many and great, and good waters, the majority of which contain gold. In the trees and fruits and plants, there is a great difference from those of Juana. In this island, there are many spices and great mines of gold and of other metals.

The people of this island, and of all the other islands which I have found and of which I have information, all go naked, men and women, as their mothers bore them, although some women cover a single place with the leaf of a plant or with a net of cotton which they make for the purpose. They have no iron or steel or weapons, nor are they fitted to use them, not because they are not well built men and of handsome stature, but because they are very marvelously timorous. They have no other arms than weapons made of canes, cut in seeding time, to the ends of which they fix a small sharpened stick. And they do not dare to make use of these, for many times it has happened that I have sent ashore two or three men to some town to have speech, and countless people have come out to them, and as soon as they have seen my men approaching they have fled, even a father not waiting for his son. And this, not because ill has been done to anyone; on the contrary, at every point where I have been and have been able to have speech, I have given to them of all that I had, such as cloth and many other things, without receiving anything for it; but so they are, incurably timid. It is true that, after they have been reassured and have lost their fear, they are so guileless and so generous with all they possess, that no one would believe it who has not seen it. They never refuse anything which they possess, if it be asked of them; on the contrary, they invite anyone to share it, and display as much love as if they would give their hearts, and whether the thing be of value or whether it be of small price, at once with whatever trifle of whatever kind it may be that is given to them, with that they are content. I forbade that they should be given things so worthless as fragments of broken crockery and scraps of broken glass, and ends of straps, although when they were able to get them, they fancied that they possessed the best jewel in the world. So it was found that a sailor for a strap received gold to the weight of two and a half *castellanos,* and others much more for other things which were worth much less. As for new *blancas,* for them they would give everything which they had, although it might be two or three *castellanos'* weight of gold or an *arroba* or two of spun cotton. . . . They took even the pieces of the broken hoops of the wine barrels, and, like savages, gave what they had, so that it seemed to me to be wrong and I forbade it. And I gave them a thousand handsome good things, which I had brought, in order that they might conceive affection, and more than that, might become Christians and be inclined to the love and service of their highnesses and of the whole Castilian nation, and strive to aid us and to give us of the things which they have in abundance and which are necessary to us. And they do not know any creed and are not idolaters, only they all believe that power and good are in the heavens, and they are very firmly convinced that I, with these ships and men, came from the heavens, and in this belief they everywhere received me, after they had overcome their fear. And this does not come because they are ignorant; on the contrary, they are of a very acute intelligence and are men who navigate all those seas, so that it is amazing how good an account they give of everything, but it is because they have never seen people clothed or ships of such a kind.

And as soon as I arrived in the Indies, in the first island which I found, I took by force some of them, in order that they might learn and give me information of that which there is in those parts, and so it was that they soon understood us, and we them, either by speech or signs, and they have been very serviceable. I still take them with me, and they are always assured that I come from Heaven, for all the intercourse which they have had with me; and they were the first to announce this wherever I went, and the others went running from house to house and to the neighbouring towns, with loud cries of, "Come! Come to see the people from Heaven!" . . .

In conclusion, to speak only of that which has been accomplished on this voyage, which was so hasty, their highnesses can see that I will give them as much gold as they may need, if their highnesses will render me very slight assistance; moreover, spire and cotton, as much as their highnesses shall command; and mastic, as much as they shall order to be shipped and which up to now, has been found only in Greece, in the island of Chios, and the Seignory sells it for what it pleases; and aloe wood, as much as they shall order to be shipped, and *slaves* [emphasis added], as many as they shall order to be shipped and who will be from the idolaters. And I believe that I have found rhubarb and cinnamon, and I shall find a thousand other things of value, which the people whom I have left there will have discovered, for I have not delayed at any point, so far as the wind allowed me to sail, except in the town of Navidad, in order to leave it secured and well established, and in truth, I should have done much more, if the ships had served me, as reason demanded.

This is enough . . . and the eternal God, our Lord, Who gives to all those who walk in His way triumph over things which appear to be impossible . . . has given this victory to our most illustrious king and queen, and to their renowned kingdoms, in so great a matter, for this all Christendom ought to feel delight and make great feasts and give solemn thanks to the Holy Trinity with many solemn prayers for the great exaltation which they shall have, in the turning of so many peoples to our holy faith, and afterwards for temporal benefits, for not only Spain but all Christians will have hence refreshment and gain.

This, in accordance with that which has been accomplished, thus briefly.

Done in the caravel, off the Canary Islands, on the fifteenth of February, in the year one thousand four hundred and ninety-three.

At your orders.

El Almirante

2

Hernando Cortés on the Island of Cozumel

BERNAL DIAZ DEL CASTILLO
(circa 1519)

Hernando Cortés (1485–1547) needs little introduction to students of history; his name will forever be synonymous with the overthrow of the Aztec Empire (1519–1521), a feat accomplished with less than three companies of soldiers and 16 horses. The manner in which this unlikely victory was achieved is related in two indispensable sources: William H. Prescott's History of the Conquest of Mexico *(Boston, 1843) and Bernal Diaz's* The Conquest of New Spain *(Spain, 1576). This selection is from Diaz's (1496–1584) account, which Prescott used extensively in writing his history. Diaz actually took part in the Conquest, and speaks authoritatively, if subjectively, about the events and the participants. In this selection Diaz relates what occurred on the island of Cozumel as the expedition proceeded en route to the mainland: although Cortés reprimands a subordinate for looting the Mayan village, he subsequently desecrates the Mayan religious shrine and erects a wooden cross in its place. Such was the paradox of the European conquest of the New World, which committed numerous acts of violence in the name of love, mercy, and forgiveness.*

From *The Conquest of New Spain,* by Bernal Diaz del Castillo (London: Hakluyt, 1908).

. . . As soon as we arrived in port we went on shore with all the soldiers to the town of Cozumel, but we found no Indians there as they had all fled. So we were ordered to go on to another town about a league distant, and there also the natives had fled and taken to the bush, but they could not carry off their property and left behind their poultry and other things and Pedro de Alvarado ordered forty of the fowls to be taken. In an Idol house there were some altar ornaments made of old cloths and some little chests containing diadems, Idols, beads and pendants of gold of poor quality, and here we captured two Indians and an Indian woman, and we returned to the town where we had disembarked.

While we were there Cortés arrived with all the fleet, and after taking up his lodging the first thing he did was to order the pilot Camacho to be put in irons for not having waited for him at sea as he had been ordered to do. When he saw the town without any people in it, and heard that Pedro de Alvarado had gone to the other town and had taken fowls and cloths and other things of small value from the Idols, and some gold which was half copper, he showed that he was very angry both at that and at the pilot for not having waited for him, and he reprimanded Pedro de Alvarado severely, and told him that we should never pacify the country in that way by robbing the natives of their property, and he sent for the two Indians and the woman whom we had captured, and through Melchorejo (Julianillo his companion was dead), the man we had brought from Cape Catoche who understood the language well, he spoke to them telling them to go and summon the Caciques [local chieftains] and Indians of their town, and he told them not to be afraid, and he ordered the gold and the cloths and all the rest to be given back to them, and for the fowls (which had already been eaten), he ordered them to be given beads and little bells, and in addition he gave to each Indian a Spanish shirt. So they went off to summon the lord of the town, and the next day the Cacique and all his people arrived, women and children and all the inhabitants of the town, and they went about among us as though they had been used to us all their lives, and Cortés ordered us not to annoy them in any way. Here in this Island Cortés began to rule energetically, and Our Lord so favoured him that whatever he put his hand to it turned out well for him, especially in pacifying the people and towns of these lands, as we shall see further on.

When we had been in Cozumel three days Cortés ordered a muster of his forces so as to see how many of us there were, and he found that we numbered five hundred and eight, not counting the shipmasters, pilots, and sailors, who numbered about one hundred. There were sixteen horses and mares all fit to be used for sport or as chargers.

There were eleven ships both great and small . . . [and] there were thirty-two cross bowmen and thirteen musketeers;—*escopeteros,* as they were then called, and ten brass guns, and four falconets, and much powder and ball. . . .

Both the natives of towns near Cape Catoche and those from other parts of Yucatan [mainland] came on pilgrimages to the Island of Cozumel, for it appeared that there were some very hideous idols kept in a certain oratory on Cozumel to which it was the custom of the people of the land to offer sacrifices at that season. One morning the courtyard of the oratory where the Idols were kept was crowded with Indians, and many of them both men and women were burning a resin like our incense. As this was a new sight to us we stood round watching it with attention, and presently an old Indian with a long cloak, who was the priest of the Idols (and I have already said that the priests in New Spain are called *Papas*) went up on the top of the oratory and began to preach to the people. Cortés and all of us were wondering what could be the result of that black sermon. Cortés asked Melchorejo, who understood the language well, what the old Indian was saying, for he was informed that he was preaching evil things, and he sent for the Cacique and all the principal chiefs and the priest himself, and, as well as he could through the aid of our interpreter, he told them that if we were to be brothers they must cast those most evil Idols out of their temple, for they were not gods at all but very evil things which led them astray and could lead their souls to hell. Then he spoke to them about good and holy things, and told them to set up in the place of their Idols an image of Our Lady which he gave them, and a cross, which would always aid them and bring good harvests and would save their souls, and he told them in a very excellent way other things about our holy faith.

The Priest and the Caciques answered that their fore-fathers had worshipped those Idols because they were good, and that they did not dare to do otherwise, and that if we cast out their Idols we would see how much harm it would do us, for we should be lost at sea. Then Cortés ordered us to break the Idols to pieces and roll them down the steps, and this we did; then he ordered lime to be brought, of which there was a good store in the town, and Indian masons, and he set up a very fair altar on which we placed the figure of Our Lady; and he ordered two of our party named Alonzo Yanez and Alvaro Lopez who were carpenters and joiners to make a cross of some rough timber which was there, and it was placed in a small chapel near the altar and the priest named Juan Diaz said mass there, and the Cacique and the heathen priest and all the Indians stood watching us with attention. . . . Cortés took leave of the caciques and priests and confided to their care the Image of Our Lady and told them to reverence the cross and keep it clean and wreathed with flowers and they would see what advantage they would gain by so doing, and the Indians replied that they would do so, and they brought four fowls and two jars of honey and they embraced him. [Cortés then departed for the mainland, but had to return immediately, as one of his flagships began to leak and sink; he spent four more days on Cozumel repairing that vessel.]

3

A Generall Historie of the Indies

GONZALO DE OVIEDO
(circa 1525)

*With the publication of Gonzalo de Oviedo's (1478–1557)
monumental* Historia Natural y General de las Indias *(1535),
we see the birth of a European natural history culture that
would, in the next century, lead to the formation of the Royal Society and other
organs of institutionalized science. While the veracity of many of Oviedo's
descriptions can be discounted, the work is modern in its attempt to be systematic, if
not skeptical as with Acosta later in the same century. Oviedo lived in the
Caribbean from 1512 through 1557 and held a number of key colonial positions,
including the governorship of Carthagena and Darien. Because of his importance
in this respect* Historia Natural y General de las Indias *was well received in his
time and was influential, although for some reason the work was not translated
into English, as was his earlier pamphlet* Oviedo dela Natural Historia delas
Indias *(1526). In its Latin translation, however, the work would have been
readily available to the cognoscenti of England, for whom Latin was an international language of scholarship. In these brief selections from his long and
fascinating account, Oviedo describes, respectively, the Arawaks of Hispaniola,
some ground-dwelling fauna of the Caribbean, and the enormous hardwood trees
of the climax rain forests of the Darien Gap. The last is particularly vivid, as he
describes what was likely a mahogany tree that "exceeded in height the Towre of
Saint Romane in the Citie of Toledo" before it began to spread its branches.
Climbing on the strangler vines around the tree, Oviedo ascends to this place and is
treated to a vision of abundance that, whether real or not in the telling, was very
real in the believing. The Caribbean, like the Garden of Eden that defined to an
extent Oviedo's view of nature, was a literal paradise to each of these New World
Adams. It promised regeneration even as it presaged destruction.*

From *Purchas His Pilgrimes* (vol. XV), edited by Samuel Purchas (Glasgow: Maclehose, 1906).

Of the Original Inhabitants of Hispaniola [and their naturalists]

Before the Inhabitants of the Iland of Hispaniola had received the Christian Faith, there was among them a Sect of men, which lived solitarily in the Desarts and Woods, and led their life in Silence and Abstinence, more streightly then ever did the Philosophers of Pythagoras Sect, abstaining in like manner from the eating of all things that live by bloud, contented onely with such Fruites, Herbes, and Rootes, as the Desarts and Woods ministred unto them to eat: the Professors of this Sect were called Piaces. They gave themselves to the knowledge of naturall things, and used certaine secret Magicall Operations and Superstitions, whereby they had familiaritie with Spirits, which they allured into their owne bodies, at such times as they would take upon them to tell of things to come. . . . If he be also demanded of the eclipse of the Sunne or Moone (which they greatly feare and abhorre) he giveth a perfect answer, and the like of tempests, famine, plentie, warre or peace, and such other things. . . . But since the Christian faith hath beene dispersed throughout the Iland, these divellish practises have ceased, and they of the members of the Divell, are made the members of Christ by Baptisme, forsaking the Divell and his works, with the vaine curiosity of desire of knowledge of things to come, whereof for the most part it is better to be ignorant, then with vexation to know that which cannot be avoided.

Of Snakes, Dragons, Spiders, and Toads

I have also seene in the firme Land a kinde of Adders, very small, and of seven or eight foot long; these are so red, that in night they appeare like burning coles, and in the day seeme as red as blood, these are also venemous, but not so much as the Vipers. There are other much lesse and shorter, and blacker: these come out of the Rivers, and wander sometimes farre on the Land, and are likewise venemous. These are also other Adders of a russet colour: these are somewhat bigger than the Viper, and are hurtful and venemous. There are likewise another sort of many colours, and very long: of these I saw one in the yeare of Christ 1515. in the Iland of Hispaniola, neere unto the Sea coasts, at the foote of the Mountaines called Pedernales. When this Adder was slain, I measured her & found her to be more than twenty foot long, and somewhat more then a mans fist in bignesse: and although she had three or foure deadly wounds with a Sword, yet dyed she not, nor stunke the same day, in so much that her blood continued warme all that time. There are also in the Marishes and desarts of the firme Land many other kinds of Lysarts, Dragons, and divers other kindes of Serpents. . . . There are also Spiders of marveilous bignesse, and I have seene some with bodie and legges bigger then a mans hand extended every way, and I once saw one of such bignesse, that onely her body was as bigge as a Sparrow, and full of that Laune whereof they make their webbes: this was of a darke russet colour, with eyes greater then the eyes of a Sparrow, they are venemous, and of terrible shape to behold. There are also Scorpions, and divers other such venemous wormes. Furthermore in the firme Land, there are many Toades, being verie noioux and hurtful by reason of their great multidue, they are not venemous, they are seene in great abundance in Dareene, where they are so big that when they die in the time of drought, the bones of some of them (and especially the ribs) are of such greatnesse, that they appeare to be the bones of Cats, or of some other beasts of the same bignesse. . . . These Toades sing after three or foure sort, for some of them sing pleasantly, other like ours of Spaine, some also whistle, and other some make another manner of noise: they are likewise of divers colours, as some greene, some russet or gray, and some almost blacke, but of all sorts they are great and filthie, and noious by reason of their great multitude, yet they are not venemous, as I have said.

On the Great Trees of the New World

. . . a league from Dariena or the Cities of Sancta Maria Antiqua, there passeth a River very large and deepe, which is called Cuti, over the which the Indians laid a great Tree, so traversing the same, that it was in the stead of a bridge, the which I my selfe with divers other that are at this present in your Majesties Court, have oftentimes passed over. . . . I [in the year 1522] caused another great Tree to bee laid in that place, which in like manner traversed the River, and reached more then fiftie foote over the further side: This Tree was exceeding great, and rested above the water more than two eubits, in the fall, it cast downe all such other Trees as were within the reach thereof. . . . This Tree, in the thickest part thereof, was more then sixteene spannes thicke, and was nevertheless but little in respect of many other trees which are found in this Province. For the Indians of the Coast and Province of Cartagenia, make Barkes or Boates thereof (which they call Canoas) of such bignesse, beeing all one whole Tree, that some containe a hundred men, some a hundred and thirtie, and some more. . . . Some of these . . . saile with two sailes . . . which they make of very good Cotton. The greatest Trees that I have seene in these parts, or in any other Regions, was in the Province of Guaturo [where] . . . I passed over a very high Mountaine, full of great Trees, in the top whereof, we found one Tree, which had three roots, or rather divisions of the roote above the Earth, in forme of a Triangle, or Trevet, so that betweene every foot of this Triangle or three feet, there was a space of twentie foot betweene each foot, and this of such height above the Earth, that a laden Cart of those wherewith they are accustomed to bring home Corne in time of

Harvest in the Kindome of Toledo in Spaine, might easily have passed through every of those partitions or windoors which were betweene the three feet of the said Tree . . . it exceeded in height the Towre of Saint Romane in the Citie of Toledo [before it began to spread its branches] . . . and when I was ascended to the place where it begunne to spread the branches, it was a marvellous thing to behold a great Countrey of such Trees. . . . This tree was easie to climbe, by reason of certain Besuchi [vines] . . . which grew wreathed about the Tree, in such sort that they seemed to make a scaling Ladder.

4

Ferdinando de Soto His Voyage to Florida

AN [ANONYMOUS] PORTUGALL OF THE COMPANIE
(circa 1539)

After witnessing Pizzaro's execution of his good friend, Incan King Atahuallpa in 1536, Ferdinando de Soto (1500–1542) returned in disgust to Spain. Shortly thereafter, however, he was persuaded to lead an expedition to Florida and the southern coast of North America, which was then terra incognita *to the conquerors of the Caribbean, the Aztec empire, and the Incan empire. It was on this trip that de Soto died of a fever and was buried in the Mississippi River to prevent his body from being disturbed by hostile natives in what is today Louisiana. In this account by "an [anonymous] Portugall of the Companie" we are told of a most unusual occurrence: having landed in the wilderness of south Florida the Spaniards shortly discover, remarkably, one of their own living in relative contentment with the local people.*

From *Purchas His Pilgrimes* (vol. XVII), edited by Samuel Purchas (Glasgow: Maclehose, 1906).

On Sunday the eighteenth of May, in the yeere of our Lord 1539. the Adelantado or President departed from Havana in Cuba with his fleet, which were nine vessels, five great shippes, two Caravels, and two Brigantines: they sayled seven dayes with a prosperous wind. The five and twentieth day of May, the day de Pasca de Spirito Santo (which we call Whitson Sunday [Hakluyt's note]) they saw the Land of Florida; and because of the shoalds, they came to an anchor a league from the shoare. On Friday the thirtieth of May they landed in Florida, two leagues from a Towne of an Indian Lord, called Ucita. They set on Land two hundred and thirteene Horses, which they brought with them, to unburden the ships, that they might draw the lesse water. He landed all his men, and only the Seamen remained in the ships, which in eight daies, going up with the tide everie day a little, brought them up unto the Towne. As soone as the people were come on shore, he pitched his Campe on the Sea side, hard upon the Bay which went up unto the Towne . . . [Several days later] they came to the Towne of Ucita, where the Governour was, on Sunday the first of June, being Trinitie Sunday. The Towne was of seven or eight houses. The Lords house stood neere the shoare upon a very high Mount, made by hand for strength. At another end of the Towne stood the Church, and on the tip of it stood a fowle made of wood with gilded eies. Here we found some Pearles of small value, spoiled with the fire, which the Indians doe pierce and string them like Beads, and weare them about their neckes and hand-wrists, and they esteeme them very much. The houses were made of Timber, and covered with Palme leaves.

From the Towne of Ucita the Governour sent Alcalde Major Baltasar de Gallegos with fortie Horsemen and eightie Footmen into the Countrie to see if they could take any Indians: and the Captaine John Rodriguez Lobillo another way with fiftie Footmen. John Rodriguez Lobillo returned to the Campe with six men wounded, whereof one died, and brought the foure Indian women, which Baltasar Gallegos had taken in the Cabbins or Cottages. Two leagues from the Towne, comming into the plaine field, he espied ten or eleven Indians, among whom was a Christian, which was naked and scorched with the Sunne, and had his armes razed after the manner of the Indians, and differed nothing at all from them. And as soone as the Horsemen saw them they ranne toward them. The Indians fled, and some of them hid themselves in a Wood, and they overtooke two or three of them which were wounded: and the Christian seeing an Horseman runne upon him with his Lance began to crie out, Sirs, I am a Christian, slay mee not, nor these Indians, for they have saved my life. And straight way hee called them, and put them out of feare, and they came forth of the Wood unto them. The Horsemen tooke both the Christian and the Indians up behind them; and toward night came into the Campe with much joy: which thing being knowne by the Governour, and them that remained in the Campe, they were received with the like.

The Christians name was John Ortiz, and hee was borne in Sivill, of Worshipfull Parentage. He was tweleve yeeres in the hands of the Indians. He came into this Countrie with Pamphilo de Narvaez; and returned in the ships to the Iland of Cuba . . . and returned backe againe to Florida [where he was captured by the Indians] while ashore . . . and those of the Brigandine sought not to land, but put themselves to Sea, and returned to the Iland of Cuba. Ucita commanded to bind John Ortiz hand and foot upon foure stakes aloft upon a raft, and to make a fire under him, that there he might bee burned: But a daughter of his desired him that he would not put him to death, alleaging, that one only Christian could do him neither hurt nor good, telling him, that it was more for his honour to keepe him as a Captive. And Ucita granted her request, and commanded him to be cured of his wounds: and as soone as he was whole, he gave him the charge of the keeping of the Temple: because that by night the Wolves did carrie away the dead corpses out of the same [Ortiz later fell into disfavor with Ucita and went to live with another tribe, the Mococo, for nine years.]

5

A Briefe Narration of the Destruction of the Indies by the Spaniards

BARTHOLOMEW DE LAS CASAS
(circa 1542)

*Bartholomew de las Casas (1474–1566) was the first promi-
nent intellectual to expose the oppression of the Amerindians
and demand the abolition of Amerindian slavery. For over half
a century after his ordination as a Dominican priest in 1512 or 1513, las Casas
worked tirelessly in the Caribbean to transform the colonial society into something
worthy of the high ideals expressed in its religion. Although his history of the
Conquest was not published—at his request—until after his death, the book
inspired later social and political reformers, including Simon Bolivar and the
leaders of the Mexican revolution. Today las Casas can be seen as the father of all
those who have since sought to provide a voice for the voiceless and to defend the
principles of universal equality and freedom. In this selection, las Casas paints a
disturbing picture of the conquest in general and of the situation on Hispaniola in
particular; the veracity of his account is underscored by the fact that las Casas was
physically present in the region during this period, and was a firsthand observer of
some of the atrocities he relates.*

From *Purchas His Pilgrimes* (vol. XVIII), edited by Samuel Purchas (Glasgow: Maclehose, 1906).

Introduction

The Indies were discovered the yeere 1492. and inhabited by the Spanish the yeere next after ensuing: so as it is about fortie nine yeeres sithence that the Spaniards some of them went into those parts. And the first Land that they entred to inhabite, was the great and most fertile Ile of Hispaniola, which containeth six hundred leagues in compasse. There are other great and infinite Iles round about, and in the Confines on all sides: which we have seene the most peopled, and the fullest of their owne native people, as any other Countrie in the World may be. The firme Land lying off from this Iland two hundred and fiftie leagues, and somewhat over at the most, containeth in length on the Sea Coast more then daily be discovered more and more, all full of people, as an Emmote hill of Emmots. Insomuch, as by that which since, unto the yeere the fortieth and one hath beene discovered: It seemeth that God hath bestowed in that same Countrie, the gulfe or the greatest portion of Mankind.

God created all these innumerable multitudes in every sort, very simple, without subtletie, or craft, without malice, very obedient, and very faithfull to their naturall Liege Lords, and to the Spaniards whom they serve, very humble, very patient, very desirous of peace making, and peacefull, without brawles and strugglings, without quarrels, without strife, without rancour or hatred, by no meanes desirous of revegement. . . . Upon these Lambes so meeke, so qualified and endued of their Maker and Creator, as that bin said, entred the Spanish incontinent as they knew them, as, Wolves, as Lions, and as Tigres most cruell of long time famished: and have not done in those quarters these fortie yeeres past, neither yet doe at this present, ought else save teare them in pieces, kill them, martyr them, afflict them, torment them, and destroy them by strange sorts of cruelties never neither seene, nor read, nor heard of the like (of the which some shall be set down hereafter) so far forth that of above three Millions of soules that were in the Ile of Hispaniola, and that we have seene, there are not now two hundred natives of the Countrey. The Ile of Cuba, the which is in length as farre as from Valladolid untill Rome, is at this day as it were all waste. Saint Johns Ile [Puerto Rico], and that of Jamayca, both of them very great, very fertill, and very faire, are desolate. . . .

At touching the maine firme land [mainland], we are certaine that our Spaniards, by their cruelties and cursed doings have dispeopled and made desolte more then ten Realmes greater then all Spaine, comprising also therewith Aragon & Portugall, and twise as much or more land then there is from Sevill to Jerusalem, which are above a thousand leagues: which Realmes

49

as yet unto this present day remaine in a wildernesse and utter desolation, having bin before time as well peopled as was possible. We are able to yeelde a good and certaine accompt, that there is within the space of the said fortie yeares, by those said tyrannies and divellish doings of the Spaniards, done to death unjustly and tyrannously more than twelve Millions of soules, men, women, and children. And I doe verily beleeve, and thinke not to mistake therein, that there are dead more then fifteene Millions of soules.

The cause why the Spanish have destroyed such an infinite of soules, hath beene onely, that they have held it for their last scope and marke to get Gold [i.e., many of these people were enslaved to work in the gold mines], and to enrich themselves in a short time, and to mount at one leape to very high estates, in no wise agreeable to their persons: or to say in a word, the cause hereof hath beene their avarice and ambition. And by this meanes have died so many Millions without faith and without Sacraments.

Of the Ile of Hispaniola

In the Ile Hispaniola, which was the first (as we have said) where the Spaniards arrived, began the great slaughters and spoyles of people: the Spaniards begun to take their wives and children of the Indies, for to serve their turne and to use them ill, and having begun to eate their victuals, gotten by their sweat and travel. . . . Now after sundry other forces, violences, and torments, which they wrought against them: the Indians began to perceive that those were not men discended from heaven. Some of them therefore hid their victuals, others hid their wives and children, some others fled into the Mountaines, to separate themselves a farre off from a Nation of so hard natured and ghastly conversation. The Spaniards buffeted them with their fists and bastonades: pressing also to lay hands upon the Lords of the Townes. And these cases ended in so great an hazard and desperatenesse, that a Spanish Captaine durst adventure to ravish forcibly the wife of the greatest King and Lord of this Ile. Since which time the Indians began to search meanes to cast the Spaniards out of their lands, and set themselves in armes: but what kinde of armes? very feeble and weake to withstand or resist, and of lesse defence. The Spaniards with their Horses, their Speares and Lances, began to commit murders, and strange cruelties: they entred into Townes, Borowes, and Villages, sparing neither children nor old men, neither women with child, neither them that lay In, but that they ripped their bellies, and cut them in peeces, as if they had beene opening of Lambes shut up in their fold. They laid wagers with such as with one thrust of a sword would paunch or bowell a man in the middest, or with one blow of a sword would most readily and most deliverly cut off his head, or that would best pierce his entrals at one stroake. They tooke the little soules by the heeles, ramping them from the mothers dugges, and crushed their heads against the clifs. Others they cast into the Rivers laughing and mocking, and when they tumbled into the water, they said, now shift for thy selfe such a ones corpes. They put others, together with their mothers, and all that they met, to the edge of the sword. They made certaine Gibbets long and low, in such sort, that the feete of the hanged on, touched in a manner the ground, every one for thirteene, in honour and worship of our Saviour and his twelve Apostles (as they used to speake) and setting to fire, burned them all quicke that were fastened. . . . And forasmuch, as all the people which could flee, hid themselves in the Mountaines, and mounted on the tops of them, fled from the men so without all manhood, emptie of all pitie, behaving them as savage beasts, the slaughters and deadly enemies of mankine: they taught their Hounds, fierce Dogs, to teare them in peeces at the first view. . . .

6

The Sea Turtles of the Caribbean Islands

PIETRO MARTIRE D'ANGHIERA
(1555)

Peter Martyr, also known as Pietro Martire d'Anghiera (dates unavailable), published The Decades of the Newe Worlde or West India *in London in 1555. The* Decades *was only the second book printed in English to describe the New World, and consists of a series of letters addressed to various Catholic officials, including Pope Leo X. The English editor of the collection was Richard Eden, who in translating and printing this book, as well as selections from Gonzalo de Oviedo, Amerigo Vespucci, and López de Gómara, anticipated the later work of Hakluyt and Purchas in assembling important accounts of travel and discovery. In this selection Martyr describes the sea turtles of Portus Bellus Island, which is located off the southern coast of Hispaniola and is today known as Isla Beata. Most ominous here is the reference to "the fleshse of these tortoyles" which, Martyr observes, is said "to be equall with veale in taste." In fact, as Archie Carr later relates in his selection, the decline of the sea turtle was directly related to the popularity of its meat, as well as its eggs, as food delicacies.*

From *The Decades of the New Worlde or West India* (London, 1555), translated by Richard Eden, 1555.

On the lefte syde of *Hispaniola* towarde the Southe, neare unto the haven *Beata,* there lythe an Islande named *Portus Bellus.* They tell marvelous thynges of the monsters of the sea aboute this Island, and especially of the tortoyies. For they saye that they are bygger then greate rounde targettes. At suche tyme as the heate of nature moveth theym too generation, they coome foorthe of the sea: And makynge a deepe pytte in the sande, they laye three or foure hudreth egges therein. When they have thus emptied their bagge of conception, they putte as much of the sande ageyne into the pytte, as maye suffyce to cover the egges: And soo resorte ageyne to the sea, nothynge carefull of their succession. At the daye appopynted of nature to the procreation of these beautes, there escapeth owte a multitude of tortoyles, as it were pis-semares swarming owte of an ante hyll: And this onely by the heate of the soonne withowte any helpe of their parentes. They saye that their egges are in maner as bygge as geese egges. They also compare the fleshse of these tortoyles, to be equall with veale in taste.

7

*T*he Voiage of Captain René Laudonniere to Florida

RENÉ LAUDONNIERE
(circa 1564)

During the middle of the sixteenth century there was a civil war in France between the Catholics and the Protestants. As a result of this conflict, the persecuted Huguenots sought to form a Protestant colony in the New World, much as the English Puritans would succeed in doing in Massachusetts in 1620. Captain René Laudonniere (no dates available), one of the earliest French explorers of the Caribbean, was placed in command of three vessels and dispatched by King Charles IX of France in 1564 as a part of this effort. The expedition, which departed Dieppe on February 15, 1562, reached the island of Dominica in the West Indies in late May, following layovers first in England and then in the Canary Islands. After encountering many difficulties in Florida—to the extent that he was provided some assistance by Sir John Hawkins later in 1564—Laudonniere finally managed to return to France in 1566, where he met with the displeasure of the throne and soon disappeared from view. The Laudonniere account is of particular interest here because, being somewhat marooned among the Floridians, the Captain and his men were compelled to come to terms with a culture alien from their own, and learn to relate to nature in a manner distinct from their previous experience. "Briefly," Laudonniere writes, "the place is so pleasant, that those which are melancholicke would be inforced to change their humour." Such is the power of nature, when viewed not from the hubris of empire but from the humility of one trying to survive.

From *Hakluyt's Voyages* (vol. ix), edited by Richard Hakluyt (Glasgow: Maclehose, 1904).

Of Dominica

Dominica is one of the fayrest Islands of the West, full of hilles, and of very good smell. Whose singularities desiring to know as we passed, and seeking also to refresh our selves with fresh water, I made the Mariners cast anker, after we had sayled about halfe along the coast thereof. As soone as we had cast anker, two Indians (inhabitants of that place) sayled toward us in two Canoas full of a fruite of great excellencie which they call Ananas. As they approached unto our Barke, there was one of them which being in some misdoubt of us, went back againe on land, and fled his way with as much speede as he could possible. Which our men perceived and entred with diligence into the other Canoa, wherein they caught the poore Indian, & brought him unto me. But the poore fellow became so astonied in beholding us, that he knew not which way to behave himselfe, because that (as afterward I understood) he feared that he was fallen into the Spaniards hands, of whom he had bene taken once before, and which, as he shewed us, had cut of his stones [testicles]. At length this poore Indian was secure of us, and discoursed unto us of many things, whereof we received very small pleasure, because we understood not his minde but by his signes. Then he desired me to give him leave to depart, and promised me a thousand presents, whereunto I agreed on condition that he would have patience untill the next day, when I purposed to goe on land, where I suffered him to depart after I had given him a shirte, and certaine small trifles, wherewith he departed very well contented from us.

The place where we went on shore was hard by a very high Rocke, out of which there ran a little river of sweet and excellent good water: by which river we stayed certaine dayes to discover the things which were worthy to be seene, and traffiqued dayly with the Indians: which above all things besought us that none of our men should come neere their lodgins nor their gardens, otherwise that we should give them great cause of jelousie, and that in so doing, wee should not want of their fruite which they call Ananas, whereof they offered us very liberally, receiving in recompence certaine things of small value. This notwithstanding, it happened on a day that certaine of our men desirous to see some new things in these strange countries, walked through the woods: and following still the litle rivers side, they spied two serpents of exceeding bignes, which went side by side overthwart the way. My souldiers went before them thinking to let them from going into the woods: but the serpents nothing at all astonied at these gestures glanced into the bushes with fearfull hyssings: yet for all that, my men drew their swords and killed them, and found them afterward 9 great foote long, and as big as a mans leg. During this combate, certaine others more undiscreete went and gathered their Ananas in the Indians gardens, trampling through them without any discretion: and not therewithall contented they went toward their dwellings; whereat the Indians were so much offended, that without regarding anything they rushed upon them and discharged their shot, so that they hit one of my men named Martine Chaveau, which remained behind. We could not know whether hee were killed on the place, or whether he were taken prisoner: for those of his company had inough to doe to save themselves without thinking of their companion [Laudioniere's party then departs Dominica and sails north toward New France, landing in Florida at about 30° north latitude on June 22, 1564. Laudionierre is introduced to the father of the local chieftain, who, he reports, is 250 years old.] . . .

Afterward they questioned with him [the local chieftain] concerning the course of his age: whereunto he made answere, shewing that he was the first living originall, from whence five generations were descended, as he shewed unto them by another olde man that sate directly over against him, which farre exceeded him in age. And this man was his father, which seemed to be rather a dead carkeis then a living body: for his sinews, his veines, his artiers, his bones, and other parts, appeared so cleerely thorow his skinne, that a man might easily tell them, and discerne them one from another. Also his age was so great, that the good man had lost his sight, and could not speake one onely word but with exceeding great paine. Monsieur de Ottigni having seene so strange a thing, turned to the yoonger of these two olde men, praying him to vouchsafe to answere him to that which he demanded touching his age. Then the olde man called a company of Indians, and striking twise upon his thigh, and laying his hand upon two of them, he shewed him by signes, that these two were his sonnes: againe smiting upon their thighes, he shewed him others not so olde, which were the children of the two first, which he continued in the same maner untill the fifth generation. But though this olde man had his father alive more olde then himself, and that both of them did weare their haire very long, and as white as was possible, yet it was tolde them, that they might yet live thirtie or fortie yeeres more by the course of nature: although the younger of them both was not less then two hundred and fiftie yeeres olde. After he had ended his communication, hee comaunded two young Egles to be given to our men, which he had bred up for his pleasure in his house. Hee caused also little Paniers made of Palme leaves full of Gourds red and blew to bee delivered unto them. For recompence of which presents he was satisfied with French toys. . . .

Now was I determined to search out the qualities of the hill [on which we were staying]. Therefore I went right to the toppe thereof, where we found nothing else but Cedars, Palme, and Baytrees of so sovereigne odour, that Baulme smelleth nothing like in comparison. The trees were environed rounde about with Vines bearing grapes in such quantitie, that the number would suffice to make the place habitable. Besides this fertilitie of the soyle for Vines, a man may see Esquine wreathed about the shurbs in great quantitie.

Touching the pleasure of the place, the Sea may bee seene plaine and open from it, and more then sixe great leagues off, neere the River Belle, a man may beholde the medowes divided asunder into Iles and Islets enterlacing one another: Briefly the place is so pleasant, that those which are melancholicke would be inforced to change their humour.

The Second Voyage Made by Sir John Hawkins Knight

JOHN HAWKINS
(circa 1564)

Sir John Hawkins (1532–1595) has some notoriety in history for being the first Englishman to bring slaves from West Africa to the Caribbean. That first voyage occurred in 1562–63, and involved some 300 Africans whom Hawkins traded to the Spanish in Hispaniola for sugar, pearls, animal hides, and ginger. It was on the larger expedition in 1564 that Hawkins relieved Captain Laudonniere, who was in some distress in Florida, before returning to Plymouth. During the 1570s and 1580s Hawkins served as treasurer and comptroller of the English Navy, and is often cited by historians as having successfully prepared that Navy for its famous encounter with the Spanish Armada in 1588. As a result of his distinguished conduct during that naval battle, Hawkins was knighted. Hawkins and Drake sailed for the West Indies in 1595 in an attempt to interdict Spanish trade; both died on that expedition, much to the dismay of the English court. These early accounts often attest to the former abundance of wildlife in the Caribbean—Hawkins relates here that on the Tortugas (Cayman Islands) he "found such a number of birds, that in halfe an houre he laded [loaded] her [his landing boat] with them; and if they had beene ten boats more, they might have done the like." Upon rescuing the Laudonierre expedition in Florida, Hawkins reports that, "The ground yeeldeth naturally grapes in great store, for in the time that the Frenchmen were there, they made 20 hogsheads of wine." The French also showed the English "pieces of unicornes hornes," which the French obtained in trade from the Indians. "Of those unicornes they have many," Hawkins observed.

From *Hakluyt's Voyages* (vol. x), edited by Richard Hakluyt (Glasgow: Maclehose, 1904).

The fifth of July we had sight of certeine Islands of sand, called the Tortugas (which is lowe land) where the captaine went in with his pinnesse, and found such a number of birds, that in halfe an houre he laded her with them; and if they had beene ten boats more, they might have done the like. These Islands beare the name of Tortoises, because of the number of them, which there do breed, whose nature is to live both in the water and upon land also, but breed onely upon the shore; in making a great pit wherein they lay egges, to the number of three or foure hundred, and covering thm with sand, they are hatched by the heat of the Sunne; and by this meanes commeth the great increase. Of these we tooke very great ones, which have both backe and belly all of bone, of the thicknes of an inch: the fish whereof we proved, eating much like veale; and finding a number of egges in them, tasted also of them, but they did eat very sweetly. Heere wee ankered six houres, and then a faire gale of winde springing, we weyed anker, and made saile toward Cuba, whither we came the sixt day. . . .

[Hawkins overshoots Havana and twelve days later reaches the southern coast of Florida, where he discovers the marooned company of French explorer Rene Laudonierre and offers assistance to them.]

The Floridians [Natives] have pieces of unicornes hornes which they weare about their necks, whereof the Frenchmen obteined many pieces. Of those unicornes they have many; for that they doe affirme it to be a beast with one horne, which comming to the river to drinke, putteth the same into the water before he drinketh. Of this unicornes horne there are of our company, that having gotten the same of the Frenchmen, brought home thereof to shew. It is therfore to be presupposed that there are more commodities as well as that, which for want of time, and people sufficient to inhabit the same, can not yet come to light: but I trust God will reveale the same before it be long, to the great profit of them that shal take it in hand. Of beasts in this countrey besides deere, foxes, hares, polcats, conies, ownces, & leopards, I am not able certeinly to say: but it is thought that there are lions and tygres as well as unicornes; lions especially; if it be true that is sayd, of the enmity betweene them and the unicornes: for there is no beast but hath his enemy, as the cony the polcat, the sheepe the woolfe, the elephant the rinoceros; and so of other beasts the like: insomuch, that whereas the one is, the other can not be missing. And seeing I have made mention of the beasts of this countrey, it shall not be from my purpose to speak also of the venimous beasts, as crocodiles, whereof there is great abundance, adders of great bignesse, whereof our men killed some of a yard and a half long. Also I heard a miracle of one of these adders, upon the which a faulcon seizing, the sayd adder did claspe her taile about her; which the

French captain [Laudonierre] seeing, came to the rescue of the faulcon, and took her slaying the adder; and this faulcon being wilde, he did reclaim her, and kept her for the space of two moneths, at which time for very want of meat he was faine to cast her off. On these adders the Frenchmen did feed, to no little admiration of us, and affirmed the same to be a delicate meat. And the captaine of the Frenchmen saw also a serpent with three heads and foure feet, of the bignesse of a great spaniell, which for want of a harquebuz he durst not attempt to slay. There be also of sea fishes, which we saw comming along the coast flying, which are of the bignesse of a smelt, the biggest sort whereof have foure wings, but the other have but two. . . . We took also dolphins which are of very goodly colour and proportion to behold, and no less delicate in taste. Fowles also there be many, both upon land and upon sea: but concerning them on the land I am not able to name them, because my abode was there so short. But for the fowle of the fresh rivers, these two I noted to be the chiefe, whereof the Flemengo is one, having all red feathers, and long red legs like a herne, a necke according to the bill, red, whereof the upper neb hangeth an inch over the nether; and an egript, which is all white as the swanne, with legs like to an hearn-shaw, and of bignesse accordingly, but it hath in her taile feathers of so fine a plume, that it passeth the estridge his feather. Of the sea-fowle above all other not common in England, I noted the pellicane, which is fained to be the lovingst bird that is; which rather then her young should want, wil spare her heart bloud out of her belly: but for all this lovingnesse she is very deformed to beholde. . . . Here I have declared the estate of Florida . . . and surely I may this affirme, that the ground of the [other parts of the West Indies] for the breeding of cattell, is not in any point to be compared to this of Florida, which all the yeere long is so greene, as any time in the Summer with us: which surely is not to be marvelled at, seeing the countrey standeth in so watery a climate: for once a day without faile they have a shower of raine; which by meanes of the countrey it selfe, which is drie, and more fervent hot then ours, doeth make all things to flourish therein. And because there is not the thing we all seek for, being rather desirous of present gaines, I doe therefore affirme the attempt thereof to be more requisit for a prince, who is of power able to go thorow the same, rather then for any subject.

9

*T*he Naturall Historie
of the West Indies

JOSEPH ACOSTA
(circa 1588)

The essence of Renaissance humanism was skepticism—to question the received wisdom, to hold the bright fact up against the dim myth, to revolt in every fashion against the otherworldliness of the Middle Ages. The writer in this collection who perhaps best exemplifies this weltanschauung is Joseph de Acosta (1540–1600), a Jesuit priest who explored the Caribbean extensively for over fifteen years before he returned to Spain and published his classic work Historia Natural Y Moral de las Indies (1588). In Acosta's daring challenge of orthodoxy regarding the origin, the dispersal, and the development of species found in the New World, as compared and contrasted with those present in the Old World, we see born the intellectual struggle that would result, three centuries later, in the publication of Charles Darwin's revolutionary work On the Origin of Species (London, 1859). For the first time in twenty centuries, a respected establishment thinker, Acosta, had the courage not only to question Aristotle, but to also, through implication, dispute the authority of the Bible:

> It were a matter more difficult, to shew, and prove, what beginning many and sundrie sorts of beasts had, which are found at the Indies, of whose kinds we have non in this Continent [Europe]. For if the Creator hath made them there, we may not then alleadge nor flie to Noahs Arke, neither was it then necessarie to save all sorts of birds and beasts, if others were to bee created anew. . . . I demand how it is possible that none of their kinde should remayne here? And how they are found there, being as it were Travellers and Strangers?

Of further importance is Acosta's division of his book into "Roots," "Metalls," and "Beastes," which anticipates the triumvirate of sciences that are the foundation of modern natural science: botany, geology, and zoology. Acosta, like Socrates before him, was forever asking simple and straightforward questions, and because of that honesty and tenacity, his book will never grow dusty on the shelf.

From *Purchas His Pilgrimes* (Vol. XV), by Samuel Purchas (London: Hakluyt, 1906).

On the Climate of the West Indies

Considering with my selfe, the pleasing temperature of many Countries at the Indies, where they know not what Winter is, which by his cold doth freeze them, nor Summer which doth trouble them with heat, but that with a Mat they preserve themselves from the injuries of all weather, and where they scarce have any neede to change their garments throughout the yeere. I say, that often considering of this, I find that if men at this day would vanquish their passions, and free themselves from the snares of covetousnesse, leaving many fruitlesse and pernicious designes, without doubt they might live at the Indies very pleasant and happily: for that which other Poets sing of the Elisean fields & of the famous Tempe, or that which Plato reports or feignes of his Atlantike Iland; men should find in these Lands, if with a generous spirit they would choose rather to command their silver and their desires, then to remayne to it slaves as they are. . . .

. . . There are some windes which blow in certaine Regions [of the West Indies], and are, as it were, Lords thereof, not admitting any entrie or communication of their contraries. In some parts they blow in that sort, as sometimes they are Conquerors, sometimes conquered; often there are divers and contrarie windes, which doe runne together at one instant, dividing the way betwist them, sometimes one blowing above of one sort, and another below of an other sort; sometimes they incounter violently one with another, which puts them at Sea in great danger: there are some windes which helpe to the generations of Creatures, and others that hinder and are opposite. There is a certaine winde, of such a qualitie, as when it blowes in some Countrie, it causeth it to raine Fleas, and in so great abundance, as they trouble and darken the aire, and cover all the Sea-shoare: and in other places it raines Frogs . . . The Meridionall [South wind] . . . commonly is raynie and boysterous, and . . . Plinie reports that in Africke it raines with the Northerne winde, and that the Southerne winde is cleere. . . . It is needfull to seeke further, to know the true and originall cause of these so strange differences [differences in moisture and temperature] which we see in the winds. I cannot conceive any other, but that the same efficient cause which bringeth forth and maketh the winds to grow, doth withall give them this originall qualitie: for in truth, the matter whereon the winds are made, which is no other thing (according to Aristotle) but the exhalation of the interior Elements, may well cause in effect a great part of this diversitie, being more grosse, more subtill, more drie, and more moist. . . . But the beginnings of these motions and influences are so obscure and hidden from men, and on the other part, so mightie and of so great force, as the holy Prophet David in his propheticall spirit, and the Prophet Jeremie admiring the greatnesse of the Lord [Psalme 134; Jeremie 10], speake thus, Qui profert ventos de thesauris suis. Hee that drawes the windes out of his Treasures. In truth these principles and beginnings are rich and hidden treasures: for the Author of all things holds them in his hand, and in his power; and when it pleaseth him, sendeth them forth for the good or chastisement of men, and sends forth such windes as he pleaseth: not as that Eolus whom the Poets doe foolishly feigne to have charge of the windes, keeping them in a Cave like unto wilde beasts.

Of Beasts and Fowles in the West Indies

They found of some sorts of beasts that are in Europe, and were not carried thither by the Spaniards. There are Lions, Tigres, Beares, Boares, Foxes, and other fierce and wilde beasts, whereof we have treated in the first Booke, so as it was not likely they should passe to the [West] Indies by Sea, being impossible to swim the Ocean: and it were a folly to imagine that men had imbarked them with them. It followes therefore that this [Old] world joynes with the new in some part: by which these beasts might passe, and so by little and little multiplyed this world. The Lions which I have seene, are not red, neither have they such haire as they usually paint them with. They are grey, and not so furious as they seeme in pictures. The Indians assemble in troupes to hunt the Lion, and make as it were a circle, which they doe call Chaco, wherewith they inviron them, and after they kill them with stones, staves, and other weapons. These Lions use to climbe trees, where being mounted, the Indians kill them with Lances and Crosse-bowes, but more easily with Harquebuzes. The Tigres are more fierce and cruell, and are more dangerous to meet, because they breake forth and assaile men in treason: They are spotted, as the Historiographers describe them. I have heard some report that these Tigres were very fierce against the Indians, yet would they not adventure at all upon the Spaniards, or very little; and that they would choose an Indian in the middest of many Spaniards, and carry him away.

The Beares which in Cusco they call Otoioncos, be of the same kinde that ours are, and keepe in the ground. There are few swarmes of Bees, for that their honycombs are found in Trees, or under the ground, and not in Hives as in Castile. . . . It seemes not hard to beleeve, but is almost certaine, that all these beasts for their lightnesse, and being naturally wilde, have passed from one World to another, by some parts where they joyne, seeing that in the great Ilands [of the West Indies] farre from the mayne land I have no heard that there are any, though I have made diligent inquirie. [Acosta then discusses birds of the New World and concludes that they, too, must have arrived via a land bridge from the Old World.] . . .

It were a matter more difficult, to shew, and prove, what beginning many and sundrie sorts of beasts had, which are found at the Indies, of whose kindes we have non in this Continent [Europe]. For if the Creator hath made them there, we may not then alleadge nor flie to Noahs Arke, neither was it then necessarie to save all sorts of birds and beasts, if others were to bee created anew. Moreover, we could not affirme, that the creation of the World was made and finished in sixe dayes, if there were yet other new kindes to make, and specially perfit beasts, and no lesse excellent then those that are known unto us: If we say then that all these kindes of Creatures were preserved in the Arke of Noah, it followes, that those beasts, of whose kindes wee fine not any but at the Indies, have passed thither from this Continent, as wee have said of other beasts that are known unto us. This supposed, I demand how it is possible that none of their kinde should remayne here? And how they are found there, being as it were Travellers and Strangers? Truly it is a question that hath long held me in suspence. I say for example, if the sheepe of Peru, and those which they call Pacos and Guanacos, are not found in any other Regions of the world, who hath carried them thither? or how came they there, seeing there is no shew nor remaynder of them in al this world? If they have not passed from some other Region, how were they formed and brought forth there? It may bee God hath made a new creation of beasts! That which I speak of these Pacos and Guanacos may be said of a thousand different kinds of birds and beasts of the Forest, which have never beene known, neither in shape nor name; and whereof there is no mention made, neither among the Latines, nor Greekes, nor any other Nations of the World. We must then say, that though all beasts came out of the Arke, yet by a naturall instinct, and the providence of Heaven, divers kins dispersed themselves into divers region, where they found themselves so well, as they would not part; or if they departed, they did not preserve themselves, but in processe of time perished wholly, as we doe see it chance in many things. For if wee shall looke precisely into it, we shall find that it is not proper and peculia alone to the Indies, but generall to many other Nations and Provinces of Asia, Europe, and Affrike, where they say there are certain kindes of Creatures, that are not found in other Regions.

. . . We may likewise consider well upon this subject, whether these beasts differ in kinde, and essentially from all others, or if this difference be accidentall, which might grow by divers accidents. . . . But to speake directly, who so would by this Discourse shewing onely thse accidentall diferences, preserve the propogation of beasts at the Indies, and reduce them to those of Europe, hee shall undertake a charge hee will hardly discharge with his honour. For if wee shall judge the kindes of beasts by their properties, those of the Indies are so divers, as it is to call an Egge a Chestnut, to seeke to reduce them to the knowne kindes of Europe.

10

The Discoverie of the Large, Rich, and Beautiful Empire of Guiana

SIR WALTER RALEIGH
(circa 1595)

Sir Walter Raleigh (1552–1618) was one of the most remarkable figures of the Elizabethan Age: poet, philosopher, historian,
explorer, soldier, courtier, colonizer. A great favorite of Queen
Elizabeth, who teasingly called him "Water" in imitation of his West England
accent, Raleigh founded the first English colony in Virginia and is believed to have
been the person who first introduced the potato and tobacco to England. In 1595 he
led the English expedition to Guiana and ascended the Orinoco River for some 450
miles in search of the elusive Manoa gold mine. Upon the death of Elizabeth in
1603, Raleigh was stripped of all his holdings and imprisoned in the Tower of
London for allegedly playing a role in Lord Cobham's conspiracy. He remained
there for the next thirteen years, writing his celebrated History of the World. After
Raleigh's second and final expedition to Guiana proved a complete failure—his
son was killed and he lost ten of his fourteen ships—he was sent to the Tower of
London and beheaded for attempting to escape. In this selection from the 1595
Discoverie of Guiana Raleigh describes the Orinoco River, which drains north
from Venezuela into the Caribbean Sea. There are Arawaks here, as well as other
Amerindians, who favorably impress Raleigh: "I never [did] behold a more goodly
or better favoured people or more manly." Despite the difficulties presented by
navigating the ever-narrowing river in the extreme tropical heat, Raleigh persists,
and is rewarded with a view of a great waterfall (perhaps Angel Falls) over twenty
miles away: "there appeared some tenne or twelve overfals in sight, every one as
high over the other as Church-tower, which fell with that furty, that the rebound of
water made it seeme . . . a smoke that had risen over some great towne."

From The Principal Navigations, Voyages, Traffiques, and Discoveries of the English Nation
(Vol. IX), by Richard Hakluyt (New York: Macmillan, 1904).

The great river of Orenoque or Baraquan hath nine branches which fall out on the North side of his owne maine mouth: on the South side it hath seven other fallings into the sea, so it disemboqueth by sixteene armes in all, betweene Ilands and broken ground, but the Ilands are very great, many of them as bigge as the Isle of Wight, and bigger, and many lesse. From the first branch on the North to the last of the South, it is at least 100 leagues, so as the rivers mouth is 300 miles wide at his entrance into the sea, which I take to be farre bigger then that of Amazones. All those that inhabit in the mouth of this river upon the severall North branches, are these Tivitivas, of which there are two chief lords which have continuall warres one with the other. . . .

These Tivitivas are a very goodly people and very valiant, and have the most manly speech and most deliberate that ever I heard, of what nation soever. In the Summer they have houses on the ground, as in other places: in the Winter they dwell upon the trees, where they build very artifiall townes and villages, as it is written in the Spanish story of the West Indies, that those people do in the low lands nere the gulfe of Uraba: for betweene May & September the river of Orenoque riseth thirty foot upright, and then are those ilands overflowen twenty foot high above the levell of the ground, saving some few raised grounds in the middle of them: and for this cause they are inforced to live in this maner. They never eat of any thing that is set or sowen: and as at home they use neither planting nor other manurance, so when they come abroad, they refuse to feed of ought, but of that which nature without labour bringeth forth. They use the tops of Palmitos for bread, and kill deere, fish, and porks, for the rest of their sustenance. They have also many sorts of fruits that grow in the woods, and great variety of birds and fowle.

And if to speake of them were not tedious, and vulgar, surely we saw in those passages of very rare colours and formes, not elsewhere to be found, for as much as I have either seene or read. Of these people those that dwell upon the branches of Orenoque, called Capuri and Macureo, are for the most part carpeneters of canoas, for they make the most and fairests canoas, and sel them into Guiana for golde, and into Trinidad for tabacco, in the excessive taking whereof, they exceed all nations; and notwithstanding the moistnesse of the aire in which they live, the hardnesse of their diet, and the great labours they suffer to hunt, fish and fowle for their living; in all my life, either in the Indies or in Europe, did I never behold a more goodly or better favoured people or a more manly. They were woont to make warre upon all nations, and especially on the Canibals, so as none durst without a good strength trade by those rivers: but of late they are at peace with their neighbours, all holding the Spaniards for a common enemy. . . . Those nations what are called Arwacas, which dwell on the South of Orenoque (of which place and nation our Indian pilot was) are dispersed in many other places, and doe use to beat the bones of their lords into powder, and their wives and friends drinke it all in their severall sorts of drinks.

After we departed from the port of these Ciawani, we passed up the river with the flood, and ankered the ebbe, and in this sort we went onward. The third day that we entred the river, our galley came on ground, and stucke so fast, as we thought that even there our discovery had ended, and that we must have left fourescore and ten of our men to have inhabited like rooks upon trees with those nations: but the next morning, after we had cast out all her ballast, with tugging and halling to and fro, we got her aflote, and went on. . . . Every day we passed by goodly branches of rivers. . . . When three dayes more were overgone, our companies began to despaire, the weather being extreame hote, the river bordered with very high trees, that kept away the aire, and the current against us every day stronger then other . . . we were now in five degrees [north latitude].

The further we went on (our victuall decreasing and the aire breeding great faintnesse) wee grew weaker and weaker, when we had most need of strength and abilities. . . . On the banks of these rivers were divers sorts of fruits good to eat, flowers and trees of such variety, as were sufficient to make tenne volumes of herbals: we relieved our selves many times with the fruits of the countrey, and sometimes with fowle and fish. We saw birds of all colours, some carnation, some crimson, orenge-tawny, purple, watchet, and of all other sorts both simple and mixt, and it was unto us a great good passing of the time to beholde them, besides the reliefe we found by killing some store of them with our fowling pieces; without which, having little or no bread, and lesse drinke, but onely the thicke and troubled water of the river, we had beene in a very hard case. . . .

On both sides of this river [Now of the Arwacas], we passed the most beautifull countrey that ever mine eyes beheld: and whereas all that we had seene before was nothing but woods, prickles, bushes, and thornes, here we beheld plaines of twenty miles in length, the grasse short and greene, and in divers parts groves of trees by themselves, as if they had beene by all the arte and labour in the world so made of purpose: and still as we rowed, the deere came downe feeding by the waters side, as if they had beene used to a keepers call. Upon this river there were great store of fowle, and of many sorts: we saw in it divers sorts of strange fishes, and of marvellous bignes: but for largartos it exceeded, for there were thousands of those ugly serpents; and the people call it for the abundance of them, The river of Largartos, in their language. I had a Negro a very proper yoong fellow, who leaping out of the galley to swim in the mouth of this river, was in all our sights taken and devoured with one of those lagartos. . . .

That night we came to an ancker at the parting of the three goodly Rivers . . . and landed upon a faire sand, where wee found thousands of Tortugas egges, which are very wholesome meate, and greatly restoring, so as our men were nowe well filled and highly contented both with the fare, and neerenesse of the land of Guiana which appeared in sight. . . .

When we were come to the tops of the first hilles of the plaines adjoyning to the river, we behelde that wonderfull breach of waters, which ranne down Caroli: and might from that mountaine see the river howe it ranne in three parts, above twenties miles off, and there appeared some tenne or twelve overfals in sight, every one as high over the other as a Church-tower, which fell with that fury, that the rebound of water made it seeme, as if it had bene all covered over with a great shower of raine: and in some places we tooke it at the first for a smoke that had risen over some great towne. For mine owne part I was well perswaded from thence to have returned, being a very ill footeman, but the rest were all so desirous to goe neere the saide strange thunder of waters, as they drew me on by little and little, till we came into the next valley where we might better discerne the same. I never saw a more beautifull countrey, nor more lively prospects, hils so raised here and there over the valleys, the river winding into divers branches, the plaines adjoyning without bush or stubble, all faire greene grasse, the ground of hard sand easie to march on, either for horse or foote, the deere crossing in every path, the birdes toward evening singing on every tree with a thousand severall tunes, cranes and herons of white, crimson, and carnation pearching in the rivers side, the aire fresh with a gentle Easterly winde, and every stone that we stouped to take up, promised either golde or silver by his complexison . . . and yet we had no meanes but with our daggers and fingers to teare them out here and there, the rockes being most hard of that minerall Sparre aforesaide, which is like flint, and is altogether as hard or harder, and besides the veines lye a fathome or two deepe in the rockies . . . yet some of these stones I shewed afterward to a Spaniard of the Caracas, who tolde me that it was El Madre del oro, that is the mother of gold, and that the Mine was farther in the ground.

 11

A Briefe Relation of the Severall Voyages

GEORGE, THE EARL OF CUMBERLAND
(circa 1596)

In A Briefe Relation of the Severall Voyages (*1598*) *of George, the Earl of Cumberland (no dates available), we have one of the earliest descriptions of the Carib people of the Lesser Antilles. Dominica, an extremely mountainous island about halfway between Guadeloupe and Martinique, was one of the last strongholds of the Caribs, who tenaciously defended their homeland well into the eighteenth century. About 1000 mixed-race descendents of the native Carib still live on the 3500-acre Carib Indian Reservation in the highlands of Dominica. In this selection, which Purchas gleaned from various Relations and Journals associated with the Cumberland forays into the West Indies, the author describes in surprising detail—considering this was a military and not a scientific expedition—the life-style of the Caribs.*

From *Purchas His Pilgrimes* (vol. XVI), edited by Samuel Purchas (New York: Macmillan, 1906).

By two in the afternoone wee were come so neere aboard the shoare [of Dominica], that wee were met with many Canoes, manned with men wholly naked, saving that they had chaines and bracelets and some bodkins in their eares, or some strap in their nostrils or lips; the cause of their comming was to exchange their Tabacco, Pinos, Plantins, Potatoes, and Pepper with any trifle if it were gawdie. They were at first supicious that wee were Spaniards or Frenchmen, but being assured that wee were English they came willingly aboard. They are men of good proportion, strong, and straight limmed, but few of them tall, their wits able to direct them to things bodily profitable. Their Canoes are of one Tree commonly in breadth, but containing one man, yet in some are seene two yonkers sit shoulder to shoulder. They are of divers length: some for three or four men that sit in reasonable distance, and in some of them eight or nine persons a rowe. Besides their Merchandise for exchange, every one hath commonly his Bowe and Arrowes; they speak some Spanish words: they have Wickers platted something like a broad shield to defend the rain, raine, they that want these, use a very broad leafe to that purpose, they provide shelter against the raine because it washeth of their red painting, laid so on that if you touch it, you shall finde it on your fingers. . . . Their Oares wherewith they rowe are not laid in bankes as Ship-boates have, but are made like a long Battledoore, saving that their palmes are much longer than broade, growing into a sharpe point, with a rising in the middest of them a good way; very like they are to blades of bigge Westerne Daggers, that are now made with graving. The shankes of these Oares are of equal bignesse, and at the top crosset, like a lame man's crutch. These they use always with both their hands, but indifferently as they finde cause to steere this way or that way. The next morning wee bore in to the North-West end of the Iland, where we found a goodly Bay able to receive a greater Navie then hath beene together in the memorie of this age. There his Lordship found the hote Bathe fast by the side of a very fine River. The Bathe is as hot as either the Crosse-bathe or Kings-bathe at the Citie of Bathe in England, and within three or foure yards runneth into the River, which within a stones cast disburdeneth it selfe into the Sea. Here our sicke men specially found good refreshing. In this place his Lordship staid some six dayes in watering the whole fleet. . . .

That evening and the next morning all our men were brought aboard, and on thursday night our sailes were cut for the Virgines [Virgin Islands]. To describe this Iland [Dominica], it lieth North-west and South-east, the soile is very fat, even in the most negelcted places, matching the Garden-plats in England for a rich blacke molde: so Mountainous (certaine in the places where we came neere the Sea-coasts) that the Vallies may better be called Pits then

Plaines, and withall so unpassably wooddie, that it is marvailous how those naked souls can be able to pull themselves through them, without renting their naturall cloathes. Some speake of more easie passages in the Inland of the Iland, which make it probable that they leave those skirts and edges of their Countrie thus of purpose for a wall of defence. These Hils are apparelled with very goodly greene Trees, of many sorts. The tallnesse of these unrequested Trees make the hils seeme more hilly then of themselves happily they are: for they grow so like good children of some happy civill body, without envie or oppression, as that they looke like a proud meddow about Oxford, when after some irruption, Tems is againe cooched low within his owne banks, leaving the earths Mantle more ruggie and flakie, then otherwise it would have bin; yea so much seeme these natural children delighted with equalitie and withall with multiplication, that having growne to a definite stature, without desire of overtopping others, they willingly let down their boughes, which being come to the earth againe take roote, as it were to continue the succession of their decaying progenitors: and yet they doe continually maintaine themselves in a greene-good liking, through the libertie partly of the Sunnes neighbourhood, which provideth them in that neerenesse to the Sea, of exceeding shores; partly of many fine Rivers, which to requite the shadow and coolenesse they receive from the Trees, give them backe againe, a continuall refreshing of very sweete and tastie water. . . . A Captaine or two watering neere the place where his Lordship first anchored, found a leasure to rowe up a River with some guard of Pikes and Musketers, till they came to a Towne of these poor Salvages; and a poore Towne it was of some twenty cottages rather than Houses, and yet was there a King, whom they found in a wide hanging garment of rich crimson taffetie, a Spanish Rapier in his hand, and the modell of a Lyon in shining Brasse, hanging upon his breast. There they saw their women as naked as wee had seene their men, and alike attired even to the boring of their lippes andeares, yet in that nakednesse, they perceived some sparkes of modestie, not willingly comming in the sight of strange and apparelled men: and when they did come, busie to cover, what should have bin better covered. The Queene they saw not, nor any of the Noble wives, but of the vulgar many; and the Maidens it should seeme they would not have so squemish, for the King commanded his Daughters presence, with whom our Gentlemen did dance after meate was taken away. This withdrawing of their wives seemeth to come of the common jelousie of these people; for (it is reported) that though they admit one man to have many wives, yet for any man to meddle with another mans wife, is punished with death, even among them. And no mervaile if the severitie of law be set instead of many other wanting hinderances. It seemeth that themselves are wearie of their nakednesse, for besides the Kings apparell, they are exceeding desirous to exchange any of their Commodities for an old Waste-coate, or but a Cap, yea or but a paire of Gloves.

It is pretie that they say is the difference twist the habit of a Wife and a Maide. The Maide weareth no garter (and indeed she needeth none) but the Wife is the first night she is married (which is not done without asking at the least the consent of her parents) so straightly gartered, that in time the flesh will hang over the list. The haire of men and women are of like length, and fashion . . . their meates are their fine fruites, yet they have Hennes and Pigges, but it should seeme rather for delight, then victuall: their drinke is commonly water, but they make drinke of their Cassain, better of their Pines (and it should seeme that might be made an excellent liquor,) but the best and reserved for the Kings cup onely of Potatoes: their Bread is Cassain. The last report of them shall bee what I have seen in experience, namely their great desire to understand the English tongue; for some of them will point to most parts of his body, and having told the name of it in the language of Dominica, he would not rest till he were told the name of it in English, which having once told he would repeate till he could either name it right, or at least till he thought it was right, and so commonly it should be, saving that to all words ending in a consonant they always set the second vowell, as for chinne, they chin-ne, so making most of the monasillables, dissillables. But it is time to leave them who are already many leagues of.

PART II

1600–1799

PARADISE LOST: THE AGE OF COLONIZATION

Natural Philosophy flourished first in the East. It was in great Perfection among the *Assyrians, Chaldeans,* and *Egyptians;* and, if their Knowledge of it had been faithfully conveyed to Posterity, we might have expected, that the next Age of Learning in Greece would have been able to have made greater Progress in that noble Science. But, alas! here Philosophy was forced to put on a poetical Dress, adorned by the Poets, its Patrons, with Fables, and enlivened with extravagant Fancies. . . . Nor did the Philosophical Part of it revive, or shew the least Spark of its native Brightness, till *Galileo* in *Italy,* and the great *Bacon* in *England,* became its Patrons. . . . But of late Years [Natural History's] greatest Promoters have been the Royal Society in *England,* and the Academy of Sciences in *France:* By their means, chiefly, has the World received more useful Discoveries and Improvements in one Century, than it had done for many Ages before . . . in pursuing the Study of Nature, and meditating upon the exact Harmony so visible in the Works of the Creation, we are sure to meet with untainted Pleasures. . . .

Griffith Hughes
The Natural History of Barbados
(1750)

1605, Cervantes publishes *Don Quixote*. 1608, Galileo builds telescope. 1611, Shakespeare's *The Tempest* is based on Strachey's account of Bermuda. 1611, King James Bible. 1618, Raleigh executed. 1620, Bermuda Assembly passes law regulating the killing of sea turtles. 1620, Dutch Masters flourish. 1620, potatoes eaten widely in Europe. 1620, eight Caribbean animals extinct since the Discovery, including the Gaudelupe violet macaw, the Puerto Rican giant heptaxodon, and the Haitian isolobodon; many islands infested with rats. 1623, English settle St. Christopher (St. Kitts). 1628, Dutch seize Spanish silver convoy off Cuba. 1634–1640, Dutch take Aruba, Bonaire, and Curacao from the Spanish. 1635, French settle Martinique and Gaudeloupe. 1645, Sugar cultivation enters intense phase, resulting in increased slave trade. 1655, Jamaica becomes a British colony. 1660s, Beginning of European scientific societies. 1665, Robert Hooker writes treatise on the microscope. 1667, Milton completes *Paradise Lost.* 1671, the Danes occupy St. Thomas. 1687, Sir Hans Sloane explores the Caribbean. 1688, the Glorious Revolution in England. 1692, severe earthquakes in Jamaica. 1718–1719, England and France declare war on Spain. 1719, Daniel Defoe publishes *Robinson Crusoe.* 1727, first coffee plantation (an Ethiopian crop) in New World. 1731, Treaty of Vienna. 1733, Molasses Act prohibits American colonies from trading with the French West Indies. 1735, Linnaeus publishes *Systema Naturae.* 1754, first iron-rolling mill in England. 1755, Johnson publishes the *Dictionary.* 1760, slave revolt in Jamaica. 1761, Rousseau publishes *Social Contract.* 1762, Mozart tours Europe as a prodigy. 1762, English occupy Cuba. 1763, Peace of Paris. 1765, St. Vincent's Botanical Gardens formed. 1772, Judge William Murray rules in Somerset case that a slave is free on landing in England. 1775, James Watt perfects the steam engine; the beginning of the Industrial Revolution. 1776, Smith publishes *The Wealth of Nations.* 1776, American colonies declare independence from England. 1779, French seize St. Vincent and Grenada. 1782, English defeat French in naval battle off Gaudeloupe. 1783, Peace of Versailles. 1787, English settlement for freed slaves founded in Sierra Leone. 1789, the French Revolution, which includes a declaration of human rights. 1790s, the beginning of the Romantic Movement.

12

A True Reportory
of the Wracke

WILLIAM STRACHEY
(circa 1610)

Little is known of William Strachey (no dates available), other than the fact that he was shipwrecked on Bermuda in 1609 with Sir George Somers, that he subsequently wrote an account of the ordeal, and that he later composed a narrative pertaining to the Virginia colony. It is generally thought that Strachey's True Reportory of the Wracke, *which reached London in the summer of 1610, influenced William Shakespeare in the composition of his last important play* The Tempest *(1611), which is also based on a shipwreck and contains a reference to the "still-vexed Bermoothes." Strachey here describes the Bermuda Islands in great detail, quickly dispensing with the "Devils Ilands" myth that persists to this day in the "Bermuda Triangle" of popular lore; the islands are, as he relates, not a place of "Devils and wicked Spirits," but, rather, a fairly decent place to live with fresh water, abundant wildlife, and a pleasant climate. Just a few years hence, however, we will see this island paradise contaminated with an infestation of rats in the Norwood selection; in fact, rats would disturb the fragile ecological equilibrium of virtually every Caribbean island. For now, though, the Bermudas represented a much-needed sanctuary from the perils of the sea for these weary Englishmen and English-women.*

From *Purchas His Pilgrimes* (vol. XIX), by Samuel Purchas (New York: Macmillan, 1906).

We found it to be the dangerous and dreaded Iland, or rather Ilands of the Bermuda: whereof let mee give your Ladyship a briefe description, before I proceed to my narration. And that the rather, because they be so terrible to all that ever touched on them, and such tempests, thunders, and other fearfull objects are seene and heard about them, that they be called commonly, The Devils Ilands, and are feared and avoyded of all sea travellers alive, above any other place in the world. Yet it pleased our mercifull God, to make even this hideous and hated place, both the place of our safetie, and meanes of our deliverance.

And hereby also, I hope to deliver the world from a foule and generall errour: it being counted of most, that they can be no habitation for Men, but rather given over to Devils and wicked Spirits; whereas indeed wee find them now by experience, to bee as habitable and commodious as most Countries of the same climate and situation: insomuch as if the entrance into them were as easie as the place it selfe is contenting, it had long ere this beene inhabited, as well as other Ilands. Thus shall we make it appeare, That Truth is the daughter of Time, and that men ought not to deny every thing which is not subject to their own sense.

The Bermudas bee broken Ilands, five hundred of them, in manner of an Archipelagus (at least if you may call them all Ilands that lie, how little soever into the Sea, and by themselves) of small compasse, some larger yet then other, as time and Sea hath wonne from them, and eaten his passage through, and all now lying in the figure of a Croissant, within the circuit of sixe or seven leagues at the moste, albeit at first it is said of them that they were thirteene or fourteene leagues; and more in longitude as I have heard. For no greater distance is it from the Northwest Point to Gates his Bay, as by this Map your Ladyship may see, in which Sir George Summers, who coasted in his Boat about them all, tooke great care to expresse the same exactly and full, and made his draught perfect for all good occassions, and the benefit of such, who either in distresse might be brought upon them, or make saile this way. . . .

These Ilands are often afflicted and rent with tempests, great strokes of thunder, lightning and raine in the extreamity of violence: which (and it may well bee) hath so sundred and torne down the Rockies, and whurried whole quarters of Ilands into the maine Sea (some sixe, some seven leagues, and is like in time to swallow them all) so as even in that distance from the shoare there is no small danger of them and with them, of the stormes continually raging from them, which once in the full and change commonly of every Moone (Winter or Summer) keepe their unchangeable round, and rather thunder then blow from every corner about them, sometimes fortie eight houres together: especially if the circle, which the Philosophers call Halo were (in our being there) scene about the Moone at any season, which bow indeed appeared there often, and would bee of a mightie compasse and breadth. . . .

Well may the Spaniards, and these Biscani Pilots, with all their Traders into the Indies, passe by these Ilands as afraid (either bound out or home-wards) of their very Meridian, and leave the fishing for the Pearle (which some say, and I beleeve well is as good there, as in any of their other Indian Ilands, and whereof we had some triall) to such as will adventure for them. The Seas about them are so ful of breaches, as with those dangers, they may well be said to be the strongest situate in the world. . . . There is one onely side that admits so much as hope of safetie by many a league, on which (as before described) it pleased God to bring us, wee had not come one man of us else a shoare, as the weather was: they have beene ever therefore left desolate and not inhabited.

The soile of the whole Iland is one and the same, the mould, dark, red, sandie, dry, and uncapable I beleeve of any of our commodities or fruits. Sir George Summers in the beginning of August, squared out a Garden by the quarter, the quarter being set downe before a goodly Bay . . . and sowed Muske Melons, Pease, Onyons, Raddish, Lettice, and many English seeds, and Kitchen Herbes. All which in some ten daies did appeare above ground, but whether by the small Birds, of which there be many kindes, or by Flies (Wormes I never saw any, nor any venomous thing, as Toade, or Snake, or any creeping beast hurtfull, onely some Spiders, which as many affirme are signes of great store of Gold: but they were long and slender legge Spiders, and whether venomous or no I know not; I beleeve not, since wee should still find them amongst our llinen in our Chests, and drinking Cans; but we never received any danger from them: A kind of Melontha, or blacke Beetell there was, which bruised, gave a savour like many sweet and strong gums punned together) whether, I say, hindred by these, or by the condition or vice of the soyle they came to no proofe, nor thrived. It is like enough that the commodi-ties of the other Westerne Ilands would prosper there, as Vines, Lemmons, Oranges, and Sugar Canes: Our Governour made triall of the later, and buried some two or three in the Garden mould, which were reserved in the wracke amonst many which wee caried to plant here in Virginia, and they beganne to grow, but the Hogs breaking in, both rooted them up and eate them: there is not through the whole Ilands, either Champion ground, Valleys, or fresh Rivers. They are full of Shawes of goodly Cedar, fairer then ours here of Virginia: the Berries, whereof our men seething, straining, and letting stand some three or foure daies, made a kind of pleasant drink: these Berries are of the same bignesse, and collour of Corynthes, full of little stones, and verie restringent or hard building. Peter Martin saith, That at Alexandria in Egypt there is a kind of Cedar, which the Jewes dwelling there, affirme to be the Cedars of Libanus, which beare old fruite and new all the yeere, being a kinde of Apple which tast like Prunes: but then, neither those there in the Burmudas, nor ours here in Virginia are of that happy kind.

Likewise there grow great store of Palme Trees, not the right Indian

Palmes, such as in Saint John Port-Rico are called Cocos, and are there full of small fruites like Almonds (of the bignesse of the graines in Pomgranates) nor of those kind of Palmes which beares Dates, but a kind of Simerons or wild Palmes in growth, fashion, leaves, and branches, resembling those true Palmes: for the Tree is high, and straight, sappy and spongious, unfirme for any use, no branches but in the uppermost part thereof, and in the top grow leaves about the head of it (the inmost part whereof they call Palmeto, and it is the heart and pith of the same Trunke, so white and thing, as it will peele off into pleates as smooth and delicate as white Sattin into twentie folds, in which a man may write as in paper) where they spread and fall downward about the Tree like an overblowne Rose, or Saffron flower not early gathered; so broad are the leaves, as an Italian Ubrello, a man may well defend his whole body under one of them, from the greatest storme raine that falls. For they being stiffe and smooth, as if so many flagges were knit together, the raine easily slideth off. Wee oftentimes found growing to these leaves, many Silkwormes involved therein, like those small wormes which Acosta writeth of, which grew in the leaves of the Tunall Tree, of which being dried, the Indians make their Cochinile so precious and marchantable. With these leaves we thatched our Cabbins, and roasting the Palmito or soft top thereof, they had a taste like fried Melons, and being sod they eate like Cabbedges, but not so offensively thankefull to the stomacke. Many an ancient Burger was therefore heaved at, and fell not for his place, but for his head: for our common people, whose bellies never had eares, made it no breach of Charitie in their hot blouds and tall stomackes to murder thousands of them. They beare a kind of Berry, blacke and round, as bigge as a Damson, which about December were ripe and luscious: being scalded (whilst they are greene) they eate like Bullases. These Trees shed their leaves in the Winter moneths, as withered or burnt with the cold blasts of the North winde, especially those that grow to the Seaward, and in March, there Burgen new in their roome fresh and tender.

Other kindes of high and sweet smelling Woods there bee, and divers colours, blacke, yellow, and red, and one which bears a round blew Berry, much eaten by our owne people. of a stiptick qualities and rough taste on the tongue like a Slow to stay or binde the Fluxe, which the often eating of the luscious Palme berry would bring them into, for the nature of sweet things is to clense and dissolve. A kind of Pease of the bignesse and shape of a Katherine Peare, wee found growing upon the Rockes full of many sharp subtill prickes (as a Thistle) which we therefore called, The Prickle Peare, the outside greene, but being opened, of a deep murrie, full of juyce like a Mulberry, and just of the same substance and taste, wee both eate them raw and baked.

Sure it is, that there are no Rivers nor running Springs of fresh water to bee found upon any of them: when wee came first wee digged and found certaine gushings and soft bublings, which being either in bottoms, or on the side of hanging ground, were onely fed with raine water, which neverthelesse soone sinketh into the earth and vanished away, or emptieth it selfe out of sight into the Sea, without any channell above or upon the superficies of the earth: for according as their raines fell, we had our Wels and Pits (which we digged) either halfe full, or absolute exhausted and dry, howbeit some low bottoms (which the continuall descent from the Hills filled full, and in those flats could have no passage away) we found to continue as fishing Ponds, or standing Pooles, continually Summer and Winter full of fresh water.

The shoare and Bayes round about, when wee landed first afforded great store of fish, and that of divers kindes, and good, but it should seeme that our fiers, which wee maintained on the shoares side drave them from us, so as wee were in some want, untill wee had made a flat bottome Gundall of Cedar with which wee put farther into the Sea, and then daily hooked great store of many kindes, as excellent Angell-fish, Salmon Peale, Bonetas, Stingray, Cabally, Snappers, Hogge-fish, Sharkes, Dogge-fish, Pilcherds-Mullets, and Rock-fish, of which bee divers kindes. . . .

Likewise in Furbushers building Bay wee had a large Sein, or Tramell Net, which our Governour caused to be made of the Deere Toyles, which wee were to carry to Virginia, by drawing the Masts more straight and narrow with Roape Yarne, and which reached from one side of the Dock to the other: with which (I may boldly say) wee have taken five thousand of small and great fish at one hale. As Pilchards, Breames, Mullets, Rocke-fish, &c. and other kindes for which wee have no names. Wee have taken also from under the broken Rockes, Crevises oftentimes greater then any of our best English Lobsters; and likewise abundance of Crabbes, Oysters, and Wilkes. True it is, for Fish in everie Cove and Creeke wee found Snaules, and Skulles in that abundance, as (I thinke) no Iland in the world may have greater store or better Fish. For they sucking of the very water, which descendeth from the high Hills mingled with juyce and verdor of the Palmes, Cedars, and other sweet Woods (which likewise make the Herbes, Roots, and Weeds sweet which grow about the Bankes) become thereby both fat and wholesome. As must those Fish needes bee grosse, slimy, and corrupt the bloud, which feed in Fennes, Marishes, Ditches, muddy Pooles, and neere unto places where much filth is daily cast forth. Unscaled Fishes, such as Junius calleth Molles Pisces, as Trenches, Eele, or Lampries, and such feculent and dangerous Snakes wee never saw any, nor may any River bee invenomed with them (I pray God) where I come. . . .

Fowle there is great store, small Birds, Sparrowes fat and plumpe like a Bunting, bigger than ours, Robbins of divers colours greene and yellow, ordinary and familiar in our Cabbins and other of less sort. White and gray Hernshawes, Bitters, Teale, Snites, Crowes, and Hawkes, of which in March wee found divers Ayres, Goshawkes, and Tassells, Oxen-birds, Cormorants, Bald-Cootes, Moore-Hennes, Owles, and Battes in great store. And upon New-yeeres day in the morning, our Governour being walked foorth with another Gentleman Master James Swift, each of them with their Peeces killed a wilde Swanne, in a great Sea-water Bay or Pond in our Iland. A kind of webbe-footed Fowle there is, of the bignesse of an English greene Plover, or Sea-Meawe, which all the Summer we saw not, and in the darkest nights of November and December (for in the night they onely feed) they would come forth, but not flye farre from home, and hovering in the ayre, and over the Sea, made a strange hollow and harsh howling. Their colour is inclining to Russet, with white bellies, (as are likewise the long Feather of their wings Russet and White) these gather themselves together and breed in those Ilands which are high, and so farre alone into the Sea, that the Wilde Hogges cannot swimme over them, and there in the ground they have their Burrowes, like Conyes in a Warren, and so brought in the loose Mould, though not so deepe: which Birds with a light bough in a darke night (as in our Lowbelling) wee caught. I have beene at the taking of three hundred in an houre, and wee might have laden our Boates. Our men found a prettie way to take them, which was by standing on the Rockes or Sands by the Sea side, and hollowing, laughing, and making the strangest out-cry that possibly they could: with the noyse whereof the Birds would come flocking to that place, and settle upon the very armes and head of him that so cryed, and still creepe neerer and neerer, answering the noyse themselves: by which our men would weigh them with their hand, and which weighed heaviest they took for the best and let the others alone. . . . In January wee had great store of their Egges, which are as great as an Hennes Egge. . . . There are thousands of these Birds, and . . . at anytime (in two houres warning) wee could . . . bring home as many as would serve the whole Company: which Birds for their blindnesse (for they see weakly in the day) and for their cry and whooting, wee called the Sea Owle: they will bite cruelly with their crooked Bills.

Wee had knowledge that there were wilde Hogges upon the Iland, at first by our owne Swine preserved from the wrack and brought to shoare: for they straying into the Woods, an huge wilde Boare followed downe to our quarter, which at night was watched and taken in this sort. . . . in the end (a little businesse over) our people would goe a hunting with our Ship Dogge, and sometimes bring home thirtie, sometimes fiftie Boares, Sowes, and Pigs in a weeke alive: for the Dog would fasten on them and hold, whilest the Hunts-men made in: and there bee thousands of them in the Ilands, and . . . they were well fed with Berries that dropped from the Cedars and Palmes, and in our quarter wee made styes for them, and gathering of these Berries served them twice aday, by which meanes we kept them in good plight. . . . The Tortoyse is a reasonable tootsom (some say) wholesome meate. I am sure our Company liked the meate of them veerie well, and one Tortoyse would goe further amongst them, then three Hogs. One Turtle (for so we called them) feasted well a dozen Messes, appointing sixe to every Messe. It is such a kind of meat, as a man can neither absolutely call Fish nor Flesh, keeping most what in the water, and feeding upon Sea-grasse like a Heifer, in the bottome of the Coves and Bayes, and laying their Egges (of which wee should find five hundred at a time in the opening of a shee turtle) in the Sand by the shoare side, and so covering them close leave them to the hatching of the Sunne, like the Manati at Saint Dominique, which made the Spanish Friars (at their first arrivall) make some scruple to eate them on a Friday, because in colour and taste the flesh is like to morsells of Veale.

13

An Act Agaynst the Killinge of Ouer Young Tortoyses

THE BERMUDA ASSEMBLY
1620

No animal was more important in the exploration of the Americas than the ubiquitous sea turtle. Mariners soon discovered that these large nutritious animals were easily captured, whether on the open sea, in turtle grass lagoons, or on the nesting beaches. This 1620 act of the Bermuda Assembly represents the first instance of governmental intervention on behalf of wildlife conservation in the New World, and predates similar laws to protect waterfowl and big game species in the American colonies by more than a century. Despite such far-sighted environmental measures, the slaughter continued unabated throughout the Caribbean and elsewhere, and today the sea turtles remain a seriously endangered group of animals worldwide.

This Act was appended to Archie Carr's *So Excellente a Fishe* (New York: Charles Scribner's Sons, 1967).

In regard that much waste and abuse hath been offered and yet is by sundrye lewd and impvident psons inhabitinge within these Islands who in their continuall goinges out to sea for fish doe upon all occasions, And at all tymes as they can meete with them, snatch and catch up indifferentlye all kinds of Tortoyses both yonge and old little and greate and soe kill carrye awaye and devoure them to the much decay of the breed of so excellent a fishe, the daylye skarringe of them from of our shores and the danger of an utter distroyinge and losse of them.

It is therefore enacted by the Authoritie of this present Assembly That from hence forward noe manner of pson or psons of what degree or condition soeuer he be inhabitinge or remayninge at any time wthin these Islands shall pseume to kill or cause to be killed in any Bay Sound or Harbor or any other place out to Sea: being wthin five leagues round about of those Islands any young tortoyses that are or shall not be Eighteen inches in the Breadth or Dyameter and that upon the penaltye for euerye such offence of the fforfeyture of fifteen pounds of Tobacco whereof the one half is to be bestowed in the publique uses the other upon the informer.

14

A **Plague of Rats**
Upon Bermuda

RICHARD NORWOOD
(circa 1622)

Richard Norwood (1590?–1675) was dispatched from London in 1616 to conduct a survey of the Bermuda Islands, which were, following the sojourn of the Somers company in 1609– 10, being settled by the newly formed Bermuda Company. This selection, taken from his Relations of Summer Ilands, *which was appended to a detailed map of the Bermudas he produced in 1622, describes a "strange annoyance of Rats," as Norwood described it in classic Elizabethan understatement. The infestation was severe enough that people died because there was no food; Captain John Smith stated in his 1614* Historie of Bermudas, or Summer Ilands *that "The Rat Tragedy was now terrible: some Fishes have been taken with Rats in their bellies, catched as they swam from Ile to Ile."[1] The colonists tried to solve the problem by releasing cats and dogs to prey upon the rodents; this eventually worked, but at a terrible price to the environment, particularly to the indigenous land birds who were decimated by the indiscriminate predation. Although a deadly infestation of rats in retrospect may seem the stuff of a 1950s science fiction movie, it was to these colonists an unbelievable nightmare, the horror of which is vividly related by Norwood.*

1. Smith, John. "Historie of Bermudas, or Summer Ilands." *Purchas His Pilgrimes* (Volume XIX). Ed. Samuel Purchas. New York: Macmillan, 1906, 201.

From *Purchas His Pilgrimes* (vol. XIX), by Samuel Purchas (New York: Macmillan, 1906).

. . . In his time, the Lord sent upon the Countrey, a very grievous scourge and punishment, thretning the utter ruine and desolation of it: That it came from God I need not strive to prove, especially considering it was generally so acknowledged by us at that time: The causes and occasions of it, I need not name, being very well knowne to us all that then lived there, which were about sixe hundred persons, though shortly after much diminished. I will onely shew the thing it selfe, which was a wonderfull annoyance, by silly Rats: These Rats comming at the first out of a Ship, few in number, increased in the space of two yeeres, or lesse, so exceedingly, that they filled not onely those places where they were first landed: But swimming from place to place, spread themselves into all parts of the Countrey. Insomuch, that there was no Iland, though severed by the Sea from all other Lands, and many miles distant from the Iles where the Rats had their originall, but was pestered with them. They had their Nests almost in every Tree, and in all places their Burrowes in the ground (like Conies) to harbour in. They spared not the fruits of Plants and Trees, neither the Plants themselves, but eate them up. When wee had set our Corne, they would commonly come by troupes the night following, or so soone as it began to grow, and digge it up againe. If by diligent watching any of it were preserved till it came to earing, it should then very hardly scape them. Yea, it was a difficult matter after wee had it in our houses, to save it from them, for they became noysome even to the persons of men. Wee used all diligence for the destroying of them, nourishing many Cats, wile and tame, for that purpose, wee used Rats-bane, and many times set fire on the Woods, so as the fire might run halfe a mile or more before it were extinct: Every man in the Countrey was enjoyned to set twelve Traps, and some of their owne accord set neere a hundred, which they visited twice or thrice in a night. Wee trayned up our Dogs to hunt them, wherein they grew so expert, that a good Dog in two or three houres space, would kill fortie or fiftie Rats, and other meanes we used to destroy them, but could not prevaile, finding them still to increase against us.

And this was the principall cause of that great distresse, whereunto wee were driven in the first planting of the Countrey, for these, devouring the fruits of the earth, kept us destitute of bread a yeere or two, so that, when wee had it afterwards againe, wee were so weaned from it, that wee should easily neglect and forget to eate it with our meat. We were also destitute at that time of Boats, and other provision for fishing . . . being destitute of food, many dyed, and wee all became very feeble and weake, whereof some being so, would not; others could not stir abroad to seeke reliefe, but dyed in their houses: such as went abroad were subject, through weaknesse, to bee sudenly surprized with a disease we called the Feages, which was neither paine nor sicknesse, but as it were the highest degree of weaknesse, depriving us of power and abilitie for the execution of any bodily exercise, whether it were working, walking, or what else. . . . About this time, or immediately before, came hither a company of Ravens, which continued with us all the time of this mortalitie, and then departed. There were not before that time, nor since (so far as I heare) any more of them seene there. . . . Yet the Rats encreased and continued almost to the end of Captaine Tuckers time, although hee was provident and industrious to destroy them, but toward the end of his time it pleased God (by what meanes it is not wel known) to take them away, insomuch that the wilde Cats and many Dogs which lived on them were famished, and many of them leaving the Woods, came downe to the houses, and to such places where they use to garbish their Fish, and became tame. Some have attributed this destruction of them to the encrease of wild Cats. . . . Others have supposed it to come to passe by the coolnesse of the weather. . . . It remaineth then, that as we know God doth sometimes effect his will without subordinate and secondary causes, and sometimes against them: So wee need not doubt, but that in the speedy encrease and spreading of these Vermine; as also, in the preservation of so many of us by such weake meanes as we then enjoyed, and especially in the sudden removall of this great annoyance, there was joyned with, and besides, the ordinary and manifest meanes, a more immediate and secret worke of God.

15

The Manatee, or Sea Cow

WILLIAM DAMPIER
(circa 1697)

The life of William Dampier (1652–1715) reads like some
fantastic adventure novel; wherever we look on the globe—
Newfoundland, Sierra Leone, Jamaica, Brazil, the Galapagos
Islands, Australia, the Philippines, China, India—we find this crusty mariner,
whose pursuits ranged from ethnography and oceanography to pirating and
buccaneering. He was court-martialed in 1702 on charges of being cruel and
oppressive to his lieutenant, but in less than a year was commanding another
privateer; he was reputed to be an alcoholic and an incompetent but always seemed
to escape disaster. Dampier's Voyage Round the World, published in 1697, was
an instant best-seller, and went through four printings in two years, and it is from
this book that we read here of the Caribbean manatee, a species that Sir Hans
Sloane would soon describe as being scarce on the island of Jamaica.

From *A New Voyage Round the World,* by Captain William Dampier (London, 1697).

This *Bluefield's* River comes out between the Rivers of Nicargua [sic] and Veranga. At its Mouth is a fine sandy Bay, where Barks may clean: It is deep at its Mouth, but a Shole within; so that Ships may not enter, yet Barks of 60 or 70 Tuns may. It had this Name from Captain Blewfield, a famous Privateer living on *Providence* Island long before *Jamaica* was taken. Which Island of *Providence* was settled by the *English,* and belonged to the Earls of *Warwick.*

In this River we found a Canoa coming down the Stream; and though we went with our Canoas to seek for Inhabitants, yet we found none, but saw in two or three Places signs that *Indians* had made on the Side of the River. The Canoa which we found was but meanly made for want of Tools, therefore we concluded these *Indians* have no Commerce with the *Spaniards,* nor with other *Indians* that have.

While we lay here, our *Moskito* Men went in their Canoa, and struck us some Manatee, or Sea-Cow. Besides this *Blewfield's* River, I have seen of the Manatee in the Bay of *Campeachy,* on the Coasts of *Bocca del Drago,* and *Bocco del Toro,* in the River of *Darien,* and among the South Keys or little islands of *Cuba.* I have heard of their being found on the North of *Jamaica* a few, and in the Rivers of *Surinam* in great Multitudes, which is a very low Land. I have seen of them also at *Mindanea* one of the *Philippine* Islands, and on the Coast of *New Holland.* This Creature is about the Bigness of a Horse, and 10 or 12 foot long. The Mouth of it is much like the Mouth of a Cow, having great thick Lips. The Eyes are no bigger than a small Pea; the Ears are only two small holes on each side of the Head. The Neck is short and thick, bigger than the Head. The biggest Part of this Creature is at the Shoulders, where it hath two large Fins, one on each side of its Belly. Under each of these Fins the Female hath a small Dug to suckle her young. From the Shoulders toward the Tail it retains its beginess for about a Foot, then groweth smaller and smaller to the very Tail, which is flat, and about 14 Inches broad, and 20 Inches long, and in the Middle 4 or 5 Inches thick, but about the Edges of it not about 2 Inches thick. From the Head to the Tail it is round and smooth without any Fin but those two before-mentioned. I have heard that some have weighed above 1200 pounds, but I never saw any so large. The Manatee delights to live in brackish Water; and they are commonly in Creeks and Rivers near the Sea. 'Tis for this Reason possibly they are not seen in the *South-Seas* [South Atlanic] (that ever I could observe) where the Coast is generally a bold Shore, that is, high Land and deep Water close home by it, with a high Sea or great Surges, except in the Bay of *Panama;* yet even there is no Manatee. Whereas the *West-Indies,* being as it were, one great Bay composed of many smaller, are mostly low Land and shoal Water, and afford proper Pasture (as I may say) for the Manatee.

Sometimes we find them in salt Water, sometimes in fresh; but never far at Sea. And those that live in the Sea at such Places where there is no River nor Creek fit for them to enter, yet do commonly come once or twice in 24 hours to the Mouth of any fresh Water River that is near their Place of Abode. They live on Grass 7 or 8 inches long, and of a narrow Blade, which grows in the Sea in many places, especially among Islands near the Main. This Grass groweth likewise in Creeks, or in great Rivers near the Sides of them, in such places where there is but little Tide or Current. They never come ashore, nor into shallower Water than where they can swim. Their Flesh is white, both the Fat and the Lean, and extraordinary sweet, wholesome Meat. The Tail of a young Cow is most esteem'd; but if old both Head and Tail are very tough. A Calf that sucks is the most delicate Meat; Privateers commonly roast them; as they also great pieces cut out of the Bellies of the old ones.

The Skin of the Manatee is of great use to Privateers, for they cut them into Straps, which they make fast on the Sides of their Canoas thro' which they put their Oars in rowing, instead of Tholes or Pegs. The Skin of the Bull, or the Back of the Cow is too thick for this use; but of it they make Horse-whips, cutting them 2 or 3 Foot long: at the Handle they leave the full Substance of the Skin, and from thence cut it away tapering, but very even and square all the four Sides. While the Thongs are green they twist them, and hang them to dry; which in a Weeks time become as hard as Wood. The *Moskito* Men have always a small Canoa for their use to strike Fish, Tortoise, or Manatee, which they keep usually to themselves, and very neat and clean. They use no Oars but Paddles, the broad Part of which doth not go tapering towards the Staff, Pole or Shandle of it, as in the Oar; nor do they use it in the same manner, by laying it on the Side of the Vessel; but hold it perpendicular, griping the Staff hard with both Hands, and putting back the Water by main Strength, and very quick Strokes. One of the *Moskitoes* (for they go but two in a Canoa) sits in the Stern, the other kneels down in the Head, and both paddle till they come to the place where they expect their Game. Then they lye still or paddle very softly, looking well about them; and he that is in the Head of the Canoa lays down his Paddle, and stands up with his striking Staff in his Hand. This Staff is about 8 Foot long, almost as big as a Man's Arm at the great End, in which there is a Hole to place his Harpoon in. At the other End of his Staff there is a piece of light Wood called Bobwood, with a Hole in it, through which the small End of the Staff comes; and on this piece of Bobwood there is a Line of 10 or 12 Fathom wound neatly about, and the End of the Line made fast to it. The other End of the Line is made fast to the Harpoon, which is at the great End of the Staff, and the *Moskito* Men keeps about a Fathom of it loose in his Hand. When he strikes, the Harpoon presently comes out of the Staff, and as the Manatee swims away, the Line runs off from the Bob; and altho' at first both Staff and Bob may be carried under Water, yet as the Line runs off it will rise again. Then the *Moskito* Men paddle with all their might to get hold of the Bob again, and spend usually a quarter of an Hour before they get it. When the Manatee begins to be tired, it lieth still, and then the *Moskito* Men paddle to the Bob and take it up, and begin to hale in the Line. When the Manatee feels them he swims away again, with the Canoa after him; then he that steers must be nimble to turn the Head of the Canoa that way that his Consort points, who being in the Head of the Canoa, and holding the Line, both sees and feels which way the Manatee is swimming. Thus the Canoa is towed with a violent Motion, till the Manatee's Strength decays. Then they gather in the Line, which they are often forced to let all go the very End. At length when the Creature's Strength is spent, they hale it up to the Canoa's side, and knock it on the Head, and tow it to the nearest Shore, where they make it fast and seek for another; which having taken, they get on shore with it to put it into their Canoa: For 'tis so heavy that they cannot lift it in, but they hale it up in shole Water, as near the Shore as they can, and then overset the Canoa, laying one side close to the Manatee. Then they roll in, which brings the Canoa upright again; and when they have heav'd out the Water, they fasten a Line to the other Manatee that lieth afloat, and tow it after them. I have known two *Moskito* Men for a Week every Day bring aboard a Manatee in this manner; the least of which hath not weighed less than 600 Pound, and that in a very small Canoa, that three *Englishmen* would scarce adventure to go in. When they strike a Cow that hath a young one, they seldom miss the Calf, for she commonly takes her young under one of her Fins. But if the Calf is so big she cannot carry it, or so frightned that she only minds to save her own Life, yet the young never leaves her till to *Moskito* Men have an opportunity to strike her.

The manner of striking Manatee and Tortoise is much the same; only when they seek for Manatee they paddle so gently, that they make no noise, and never touch the side of their Canoa with their Paddle, because it is a Creature that hears very well. But they are not so nice when they seek for Tortoise, whose Eyes are better than his Ears. They strike the Tortoise with a square sharp Iron Peg, the other with a Harpoon. The *Moskito* Men make their own striking Instruments, as Harpoons, Fish-hooks, and Tortoise-Irons or Pegs. These Pegs, or Tortoise-Irons, are made 4 square, sharp at one End, and not much above an Inch in length, of such a Figure as you see in the Margin. The small Spike at the broad end hath a Line fasten'd to it, and goes also into a Hole at the End of the striking Staff, which when the Tortoise is struck flies off, the Iron and the end of the Line fastened to it going quite within the Shell, where 'tis so buried that the Tortoise cannot possibly escape.

They make ther Lines both for fishing and striking the Bark of the *Maho;* which is a sort of Tree or Shrub that grows plentifully all over the *West*-Indies, and whole Barke is made up of Strings, or Threads very strong. You May draw it off either in Flakes or small Threads, as you have Occassion. 'Tis fit for any manner of Cordage; and Privateers often make their Rigging of it. So much by way of Digression.

16

A New Voyage and Description of the Isthmus of America

LIONEL WAFER
(circa 1699)

Lionel Wafer (1660?–1705?) is reminiscent of Woody Allen's Zelig in the comic film by the same name; for he was a man who was fairly well known in his own time but who is now almost completely forgotten. Wafer is chiefly remembered for his New Voyage and Description of the Isthmus of America, *which was published in 1699, some nine years after his return from the Caribbean. While in the New World he had found employment as a ship's surgeon to several bands of buccaneers; in 1680 he made a crossing of the Panamanian Isthmus in a raid on some Spanish holdings. Wafer seems to have known many of the piratical celebrities of this era, including Sir Henry Morgan and William Dampier. There is some evidence to suggest that Wafer spent time in a Virginia prison (1687–90) for committing acts of piracy. Wafer later returned to London and published the journal that related his exploits in the Caribbean. This book is of interest to anthropologists specializing in the Cuna Indians of Panama because Wafer lived among the Cuna and wrote of their culture, as is evident here. Wafer also describes the pineapple (an indigenous New World fruit), the Panamanian monkeys (in characteristic humor), and the exotic birds of the Darien region (noting that the Cuna kept them as pets). The significant role that nature plays in Wafer's adventure narrative anticipates the later travel writings of William Bartram, in which this form of personal writing would evolve one step closer to becoming a distinctive literary genre, the modern nature book.*

From A *New Voyage Description of the Isthmus of America*, by Lionel Wafer (Oxford: Hakluyt Society, 1934).

The Pineapple

On the *Isthmus* grows that delicious Fruit which we call the Pine-Apple, in shape not much unlike an Artichoke, and as big as a Mans Head. It grows like a Crown on the top of a Stalk about as big as ones Arm, and a Foot and a half high. The Fruit is ordinarily about six Pound weight; and is inclos'd with short prickly Leaves like an Artichoke. They do not strip, but pare off these Leaves to get at the Fruit; which hath no Stone or kernel in it. 'Tis very juicy; and some fancy it to resemble the Tast of all the most delicious Fruits one can imagine mix'd together. It ripens at all times of the Year, and is rais'd from new Plants. The Leaves of the Plant are broad, about a Foot long, and grow from the Root.

The Monkeys

There are great Droves of *Monkeys,* some of them white, but most of them black; some have Beards, others are beardless. They are of a middle Size, yet extraordinary fat at the dry Season, when the Fruits are ripe; and they are very good Meat, for we ate of them very plentifully. The *Indians* were shy of eating them for a while; but they soon were persuaded to it, by seeing us feed on them so heartily. In the Rainy Season they have often Worms in their Bowels. I have taken a handful of them out of one Monkey we cut open; and some of them 7 or 8 Foot long. They are a very waggish kind of Monkey, and plaid a thousand antick Tricks as we march'd at any time through the Woods, skipping from Bough to Bough, with the young ones hanging at the old ones Back, making Faces at us, chattering, and, if they had opportunity, pissing down purposely on our Heads. To pass from top to top of high Trees, whose Branches are a little too far asunder for their Leaping, they will sometimes hang down by one anothers Tails in a Chain; and swinging in that manner, the lowermost catches hold of a Bough of the other Tree, and draws up the rest of them.

The Parrots, Parakeets, and Macaws

They have *Parrots* good store, some blue and some green, for Shape and Size like the generality of the Parrots we have from *Jamaica*. There is here great variety of them, and they are very good Meat.

They have also many *Parkites* [sic], most of them Green; generally much the same as in other Places. They don't sort with the Parrots, but go in large Flights by themselves.

Macaw-birds are here also in good plenty. 'Tis shap'd not much unlike a Parrot, but is as large again as the biggest of them. It has a Bill like a Hawk's; and a busy Tail, with two or three long stragling Feathers, all Red or Blue. The Feathers all over the Body are of several very bright and lovely Colours, Blue, Green, and Red. The Pinions of the Wings of some of them are all Red, of others all Blue, and the Beaks yellow. They make a great Noise in a Morning, very hoarse and deep, like Men who speak much in the Throat. The *Indians* keep these Birds tame, as we do Parrots, or Mag-pies. But after they have kept them close some time, and taught them to speak some Words in their Language, they suffer them to go abroad in the Daytime into the Woods, among the wild ones; from whence they will on their own accord return in the Evening to the *Indian's* Houses or Plantations, and give notice of their arrival by their fluttering and prating. They will exactly imitate the *Indian's* Voices, and their way of Singing, and they will call *Chicaly-Chicaly* in its own Note, as exactly as the *Indians* themselves, whom I have observ'd to be very expert at it. 'Tis the most beautiful and pleasant Bird that I ever saw; and the Flesh is sweet-tasted enough, but black and tough.

The Villages of the Cuna Indians

Their Houses lie mostly thin and scattering, especially in New Plantations, and always by a River-side. But in some Places there are a pretty many together, so as to make a Town or Village, yet not standing close or orderly, in Rows or Streets, but dispers'd here and there, like our Villages on Commons, or in Woodlands. They have Plantations lying about them, some at a nearer, others at a greater distance; reserving still a Place to build the common War-house [meeting hall] on. They change not their Seats or Houses, unless either for fear of the Neighbouring Spaniards, if they think them too much acquainted with the place of their Abode; or to mend their Commons, when the Ground is worn out of Heart; for they never manure not.

In building, they lay no Foundations, only dig Holes two or three Feet asunder; in which they set small Posts upright, of an equal heighth, of 6, 7, or 8 Foot high. The Walls are walled up with Sticks, and daub'd over with Earth, and from these Walls the Roof runs up in small Rafters, meeting in a Ridge, and cover'd with Leaves of some Trees of the Palm kind.

The Building is all irregular. the Length is about 24 or 25 Foot; the Breadth proportionable. There is no Chimney, but the Fire is made in the middle of the House, on the Ground; the Smoke going out at a hole on the top, or at Crevises in the Thatch. The House is not so much parted into Rooms, as all of it a Cluster of Hovels, joining together into one House. No Stories, no Doors, nor Shelves; nor other Seats, than Logs of Wood. Every one of the Family has a Hammock tied up, hanging from end to end of the Hovel or Room.

Several Houses in a Village or Neighbourhood, have one War-house or

Fort in common to them; which is generally at least 120 or 130 Foot long, about 25 broad, the Wall about 9 or 10 Foot high; and in all to the top of the Ridge about 20 Foot; and cover'd with Leaves as their other Houses. . . . The War-houses serve them also to hold their Councils, or other general meetings.

17

A Voyage to the Islands

SIR HANS SLOANE
(circa 1707)

Sir Hans Sloane (1660–1753) was one of the foremost naturalists of eighteenth-century England. A physician by profession, Sloane succeeded to the presidency of the Royal Society
upon the death of Sir Isaac Newton in 1727 and served in that office until 1741.
After a fifteen-month expedition to the West Indies from 1687–89, Sloane returned to London with 800 species of plants and began to write his masterpiece A
Voyage to the Islands of Madera, Barbadoes, Nieves, St. Christopher's and
Jamaica, with the Natural History of the Last, which was published in two
volumes (1707; 1725). On the basis of the first volume Sloane was elected to the
French Academy of Sciences, the Imperial Academy of St. Petersburg, and the
Royal Academy of Madrid. In 1716 Sloane was made a baronet and was
subsequently appointed first physician to King George II in 1727. Sloane's will
bequeathed his prodigious natural history collection—valued at 50,000 pounds—
to the English nation, and it was this "cabinet of curiosities," together with his
extensive library, that was utilized to form what is now known as the British
Museum. These selections from A Voyage to the Islands describe, successively,
diving for lost Spanish treasure, the Caribbean crocodile, the Caribbean manatee,
and the parrot fish. Both the crocodile and the manatee are now rare in the
Caribbean, while the parrot fish continues to be plentiful. Sloane was the first
prominent scientist of England to devote himself significantly to natural history;
in so doing he conveyed a respectability to the field that probably helped to persuade
other intellectuals—Mark Catesby, Griffith Hughes, William Bartram—to follow
his lead later in the century.

From A *Voyage to the Islands,* by Sir Hans Sloane (London, 1707 and 1725).

Diving for a Wreck

I perused here at *Jamaica,* a Journal of Sir *William Phipps,* which gave an account of the first finding of the great Plate-Wreck to the North-East of *Hispaniola.* After Sir *William Phipps* had been at *Samana,* on the North-side of *Hispaniola,* he went with one *Rogers,* master of a small ship to *Porto Plata,* and there discharging three Guns to get the *Spaniards* to Trade, they came down, and the *English* sold small Bables, and Searges for Hides, and jirked Hogs taken by the Hunters there. In the mean time *Rogers* had been on the Wreck, discover'd it by means of a Sea-Feather [sea fan], growing on the Planks of the Ship lying under water, and brought from thence the news of its being found. They went thither, found it grown over with Coral, and *Lapis Aftroites* [unknown reference], and took up Silver as the Weather and their Divers held out, some days more, and some less. The small Ship went near, the great one rode afar off. At last they got in Bullion 22196 pounds in Coin 30326 of which were Sows, and great Bars 336. After they sail'd for *Turks* Islands for Salt, and going thither, after several hours sailing, had almost been a-ground and wreck'd on the Handkercher Shoal. They about the Wreck were sometimes in seven Fathom water, and immediately almost out of reach of the bottom of sounding.

This Wreck had been a *Spanish* Galeon lost on these Shoals, near the *Abreojos* or *Handkercher* Shoals, to the North East of *Hispaniola,* about the year 1659, bound for *Spain.* The Inhabitants of *Hispaniola,* who used to Trade with Sir *William Phipps,* had acquainted him with it. He proposed the taking up of this Silver to the Duke of *Albemarle,* who together with Sir *James Hayes,* Mr. *Nicholson,* and others, set out two Ships, a greater and a lesser, laden with Goods to Trade with *Hispaniola,* and the *Spaniards* in the *West Indies,* in case they failed of the Wreck. They found this Wreck, as is above related, and wrought on it till the Ships Crew grew scarce of Provisions, when they had taken up about Twenty six Tuns of Silver. A Sloop from *Bermudas* came to their help: when they sail'd for *England* the Sloop return'd to *Bermudas,* and they disclosed the Matter, which soon went to the other islands. From these parts, and *Jamaica,* Sloops and *Divers* were sent, who took up a vast quantity more of Plate and Money, so that before a second Fleet came from *England,* the greatest part of what Silver remain'd unfish'd was taken up. Not only the *English* from the Plantations and England, but the Prince of *Orange,* afterwards King *William,* from *Holland,* equip'd a Ship which was sent thither, but they came too late. Those who commanded the *Dutch* Ship, and Sir *John*

Norborough, who was in the *English,* return'd without any considerable Cargoes of Silver. It happened so not only to the first Patentees, but to many other People, who by the example of this Project (where the Duke of *Albemarle* received Fifty thousand Pound to Eight hundred, and others in proportion) hoping for the same Success, took out Patents for Wrecks lying at the bottom of the Seas in all places, especially in the *West Indies,* where any Traffick is used, not considering that though there have been lost divers Ships laden with Money, on many Shoals of the *West Indies,* such as the *Serranillas* between *Jamaica* and the Continent, the *Bahama* Shoals, etc. yet in most parts there is such a Vegetation of Coralline matter out of the Sea-water, as that the bottom of the Sea incrustated with it, and the Wrecks hid by them. The Pieces of Eight in the Silver-Wreck above mention'd, that was lost in 1659 were covered with this Matter about a quarter of an Inch thick, and I have a piece of the Timber of the Ship, with an Iron Bolt in it, grown over with the *Corallium asperum candicans adulternum* [pre-Linnean classification] J.B. and some of the Pieces of Eight incrustated, others almost covered with *Astroites* [reference unknown]. Those underneath were corroded with the Sea-water, so that many of them stuck together.

The Allagator

They are very common on the Coasts and deep Rivers of *Jamaica,* one of nineteen Feet in Length, I was told was taken by a Dog, which was made use of as a Bait, with a piece of Wood ty'd to a Cord, the farther End of which was fastened to a Bed Post. The crocodile coming round as usual every Night, seiz'd the Dog, was taken by the Piece of Wood made fast to the Cord, drew the Bed to the Window and wak'd the People, who kill'd the Allagator which had done them much Mischief. The Skin was stuffed and offer'd to me as a Rarity and Present, but I could not accept of it because of its Largeness, wanting Room to stow it.

The Manati

This is sometimes taken in the quieter Bays of this Island [Jamaica], tho' rarely now a Days: They have formerly been frequent, but are, by the multitude of People and Hunters catching them, destroy'd. They are caught by the *Indians* who are reckon'd the best Hunters, knowing the Haunts and Customs of their Game, and being very dexterous at it, especially those of the *Musquitoes,* or *Costa Ricca.* The *Manatis* are reckon'd extraordinary Food and are likewise salted as Beef, and eaten as Provision. The powdered hard Stone, or rather Bone is reckoned an extraordinary Medicine in the Stone or Stoppage of Water. . . . They are so large as to require a pair of Oxen in a Cart to carry them, the best Fish in the World, and appear like Beef or Veal. . . .

The Parrot Fish

This was about a Foot long, and nine Inches broad, where broadest near the Head, the *Mandibles* were each two Bones join'd together before, of a fine blue and green Colour. . . . The Stomach and Guts were one, tho' here and there widened, *duct,* the Guts were full of Sand and *Fuci* [unknown reference]. . . . This Fish hath its Name from its Mouth, being like that of a Parrot. It feeds on *submarine* Plants growing on the Rocks. It feeds likewise on Shell-fish, which it bruises with its Mandibles.

18

Robinson Crusoe

DANIEL DEFOE
(circa 1719)

When Daniel Defoe (1660–1731) began to write Robinson
Crusoe *(1719) he was in his late fifties and had suffered
through a long, difficult life that included imprisonment, bank-
ruptcy, and being put in a public pillory. Defoe's famous story of adventure and
survival, which takes place "within the circle of the Caribbee Islands," can be read
at one level as an allegory not only of Defoe's struggle to endure, but also that of his
class, the tradesman and small merchants at the hub of eighteenth-century English
society. What is probably most remarkable about the novel is that Defoe never
visited the Caribbean and vividly created the tropical island solely from his
imagination. In this passage the protagonist explores his island and discovers not
a "howling wilderness" but rather an Edenic garden of profusion in which he
might live in solitary comfort, discovering a happiness far in excess of that which
he had previously enjoyed in society. Nature here is seen as the benefactor of
humanity, and not as its antagonist.*

From *Robinson Crusoe*, by Daniel Defoe (London, 1719).

July 4.

In the morning I took the Bible; and beginning at the New Testament, I began seriously to read it, and imposed upon myself to read awhile every morning and every night. . . . Now I began to construe the words mentioned above, "Call on Me, and I will deliver you," in a different sense from what I had ever done before; for then I had no notion of anything being called deliverance. . . . But now I learned to take it in another sense; now I looked back upon my past life with such horror, and my sins appeared so dreadful, that my soul sought nothing of God but deliverance from the load of guilt that bore down all my comfort.

My condition began now to be, though not less miserable as to my way of living, yet much easier to my mind; and my thoughts being directed, by a constant reading of the Scripture, and praying to God, to things of a higher nature. . . .

From the 4th of July to the 14th, I was chiefly employed in walking about with my gun in my hand, a little and a little at a time, as a man that was gathering up his strength after a fit of sickness; for it is hardly to be imagined how low I was, and to what weakness I was rescued. . . . I had been now in this unhappy island above ten months . . . [and] had a great desire to make a more perfect discovery of the island, and to see what other productions I might find, which I yet knew nothing of.

It was the 15th of July that I began to take a more particular survey of the island itself. I went up the creek, first, where, as I hinted, I brought my rafts on shore. I found after I came about two miles up, that the tide did not flow any higher, and that it was no more than a little brook of running water, and very fresh and good. . . . On the bank of this brook I found many pleasant savannas or meadows, plain, smooth, and covered with grass; and on the rising parts of them, next to the higher grounds, where the water, as might be supposed, never overflowed, I found a great deal of tobacco, green, and growing to a great and very strong stalk. There were divers other plants, which I had no notion of, or understanding about, and might perhaps have virtues of their own which I could not find out.

I searched for the cassava root, which the Indians, in all that climate, make their bread of, but I could find none. I saw large plants of aloes, but did not then understand them. I saw several sugar-canes, but wild, and, for want of cultivation, imperfect. . . . I found [the next day that] the brook and the savannas began to cease, and the country became more woody than before. In this part I found different fruits, and particularly I found melons upon the ground in great abundance, and grapes upon the trees. The vines had spread over the trees, and the clusters of grapes were just now in their prime, very ripe and rich. This was a surprising discovery . . . [and] I found an excellent use for these grapes; and that was, to cure or dry them in the sun, and keep them as dried grapes or raisins are kept. . . . [On the next day] I came to an opening, where the country seemed to descend to the west; and a little spring of fresh water . . . ran . . . and the country appeared so fresh, so green, so flourishing, everything being in a constant verdure or flourish of spring, that it looked like a planted garden.

I descended a little on the side of that delicious vale, surveying it with a secret kind of pleasure . . . to think that this was all my own; that I was king and lord of all this country indefeasibly, and had a right of possession; and, if I could convey it, I might have it in inheritance as completely as any lord of a manor in England. I saw here abundance of cocoa trees, orange, and lemon, and citron trees; but all wild, and very few bearing any fruit, at least not then. . . .

When I came from this journey, I contemplated with great pleasure the fruitfulness of that valley, and the pleasantness of the situation; the security from storms on that side, the water and the wood; and concluded that I had pitched upon a place to fix my abode, which was by far the worst part of the country. Upon the whole, I began to consider of removing my habitation . . . [to] that pleasant fruitful part of the island . . . I fancied now I had my country house and my sea-coast house. . . .

19

Of the Aborigines of America

MARK CATESBY
(circa 1743)

Not only was Mark Catesby (1679?–1749) an important eighteenth-century naturalist, but he was also one of England's finest artists and writers. At the encouragement of Sir Hans Sloane and others, Catesby traveled extensively in South Carolina, Georgia, Florida, and the Bahamas from 1722 through 1726, gathering specimens of fauna and flora and making the preliminary sketches that would serve to illustrate his masterpiece The Natural History of Carolina, Florida, and the Bahama Islands *(London, 1731–48). This book helped to introduce the wealthy literati of France and England—the text was bilingual—to the wonders of nature in the American subtropics, and anticipated the later illustrated books of John James Audubon, as well as the exhibit format series of photographic nature books published by the Sierra Club in this century. In this selection from Catesby's* Natural History *we see an Enlightenment mind wrestling with the geographic origins of the American Indians, speculating on the existence of a point of contact between Asia and America, and noting that "the inhabitants [in America] seem to be the same people." Curiously, this otherwise well-informed thinker doubts the veracity of the Spanish accounts of the Aztecs, and provides some insight into the general state of knowledge during this period.*

From *The Natural History of Carolina, Florida, and the Bahama Islands,* by Mark Catesby (London, 1743).

Concerning the first peopling of *America,* there has been various conjectures how that part of the Globe became inhabited. The most general opinion is, that it was from the Northern Parts of Asia. The distance between the Western Parts of the old World and *America* is too well known to suppose a passage that was practicable from one Continent to the other. The difference from the Eastermost Part of the old World to *America* not being known, there is a probability that the Continent of the North-East Part of *Asia* may be very near, if not contiguous to that of *America;* or according to the *Japonese* Maps in *Sir Hans Sloane's* Museum, the passage may be very easy from a chain of islands at no great distance from each other there laid down. The great affinity of the *Americans* with the *Eastern Tartars* in the resemblances of their features, hair, customs, &c. adds some weight to this conjecture. But, without taking upon me to determine this point, I shall attempt to give some account of these *American Aborigines* as they now exist.

. . . The inhabitants [in America] seem to be the same people . . . this affinity in the *Aborigines* of *America* with one another, holds not only in regard to resemblance, in form and features, but their customs, and knowledge of arts in a manner the same; some little differences may be in the industry of one nation more than others, and a small mechanick knowledge that some may have more than others. I am the more persuaded to this opinion, having had many opportunities of seeing and observing the various nations of *Indians* inhabiting the whole eatent of North *America* from the *Equinoctial* to *Canada,* particularly the *Charibeans, Muskitos, Mexicans, Floridans,* and those extending on the back of all our colonies, the Northermost of which differ no otherwise from the *Charibeans* (who inhabit near the *Equinoctial*). . . .

I have not the like knowledge of the inhabitants of South *America;* but from what I could ever learn of them, the characters of their persons, customs, &c. differ but little from those of the North.

If the relations of *Herrera, Solis,* and other *Spanish* Authors could be relied on, they were, I confess, enough to excite in us an high opinion of the knowledge and politeness of the *Mexicans,* even in the more abstruse arts of Sculpture and Architecture, the darling sciences of the Ancients, and which added such glory to the *Greeks* and *Romans,* whose unparallel'd frabricks still remain a testimony of their superior knowledge in those arts, though above 2000 years have passed since the finishing of some of them. Yet that all those stupendous buildings which the *Spanish* Authors describe, standing at the time of their conquering the city and territory of *Mexico,* should be so totally destroyed, than an hundred years after its conquest there should remain not the least fragment of art or magnificence in any of their buildings; hard fate!

For my own part I cannot help my incredulity, suspecting much the truth of the above-mentioned relations, which (agreeable to the humour of that nation) seems calculated to aggrandize their achievements in conquering a formidable people, who in reality were only a numerous herd of defenceles *Indians,* and still continue as perfect Barbarians as any of their neighbours.

20

Selections from
The Natural History
of Barbados

GRIFFITH HUGHES
(circa 1750)

Griffith Hughes (no dates available), the rector of St. Lucy's Parish on Barbados and a Fellow of the Royal Society, published The Natural History of Barbados *by subscription in* 1750. *Among the subscribers to this fascinating work of natural history were Samuel Johnson in England and William Fairfax and John Lee in the American colonies. Hughes' work transcended its simple herbal/bestiary format and, in its highly literary quality, anticipated Gilbert White's 1789* The Natural History and Antiquities of Selborne, *which has often been cited by scholars as being the first nature book, in the modern sense of the genre. Hughes' Preface to* The Natural History of Barbados *represents one of the first attempts to historically contextualize natural history and natural history writing; Hughes comments on the craft of nature writing:*

> *The historical Description of a Country, like its natural Appearance, must needs be attended with Variety. And as, in travelling over it, we must climb high rocky Hills, and pass through dreary Desarts, as well as open Lawns, and flowery Meads; so the Reader must not always expect to be entertained with beautiful Images and a Loftiness of Style. In Variety of Subjects, this must alter with the Nature of the Things to be described. . . . This I can with Truth say, that I have not represented one single Fact, which I did not either see myself, or had from Persons of known Veracity.*

In the first passage included here Hughes' Deism is evident—the belief that every thing in the Universe had been designed with a specific purpose by the Creator. In the "Doctrine of Design" proof of God, the Deists believed the perfection of physical nature was proof that a benevolent, all-powerful deity had created the kosmos. *Hughes also writes here on the Royal Palm, on corals (thought to be plants), on the "animal flower" (sea anemones were thought to be a cross between plant and animal), and on sharks (an account just incredible enough to be true). There is much in Hughes that is modern, and, prior to William Bartram and Gilbert White, he comes closest to creating the new prose genre of nature writing.*

From *The Natural History of Barbados*, by Griffith Hughes (London, 1750).

Of Land Animals

Animals are sensitive organic Bodies, endued with spontanoues motion. By animals, in the following Book, I would be understood to mean, without descending to minuter unnecessary Divisions, such only as are generally termed Quadrupeds, Volatiles, and Insects.

In each of these may be traced the Workmanship of a Divine Architecture, each formed in Number, Weight, and Measure; without Defect, without Superfluity, exactly fitted and enabled to answer the various Purposes of their Creation, to execute the Will of their Creator, to minister to the Delight and Service of Man, and to contribute to the Beauty and Harmony of the universal System.

How surprising an Instance of Almighty Power, and how wonderful a Piece of Mechanism, is to be seen in some of the minutest Animals! For Instance, the Potato-Louse, an Insect bred upon Vegetables in this Island [Barbados], which is so small, that it is scarce discernible by the naked Eye! Yet this is every way as perfect as an Ox, a Whale, or an Elephant. What less than infinite Wisdom and Power, could dispose a little Portion of Matter, almost too small to be viewed by the naked Eye, into that infinite Variety of Parts that are necessary to form an organic body!

Let us consider how inexpressibly fine, slender, and delicate must the several Parts be, that are necessary to form the Organs, to proportion the Structure, to direct the Machinery, and preserve and supply the vital and animal Action, in one of these very small Animals: Yet every Part that is necessary to animal Life is as truly found in one of them as in *Behometh* and *Leviathan.* I very much doubt, whether any wisdom, but that which framed them, can fully comprehend the Structure, the Symmetry, the Beauties, of such almost imperceptible Generations: and I think it must needs exceed any finite Understanding to conceive, much less explain, how such an infinite Variety of Parts, and Exercise of Powers, could be contained or exerted within so narrow a space.

The Cabbage-tree; *Latin* Palma Maxima [*non-Linnean*]

This Tree is by some Authors called *The Palmeto Royal* [Hughes refers to what is today known as the Royal Palm]. And well may it be called Royal from its great Height, majestic Appearance, and Beauty of its waving Foilage: Neither the tall Cedars of *Lebanon,* nor any of the Trees of the Forest, are equal to it in

Height, Beauty or Proportion; so that it claims among Vegetables [Hughes refers to plants that do not bear fruit as vegetables] that Superiority which *Virgil* gives to *Rome,* among the Cities of *Italy*:

> *Verum haec tantum alias inter caput extulit urbes,*
> *Quantum lenta folent inter viburna cupressi.*
> —First Eclogue

> Imperial *Rome* o'er other Cities tow'rs,
> As lofty Cypress humble Shrubs o'erpow'rs.

Its roots are innumerable, resembling so many round Thongs, of a regular determinate Bigness, seldom exceeding the Size of the little Finger, but of a great Length, penetrating some Yards into the Earth, especially where the Soil is sandy, or otherwise porous: These Roots are of a dark-brown colour.

The Trunk jets or bulges out a little near the Ground, by which means it hath the becoming Appearance of a substantial basis to support its towering Height. It is generally as strait as an Arrow; and scarce can a Pillar of the nicest Order in Architecture be more regular, especially when it is of about Thirty Years Growth: And as there is a natural involuntary Pleasure arising from the Harmony of just geometrical Proportions, striking the Eye of the most unskilful and ignorant Beholder, it is not strange that these Trees are universally admired.

Writers of Wonders represent some of them to be Three hundred Feet in Height: However, the highest in this, where they are more numerous than in any of our neighbouring Islands, is but an Hundred and Thirty-Four Feet. . . .

As there are many Thousand Leaves upon one Tree, every Branch bearing many Scores upon it, and every Leaf being set at a small and equal Distance from one another, the Beauty of such a regular lofty Group of waving Foliage, susceptible of Motion by the most gentle Gale of Wind, is not to be described. . . .

Of Corals

Though these, in general, are Vegetables; yet we are not to look upon them among the lowest Class of this Kind, because they bear, at least here, neither Leaves, Flowers, nor Fruit, having likewise their Consistencies so brittle, that they are neither malleable, nor any ways pliable: However, their innumerable Shoots and Branches are not void of Beauty, nor useless in medicinal Preparations; the white Sort being, when pulverized, esteemed good to free the Stomach from acid sour Juices; and the red Coral is not less efficacious in stopping Fluxes: From the Growth of these, we may likewise observe, that Providence is not tied down in its Operations to mechanical Rules: For among Vegetables, which flourish upon the Surface of the Earth, all our Art and

Contrivance are in vain, unless we can procure them either natural or artificial Heat, and a Communication of Air; whereas these grow to a great Length in above forty Fathom Water, where the Heat of the Sun cannot penetrate. . . .

The Sea-Ginger, or the Palmated Harts-Horn [possibly the Staghorn coral]: This is a digitated Sea-Coral, and is called Ginger from its very hot quality; for if a Piece, newly broken, be apply'd to the Tongue, it tastes excessively hot. It is found in great Plenty upon the Shores in the Island of *Antigua,* as well as among many other Places upon the *Pelican shoal* in this Island [Barbados].

The Hart's-Horn Coral [possibly the Elkhorn coral]: This takes its Name from the great Resemblance its wide-extended Branches have to an Hart's horn, both in Colour and Shape: They grow upon Rocks, at different Depths under Water: The Branches are of a brownish White, but always at the Top sharp-pointed, and tipped with a clear White: They are of so close a Texture, that, when struck by any Piece of hard Wood or Iron, they afford a metallic vibrating Sound: This Sort grows to be often above five Feet in Length. I have likewise seen a lesser Sort, resembling the palmed Hart's-Horn.

The Common Brain-Stone Coral [possibly Brain coral]: *Fungus coralloides encephaloides, gyris in medio fulcatis, lamellatis, ferratis.* Boerh. Ind. Plant. p. 1. *Lapis fungites cerebriformis.* Ray's Hist. App. p. 1850. This, as do many others of the same Species, derives its Name from its Resemblance to the human Brain, the waving white Ribs rising higher than the intermediate Spaces: These Stones are to be seen very common on all our Sea-Shores, as well as on the Land, especially about *Black Rock,* in *St. James's* Parish, and generally near the Sea.

The Animal Flower

As in Man, the most perfect Part of the sublunary Creation, there are apparently seen several different Degrees of Perfection of Body and Mind; and in Animals the Sagacity of some is evidently superior to that of others; so likewise in this seemingly confused Species of animal Life, and vegetable Appearance, the Chain gradually descends with a surprising Mixture and Connexion.

Whoever hath Leisure and Abilities to pursue a general Inquiry of this Nature, will soon find, that this progressive Series runs through the whole Creation—From the most exalted Genius to the almost senseless Idiot—From the most sagacious sensible Creature to the almost insensible Mussel—From the towering Cedar to the Hyssop springing from the Wall, or the humble Moss.

Such is that universal Harmony and Connexion, that runs through the numberless Ranks and Orders of Beings, till we come at last to inanimate matter.

This surprising Creature, that I am to treat of, hath, for a long time been the Object of my own silent Admiration; and it would even now be thought chimerical to mention, much more describe, the Qualities of so strange a Phaenomenon, if the *Polypus* of late Years had not afforded a surprising Instance of Almighty Power.

The Cave that contains this Animal, is near the Bottom of an high rocky Cliff facing the Sea, in the North Part of the Island, in the Parish of *St. Lucy:* the Descent to it is very steep and dangerous, being in some Places almost perpendicular; and what adds an Horror to this dreadful Situation, is, that the Waves from below almost incessantly break upon the Cliff, and sometimes reached its highest Summit.

As soon as you are freed from this complicated Apprehension of Danger (in your Way down) you enter a Cave spacious enough to contain five hundred People. The Roof of this is in some Places imbossed with conglaciated incrustrations intermixed with small Tubes, through whose Extremities a small Quantity of the most limpid Water drops.

From this you enter another Cave, small in Comparison of the former. . . . In the Middle of this Bason there is a fit Stone, or Rock (as I shall call it), which is always under Water.

Round its Sides, at different Depths (seldom exceeding eighteen Inches) are seen at all Times of the Year several seemingly fine radiated Flowers of a pale Yellow, or a bright Straw-colour slightly tinged with Green:

These have in Appearance a circular Border of thick-set Petals, about the Size of, and much resembling, those of a single Garden Marigold, except that the Whole of this seeming Flower is narrower at the *Discus,* or Setting on of the Leaves, than any Flower of that Kind.

I have often attempted to pluck one of these from the Rock to which they are always fixt; but could never effect it. For as soon as my Fingers came within two or three Inches of it, it would immediately contract, and close together its yellow Border, and shrink back into the Hole in the Rocky; but, if left undisturbed for the Space of about four Minutes, it would come gradually in Sight, expanding, though at first very cautiously, its seeming Leaves, till at last it appeared in its former Bloom: However, it would again recoil with a surprising Quickness, when my Hand came within a small Distance of it. . . .

There were strong Appearances of Animal Life; yet, as its Shape, and want of local Motion, classed it among Vegetables, I was for some time in Suspense, and imagined it might be an acquatic Sensitive Plant. . . . This was my Opinion, till a subsequent Visit cleared my Doubts; for I plainy saw four dark-coloured Resemblances of Threads something like the Legs of a Spider, rising out of the Centre of what I have termed a Flower. Their quick spontaneous Motion from one side to the other . . . and their closing together in Imitation of a *Forceps,* as if they had hemmed in their Prey (which the yellow Border likewise soon surrounded and closed to secure), fully convinced me, that it was a living Creature. . . .

But in what manner the Rays of Light affect these Animals, whether by its Motion acting upon their whole exceedingly delicate nervous System, which, like the *Retina* of the human Eye, is in every Part sensitive, is, I believe, inexplicable. . . . Such is the insensible Gradation, which is progressively continued by imperceptible Degrees thro' the whole Creation, from animate to inanimate, rational to irrational, that we know not where precisely to determine their respective Boundaries.

The Shark

About the latter End of Queen *Anne's* Wars, Captain *John Beams* Commander of the *York Merchant,* arrived at *Barbados* from *England.* Having disembark'd the last Part of his Loading, which was Coals, the Sailors, who had been employ'd in that dirty Work, ventured into the Sea to wash themselves; there they had not been long, before a Person on Board 'spyed a large *Shark* making towards them, and gave them Notice of their Danger; upon which they swam back and reach'd the Boat, all but one; him the Monster overtook almost within Reach of the Oars, and griping him by the Small of the Back, his devouring Jaws soon cut asunder, and as soon swallow'd the lower Part of his Body; the remaining Part was taken up and carried on Board, where his Comrade was. His Friendship with the deceased had been long distinguished by a reciprocal Discharge of such endearing Offices, as imply'd an Union and Sympathy of Souls. When he saw the sever'd Trunk of his Friend, it was with an Horror and Emotion too great for Words to paint. During this affecting Scene, the insatiable *Shark* was seen traversing the bloody Surface in Search after the Remainder of his Prey; the rest of the Crew thought themselves happy in being on Board; he—alone unhappy, that he was not within Reach of the Destroyer. Fired at the Sight, and vowing that he would make the Devourer disgorge, or be swallowed himself into the same Grave,—He plunges into the Deep, arm'd with a large sharp-pointed Knife. The *Shark* no sooner saw him, but he made furiously towards him,—both equally eager, the one of his Prey, the other of Revenge. The Moment the *Shark* open'd his rapacious Jaws, his Adversary dextrously diving, and grasping him with his left Hand somewhat below the upper Fins, successfully employs his Knife in his right Hand, giving him repeating Stabs in the Belly: the enraged *Shark,* after many unavailing Efforts, finding himself overmatch'd in his own Element, endeavours to disengage himself, sometimes plunging to the Bottom, then mad with Pain, rearing his uncouth Form (now stain'd with his own streaming Blood) above the foaming Waves. The Crews of the surrounding Vessels saw the unequal Combat, uncertain from which of the Combatants the Streams of Blood issued; till at length, the *Shark,* much weaken'd by the Loss of Blood, made towards the Shore, and with him his Conqueror; who, flush'd with an Assurance of Victory, pushes his Foe with redoubled Ardour, and, by the Help of an ebbing Tide, dragging him on Shore, rips up his Bowels; and unites and buries the sever'd carcase of his Friend in one hospitable Grave.

The Story, I confess, is of so extraordinary a Nature, that I would not have dared to give it my Reader, had I not been authorized thereto by the Testimony of a very credible Gentleman (Lieutenant Colonel *Hillary Rowe,* of *St. Lucy's*

Parish, who was not far from the Place when this happened), who is ready to confirm by Oath, the Truth of what is here related. This action, intrepid as it is, will unquestionably fall under the Censure of those, who are accustomed to judge by the Rules of moral of political Fitness; it not being prudent in any Man to expose himself to Danger, from which he must owe his Escape as much to Chance as to Valour. . . . And yet if such an Action had been recorded of *Scipio* or *Alexander* in the defense of *Laelius* or *Hephaestion,* whether it would not have been celebrated by their Admirers, among the most shining and magnanimous Achievements of those renowned Heroes and Friends.

21

A Country Walk in Antigua

JANET SCHAW
(circa 1776)

Janet Schaw's (1731–1801) Journal of a Lady of Quality *chronicles the journey of a middle-aged Scotswoman to the West Indies, the American Colonies, the Azore Islands, and Portugal in the years 1774 to 1776. This work was not published in the author's life-time, but was discovered over a century later in the collections of the British Museum. Schaw provides an interesting description of Antigua here, making observations not only on nature, but also on colonial society as well. Something of the oppressed status of women in the eighteenth century is indicated in the resistance offered to her request to take a walk outside after tea. Schaw prevails, however, and provides us with a lively picture of the countryside, including groves and gardens, the royal palms, and the cane fields; she seems oblivious to the sufferings that made such opulence possible.*

From *Journal of a Lady of Quality* (London, 1776).

Tea being finished, the Doctor and his Lady left us, and we surprised the Gentlemen, by proposing a walk out of town.

This was at first opposed, but on our persisting, Mr. Baird swore we were the finest creatures he had met these twenty years. "Zounds," said he, taking my arm under his, "I shall fancy myself in Scotland." Our walk turned out charmingly, the evening had now been cooled by the sea breeze, and we were not the least incommoded. We walked thro' a market place, the principal streets, and passed by a large church, and thro' a noble burying place. Here we read many Scotch names, among others, that of poor Jock Trumble of Curry [Scotland], who died while here with his regiment. A little above the town is the new Barracks, a long large building in the middle of a field. I do not think its situation, however, so pretty as that of the Old Barracks. A little beyond that we met a plantation belonging to a Lady, who is just now in England . . . her house, for she is a widow, is superb, laid out with groves, gardens and delightful walks of Tamarind trees, which give the finest shade you can imagine.

Here I had an opportunity of seeing and admiring the Palmetto [royal palm] tree, with which this Lady's house is surrounded, and entirely guarded by them from the intense heat. They are in general from forty to sixty feet high before they put out a branch, and as straight as a line. If I may compare great things with small, the branches resemble a fern leaf, but are at least twelve or fifteen feet long. They go round the boll of the tree and hang down in the form of an Umbrella; the great stem is white, and the skin like Satin. Above the branches rises another stem, of about twelve or fourteen feet in height, coming to a point at the top, from which the cabbage springs, tho' the pith or heart of the whole is soft and eats well. This stem is the most beautiful green that you can conceive, and is a fine contrast to the white Boll below. The beauty of this tree, however, rather surprised than pleased me. It had a stiffness in its appearance far from being so agreeable as the waving of our native trees, and I could not help declaiming that they did not look as if they were of God's making.

We walked thro' many cane pieces, as they term the fields of Sugar-canes, and saw different ages of it. This has been a remarkable fine season, and every body is in fine spirits with the prospect of the Crop of Sugar. You have no doubt heard that Antigua has no water, but what falls in rain; A dry season therefore proves destructive to the crops, as the canes require much moisture.

We returned from our walk, not the least fatigued, but the Musquetoes [sic] had smelt the blood of a British man, and my brother had his legs bit sadly. Our petticoats, I suppose, guarded us, for we have not as yet suffered from these gentry. We supped quite agreeably, but it was quite in public. No body here is ashamed of what they are doing, for all the parlours are directly off the street, and doors and windows constantly open. I own it appears droll to have people come and chat in at the windows, while we are at supper, and not only so, but if they like the party, they just walk in, take a chair, and sit down. I considered this as an inconveniency from being in a hotel, but understand, that every house is on the same easy footing. Every body in town is on a level as to station, and they are all intimately acquainted, which may easily account for this general hospitality.

 *22*

The Alligator

WILLIAM BARTRAM
(circa 1791)

William Bartram (1739–1823) was born in pre-Revolution Philadelphia, the son of famous botanist John Bartram, who founded Bartram's Botanical Gardens. Because of William Bartram's precocious artistic talents, Ben Franklin encouraged the young man to become an engraver or printer, but William preferred to study and write about nature. William Bartram's Travels Through North and South Carolina, Georgia, East and West Florida *(Philadelphia, 1791) chronicles his adventures in the southeast from 1773 to 1778. This book, much celebrated in its time, now offers a wealth of firsthand information on the Old South: the wild orange groves of Florida, the tropical reptiles, the acquatic birds, and the culture and customs of Cherokee, Seminole, and Creek Indian Nations. Bartram's* Travels *influenced Coleridge in his lyric poem "Kubla Khan," Chateaubriand in his novels* Atala *and* René, *and Wordsworth in his poem "Ruth." The book remains popular two centuries after its publication.*

This dramatic passage from Bartram's Travels *describes the alligators of Florida's eastern coast with exuberance and accuracy. Alone in a wild cypress swamp near dark, Bartram observes two large male alligators engaged in single combat—probably a territorial or breeding dispute—and, canoeing back to camp, is set upon by numerous other alligators. Once in camp peacefully writing his notes Bartram is disturbed by "two very large [black] bears." Such were the adventures of a naturalist in colonial America. Much of the natural history in Bartram's* Travels *stands up under modern scrutiny and is well rooted in fact.*

From *Travels Through North and South Carolina, Georgia, East and West Florida* (Philadelphia, 1791).

144

The verges and islets of the lagoon were elegantly embellished with flowering plants and shrubs; the laughing coots with wings half spread were tripping over the little coves, and hiding themselves in the tufts of grass; young broods of the painted summer teal, skimming the still surface of the waters, and following the watchful parent unconscious of danger, were frequently surprised by the voracious trout; and he, in turn, as often by the subtle greedy alligator. Behold him rushing forth from the flags and reeds. His enormous body swells. His plaited tail brandished high, floats upon the lake. The waters like a cataract descend from his opening jaws. Clouds of smoke issue from his dilated nostrils. The earth trembles with his thunder. When immediately from the opposite coast of the lagoon, emerges from the deep his rival champion. They suddenly dart upon each other. The boiling surface of the lake marks their rapid course, and a terrific conflict commences. They now sink to the bottom folded together in horrid wreaths. The water becomes thick and discoloured. Again they rise, their jaws clap together, re-echoing through the deep surrounding forests. Again they sink, when the contest ends at the muddy bottom of the lake, and the vanquished makes a hazardous escape, hiding himself in the muddy turbulent waters and sedge on a distant shore. The proud victor exulting returns to the place of action. The shores and forests resound his dreadful roar, together with the triumphing shouts of the plaited tribes around, witnesses to the horrid combat.

My apprehensions were highly alarmed after being a spectator of so dreadful a battle. It was obvious that every delay would but tend to increase my dangers and difficulties, as the sun was near setting, and the alligators gathered around my harbour from all quarters. From these considerations I concluded to be expeditious in my trip to the lagoon, in order to take some fish. Not thinking it prudent to take my fusee [rifle] with me, lest I might lose it overboard in case of a battle, which I had every reason to dread before my return, I therefore furnished myself with a club for my defence, went on board, and penetrating the first line of those which surrounded my harbour, they gave way; but being pursued by several very large ones, I kept strictly on the watch, and paddled with all my might towards the entrance of the lagoon, hoping to be sheltered there from the multitude of my assailants; but ere I had half-way reached the place, I was attacked on all sides, several endeavouring to overset the canoe. My situation now became precarious to the last degree: two very large ones attacked me closely, at the same instant, rushing up with their heads and part of their bodies above the water, roaring terribly and belching floods of water over me. They struck their jaws together so close to my ears, as almost to stun me, and I expected every moment to be dragged out of the boat and instantly devoured. But I applied my weapons so effectually about me, though at random, that I was so successful as to beat them off a little; when, finding that they designed to renew the battle, I made for the shore, as the only means left me for my preservation . . . as soon as I gained the shore, they drew off and kept aloof. This was a happy relief . . . I [finally] made good my entrance into the lagoon . . . [and] soon caught more trout than I had present occassion for . . . [Once back in camp after dinner] I rekindled my fire for light, and whilst I was revising the notes of my past day's journey, I was suddenly roused with a noise behind me toward the main land. I sprang up on my feet, and listening, I distinctly heard some creature wading the water of the isthmus. I seized my gun and went cautiously from my camp, directing my steps towards the noise: when I had advanced about thirty yards, I halted behind a coppice of orange trees, and soon perceived two very large bears, which had made their way through the water, and had landed in the grove, about one hundred yards distance from me, and were advancing towards me. I waited until they were within thirty yards of me: they there began to snuff and look towards my camp: I snapped my piece, but it flashed, on which they both turned and galloped off, plunging through the water and swamp, never halting, as I suppose, until they reached fast land, as I could hear them leaping and plunging a long time. . . .

 **PART III**

1800–1991
PARADISE RECALLED: THE AGE OF CONSCIENCE

Natural philosophy has brought into clear relief the following paradox of human existence. The drive toward perpetual expansion—or personal freedom—is basic to the human spirit. But to sustain it we need the most delicate, knowing stewardship of the living world that can be devised. Expansion and stewardship may appear at first to be conflicting goals, but they are not. The depth of the conservation ethic will be measured by the extent to which each of the two approaches to nature is used to reshape and reinforce the other. The paradox can be resolved by changing its premises into forms more suited to ultimate survival, by which I mean protection of the human spirit.

Edward O. Wilson
"The Conservation Ethic"
Biophilia
(1984)

1801, Toussaint L'Overture leads independence uprising on Hispaniola. 1801, Alexander von Humboldt
visits the Caribbean. 1806–1825, Latin American independence movements led by Simon Bolivar. 1807, England declares
slave trade illegal. 1815, Napoleon defeated at Waterloo; the Second
Treaty of Paris clearly defines colonial holdings in the Caribbean.
1823, the Monroe Doctrine. 1834, England abolishes slavery. 1841,
Marx and Engels publish the *Communist Manifesto*. 1848, French
abolish slavery on their islands. 1851, Cuba declares independence.
1859, Darwin publishes the *Origin of Species*. 1863, the Dutch abolish
slavery on their islands. 1860–1865, U. S. Civil War. 1863, Emancipation Proclamation. 1874, Santo Domingo prohibits destruction of trees
near springs or at the heads of streams. 1876, Spain declares El Yunque
a forest reserve. 1885, painter Winslow Homer makes his first trip to
the Caribbean. 1886, Cuba abolishes slavery. 1898, U. S. defeats
Spanish in the Spanish American War. 1898, Mexico forms first forest
reserve. 1901, Cuba becomes an independent republic. 1902, Pelée
eruption on Martinique kills 30,000. 1903, Pelican Island Wildlife
Refuge established in Florida. 1903, Puerto Rico establishes the
Lugillo National Forest. 1907, Columbia establishes first forest reserve. 1914–1918, First World War. 1915, Venezuela establishes first
forest reserve. 1916, first oil refinery in the Caribbean is built on
Curacao. 1917, U. S. purchases Danish West Indies. 1922, British
Honduras establishes first forest reserve. 1928, Hemingway arrives in
Key West. 1930, Trujillo becomes president of the Dominican Republic. 1934, Beebe sets new world diving record in submarine off
Bermuda. 1940–1945, Second World War. 1947, Everglades National Park formed. 1954, Hemingway awarded Nobel Prize for *The
Old Man and the Sea*. 1955, Guatemala initiates national park program.
1957, Duvalier rules Haiti. 1958, Virgin Islands National Park
formed. 1959, Gaudeloupan Saint-John Perse awarded Nobel Prize.
1959, Castro rules Cuba. 1961, Hemingway's home made into Cuban
national museum. 1961, Bay of Pigs invasion. 1962, Cuban Missile
Crisis. 1962, U. S. launches astronauts into space from Cape Cana-
veral. 1962, Jamaica, Trinidad, and Tobago gain independence. 1966,
Barbados and British Guiana gain independence. 1966, Panama initi-

ates national park program. 1967, Guatemalan Miguel Asturias awarded Nobel Prize. 1969, Costa Rica initiates national park program. 1969, U. S. lands two men on the moon. 1970s, the Reggae music of Jamaican songwriters Jimmy Cliff, Bob Marley, and Peter Tosh gains worldwide recognition. 1972, earthquake in Managua, Nicaragua, kills 10,000. 1973, the Bahamas gain independence. 1974, Grenada gains independence. 1982, Columbian Gabriel Marquez awarded Nobel Prize. 1978–1983, Dominica, St. Lucia, St. Vincent, Antigua, Barbuda, St. Kitts, Nevis, and the Grenadines gain independence. 1980, Panama establishes Darien National Park. 1983, U. S. intervenes in Grenada. 1987, 1 million tourists visit Cancun, established in 1974. 1988–1989, equinoctial hurricanes devastate the Caribbean. 1989, Guatemala approves 44 new national parks and conservation areas; Mexico and Guatemala establish two adjoining biosphere reserves totalling 1.9 million hectares (1 hectare = 2.47 acres). 1990, Mexico outlaws the killing of sea turtles. 1990, Lethal Yellowing Disease kills hundreds of thousands of palm trees in the Caribbean. 1991, Puerto Rican plebiscite on U. S. statehood. 1992, since the Discovery 46 Caribbean animals have become extinct, including the Atalaye nesophontes, the Jamaican least pauraque, and the Guadeloupe conure; 41 Caribbean animals in IUCN Red Data Book of species presently endangered. 1992, conservation areas in the Caribbean total 137 with a combined protected area of 13,854,149 hectares.

 **23**

Cay Bonito, Cuba

ALEXANDER VON HUMBOLDT
(circa 1801)

Alexander von Humboldt (1769–1859) was a German naturalist and explorer who made seminal contributions to the then-nascent disciplines of physical geography and biogeography. Following in the intellectual path of pioneers like Buffon, von Humboldt traveled widely and wrote prodigiously on the distribution of fauna and flora around the world, as well as on the influence of landforms and climate on living systems. From 1799 through 1804 von Humboldt undertook an extensive scientific exploration of the New World. By 1827 he had published some 30 volumes based on this expedition. Like contemporary scientist-lecturer Carl Sagan, who has used television as a means of educating the masses, Alexander von Humboldt was a great popularizer of science in his time, and lectured throughout Europe. Interestingly, von Humboldt's most important work of popularization was entitled Kosmos; *the title of Carl Sagan's television series was "Cosmos," as was his later book based on that series (New York: Random House, 1980). In this selection from* The Island of Cuba *(New York: Derby and Jackson, 1856) von Humboldt expresses his dismay at the cruelties inflicted on a sea-bird colony by a group of sailors: "The ground was covered with wounded birds, struggling with death, so that this retired spot, which before our arrival was the abode of peace, seemed now to exclaim, Man has entered here."*

From *The Island of Cuba,* by Alexander von Humboldt (New York: Derby and Jackson, 1856).

Cay Bonito (Beautiful Cay), which was the first I visited, is worthy of its name from the force of its vegetation. Everything indicates that it has been a long time above the surface of the ocean, for the interior of the cay is hardly lower than its margin. From a layer of sand and broken shells, covering the fragmentary coral rock to the depth of five or six inches, a forest of mangroves rises, which when seen from a distance, seem from their height and foliage to be laurel trees. The avicennia nitida, batis, small euphorbia, and several grassy plants, serve to fix the movable sand with their roots. But what particularly characterizes the flora of these coral islands is the beautiful silver-leaved tournefortia gnaphaliodes of Jacquin, which I first found there. It is not a solitary plant, and forms a tree four or five feet in height, its flowers having an agreeable odor. It also adorns Cay Flamenco, Cay de Piedras, and perhaps the greater part of the low islands of the Jardinillos.

While we were engaged in botanizing our sailors sought for sea crabs, and irritated with ill success, they soothed their anger by climbing the mangrove trees, and committing terrible havoc among the young *alcatraces,* which were snugly ensconced in pairs in the nest. Through Spanish America, this name is applied to the blackish, swan-sized pelican of Buffon [the French naturalist]. the *alcatraz,* with that indolence and stupid confidence with characterizes the larger sea birds, forms its nest by twining together a few twigs only, and we often found four or five of these in one tree. The young birds defended themselves valiantly with their bills, which were already six or seven inches long, while the old ones flew above our heads uttering hoarse and mournful cries; but the streams of blood continued to trickle down the trees, for the sailors were armed with clubs and cutlasses. Though we expostulated with them against this cruelty and useless tormenting, they would not desist; these men, accustomed to long obedience in the solitude of the sea, take a singular pleasure in exercising a cruel dominion over the animal creation whenever an opportunity presents itself. The ground was covered with wounded birds, struggling with death, so that this retired spot, which before our arrival was the abode of peace, seemed now to exclaim, Man has entered here.

24

Notes on the West Indies

GEORGE PINKARD
(circa 1806)

George Pinkard (no dates available) was chief surgeon on the expedition of Sir Ralph Abercromby to the West Indies; his three volume chronicle of that journey Notes on the West Indies *was published in 1806 (London: Longman, Hurst, Rees, and Orme). This book includes Pinkard's observations on Grenada, St. Vincent, Barbados, and Dutch Guiana. The doctor shows some facility for characterization and natural description; his distaste for colonialism and abhorrence for slavery are evident throughout. In the first selection ("The Electric Eel") Pinkard writes humorously of a practical joke played upon two sailors by a mischievious cook—at that time electricity, first studied by Benjamin Franklin in his famous kite experiment, was a little understood phenomena of nature. In the second selection ("The Death of a Slave") Pinkard relates the horrors of slavery as it was practiced in Dutch Guiana. Slavery, he concludes, "is a violation of nature, in which humanity is outraged and our species degraded!"*

From *Notes on the West Indies,* by George Pinkard (London: 1806).

156

The Electric Eel

The Governor has a large electric eel, which he has kept for several years in a tub, made for that purpose, placed under a small shed near to the house. This fish possesses strong electric powers, and often causes scenes of diversion among the soldiers and sailors, who are struck with astonishment at its qualities, and believe it to be in league with some evil spirit. Two sailors wholly unacquainted with the properties of the fish, were one day told to fetch an eel, which was lying in the tub in the yard, and give it the cook to dress for dinner. It is a strong fish of seven or eight pounds weight, and gives a severe shock on being touched, particularly if at all irritated or enraged. The sailors had no sooner reached the shed, than one of them plunged his hand to the bottom of the tub to seize the eel, when he received a blow which benumbed his whole arm; and without knowing what it was, he started from the tub shaking his fingers, and holding his elbow with his other hand, crying out "Damme, Jack, what a thump he fetched me with his tail." His messmate laughing at "such a foolish notion," next put down his hand to reach out the eel, but receiving a similar shock, he snapped his fingers likewise, and ran off crying out "Damme, he did give you a thump! He's a fighting fellow: he has fetched me a broadside too!—Damme, let's both have a hawl at him together, Jack, then we shall board his d——d slipper carcase [sic] spite of his rudder." Accordingly they both plunged their hands into the tub, and seized the fish, by a full grasp round the body. This was roughed treatment than he commonly experienced, and he returned with a most violent shock, which soon caused them to quit their hold. For a moment they stood aghast, then rubbing their arms, holding their elbows, and shaking their fingers, they capered about with pain and amazement, swearing that their arms were broke, and that it was the devil in the tub in the shape of an eel. They now perceived that it was not a simple blow of the tail, which they had felt before; nor could they be prevailed upon to try again to take out the fish, but stole away rubbing their elbows, swearing the devil was in the tub, and cursing "the trick about the cook and the eel."

You have, no doubt, seen drawings of this fish, and have met with preparations of it the different museums and collections of the curious. Its form is not so round as that of the common eel. The head is flatter, as is likewise the tail, and much broader; the sides are less convex and deeper; the back is wide, and the body tapers down somewhat abruptly, terminating at the belly in a thin membrane, forming a kind of fin. I have preserved the skin of one, which I hope to shew you in England at the end of the war. The shock they communicate is sometimes very powerful, and precisely resembles that from the electrical machine. I have received it both from contact, and by means of conductors. The fish at Governor Van Battenburg's once gave me a severe blow from touching it, in the water, with the end of a polished ramrod belonging to one of the soldier's firelocks.

The Death of a Slave

Two unhappy negroes, a man and a woman, having been driven by cruel treatment to abscond from the plantation Lancaster, were taken a few days since, and brought back to the estate, when the manager, whose inhuman severity has caused them to fly from his tyrannic government, dealt out to them his avenging despotism with more than savage brutality. Taking with him two of the strongest drivers, armed with the heaviest whips, he led out these trembling and wretched Africans, early in the morning, to a remote part of the estate, too distant for the officers to hear their cries; and, there, tying down first the man, he stood by, and made the drivers flog him with many hundred lashes, until, on releasing him from the ground, it was discovered that he was nearly exhausted [dead]: and in this state the inhuman monster struck him on the head, with the butt end of a large whip, and felled him again to the earth; when the poor negro, escaping at once from his slavery and his sufferings, expired at the murderer's feet. But not satiated with blood, this savage tyrant next tied down the naked woman, on the spot by the dead body of her husband, and with the whips, already deep in gore, compelled the drivers to inflict a punishment of several hundred lashes, which had nearly released her also from a life of toil and torture.

Hearing of these acts of cruelty, on my return from the hospital, and scarcely believing it possible that they could have been committed, I went immediately to the sick-house to satisfy myself by ocular testimony: when, alas! I discovered that all I had heard was too fatally true; for, shocking to relate, I found the wretched and almost murdered woman lying stark-naked on her belly, upon the dirty boards, without any covering to the horrid wounds which had been cut by the whips, and with the still warm and bloody corpse of the man extended by her side, upon the neck of which was an iron collar, and a long heavy chain, which the now murdered negro had been made to wear from the time of his return to the estate. . . . The following day we witnessed . . . the funeral. . . . It was conducted . . . with all the mirthful ceremonies of African burial, forming a scene of gaiety, which consisted of music, dancing, singing, and loud noise. They all seemed to rejoice more in his escape from pain and misery, than they sorrowed for his loss. . . . [Slavery] is a violation of nature, in which humanity is outraged and our species degraded!

25

A Horseride over
the Portland Mountains,
Jamaica

**JOSEPH STURGE
AND THOMAS HARVEY**
(circa 1838)

*In 1837, following the 1834 Imperial Abolition Act, Quakers
Joseph Sturge and Thomas Harvey (no dates available) traveled to the British West India Colonies—Antigua, Montserrat,
Dominica, St. Lucia, Barbados, and Jamaica—for "the purpose of ascertaining
the actual condition of the negro population of those islands." There was at that
time some concern as to compliance with the parliamentary act in the remote
Caribbean islands, and Sturge and Harvey wrote a detailed account of their
journey,* The West Indies in 1837 *(London: Hamilton, Adams, and Company,
1838) for the edification of readers in England. In this passage the authors write
vividly of the beauty of the Jamaican countryside in a prose style that owes much to
the nature description of the Romantic Age.*

From *The West Indies in 1837,* by Joseph Sturge and Thomas Harvey (London: Hamilton,
Adams, and Company, 1838).

Very early this morning we rode over to Altamont, the new immigrant settlement situated in the heart of the Portland mountains, about eleven miles from Bath, and fifteen from Port Antonio. We proceeded by a bridle path over a ridge three thousand feet high, called the Coonah-Coonahs. After the first four or five miles all traces of human interference with the wild domain of nature had disappeared excepting only the track we followed. Below us was a valley of immense depth formed by a long ridge on the opposite side, and by the one impending over our heads. All was one vast forest, whose solitude was broken only by the deep-toned voices of birds. That delightful and cheerful songster, the mocking bird is a lover of human haunts, and its wild and merry notes cease to be heard in these deep recesses of the mountain forests. Here the multitude of mountain springs and rivers give ten-fold luxuriance to the productions of a fertile soil vivified by a tropical sun. On the side of the precipice, above which we were travelling, were huge trees, rooted at a great depth below us, but far over shadowing our heads with their arms and foliage. Above us on the other side was a canopy sometimes so dense as to exclude the sky. Among other beautiful trees, we observed the down tree, with full crops of its curious pods of vegetable beaver, and the tree fern frequently covered the sides of the hills for a considerable extent. Our path was as thickly strewn with decayed leaves as in a northern autumn, while all else bore the aspect of summer; for in this climate few of the trees become wholly or even partially denuded. After a long and difficult ascent of several miles, and a still steeper descent, we came to a place where the valley opened into a wider basin, in which traces of cultivation began to appear. We crossed a mountain torrent, the commencement of the Rio Grande, and entering a beautiful glade covered with turf on which cattle were grazing, we came to a farm house belonging to a person of color, near which is the settlement of Altamont. A single family have been sole tenants of this wilderness, for a long period, during which their only neighbours were the Maroons, living at Moore Town, about four miles distant.

26

*T*he *Most Remarkable Reef in the West Indies*

CHARLES DARWIN
(circa 1842)

Charles Darwin (1809–1882) will forever be associated with the theory of evolution put forward in his book The Origin of Species, by Means of Natural Selection (*London: John Murray, 1859*). *A geologist by profession, Darwin relied upon information gleaned from his world travels on H.M.S.* Beagle (*1831–1836*) *and his encyclopedic knowledge of fossils to propose and document a simple and straightforward explanation of the mechanism that guides the development of life on this planet. Not since Copernicus proposed that the earth orbited around the sun had such a revolutionary idea been put forward; its reverberations are still being felt, and it is safe to say that Darwin, together with Aristotle, Copernicus, Galileo, Kepler, and Einstein, constitute the most influential scientists in history. Before* The Origin of Species, *Darwin was most well known for his theory of the formation of coral reefs, and it is from his pioneering work* The Structure and Distribution of Coral Reefs (*London, 1842*) *that this selection is taken. While Darwin did not visit the Caribbean—the* Beagle *made landfall to the south on the coast of Brazil—he was familiar with scientific reports from the region and subsequently wrote this descriptive analysis of the Yucatan/Belize barrier reef in 1842. The reef is second only to the Great Barrier Reef of eastern Australia in length.*

From *The Structure and Distribution of Coral Reefs,* by Charles Darwin, third ed. (New York: Appleton, 1897).

. . . South of latitude 18°, there commences the most remarkable reef in the West Indies: it is about 130 miles in length, ranging in a north and south line, at an average distance of fifteen miles from the coast. The islets on it are all low, as I have been informed by Captain B. Allen; the water deepens suddenly on the outside of the reef, but not more abruptly than off many of the sedimentary banks: within its southern extremity (off *Honduras*) the depth is 25 fathoms; but in the more northern parts, the depth soon decreases to 10 fathoms, and within the northernmost part, for a space of 20 miles, the depth is only from one or two fathoms. In most of these respects we have the characteristics of a barrier-reef; nevertheless, from observing, first, that the channel within the reef is a continuation of a great irregular bay, which penetrates the mainland to the depth of 50 miles; and secondly, that considerable spaces of this barrier-like reef (for instance, in latitude 16° 45' and 16° 12') are described in the charts as formed of pure sand; and thirdly, from knowing that sediment is accumulating in many parts of the West Indies in banks parallel to the shore; I have not ventured to colour this reef as a barrier. To add to my doubts, close outside this barrier-like reef, *Turneffe, Lighthouse,* and *Glover* reefs are situated, and these have so completely the form of atolls, that if they had occurred in the Pacific, I should not have hesitated to colour them blue [Darwin makes reference to a map in the volume]. *Turneffe Reef* seems almost entirely filled up with low mud islets; and the depth within the other two reefs is only from one to three fathoms. From this circumstance, and from their similarity in form, structure, and relative position, both to the bank called *Northern Triangles,* on which there is an islet between 70 and 80 feet in height, and to *Cozumel* Island, the level surface of which is likewise between 70 and 80 feet high, it is probable that the three foregoing banks are the worn-down bases of upheaved shoals, fringed with corals; left uncoloured [reference is again made to a map in the volume].

In front of the eastern *Mosquito* coast there are, between 12° and 16°, some extensive banks (already mentioned), with high islands rising from their centres, and others wholly submerged, both kinds being bordered, near their windward margins, by crescent-shaped coral-reefs. But it can hardly be doubted that these banks owe their origin, like the great bank extending from the Mosquito promontory, almost entirely to the accumulation of sediment, and not to the growth of corals; hence I have not coloured them [as barrier or fringing reefs on the map in the volume].

27

Cancun and Cozumel

JOHN L. STEPHENS
(circa 1843)

John L. Stephens (1805–1852) belongs to that illustrious group of nineteenth-century amateur archaeologists of which Heinrich Schliemann, who discovered Troy in 1873, was also a member. In 1839 Stephens, a lawyer and travel writer, was sent by President Van Buren on an obscure mission to Central America. Characteristically, he soon found himself exploring the ruins of the Mayan civilization. In Chiapis he studied Palenque. In the Yucatan he visited Uxmal, Chichen-Itza, and Tulum. In El Salvador he purchased the ruins at Copan for fifty dollars. Always the popularizer, Stephens published Incidents of Travel in Central America, Chiapis, and Yucatan *in two volumes in 1841 (New York: Harper and Brothers); a subsequent visit in 1841 resulted in* Incidents of Travel in Yucatan *(New York: Harper and Brothers, 1843). In this passage from the latter book the author describes his arrival on the same island of Cozumel that Cortés had visited three centuries before, and to which hundreds of thousands of tourists now fly each winter. "Toward evening," Stephens writes, "we strolled for a great distance along the shore, picking up shells, and at night we had a luxurious swing in our hammocks."*

From *Incidents of Travel in the Yucatan* (vol. II), by John L. Stephens (New York: Harper and Brothers, 1843).

In the afternoon we steered for the mainland, passing the island of Kancune [sic], a barren strip of land, with sand hills and stone buildings visible upon it. The whole of this coast is lined with reefs of rocks, having narrow passages which enable a canoa to enter and find shelter; but it is dangerous to attempt the passage at night. We had a good wind, but as the next harbour was at some distance, the patron came to anchor at about four o'clock under the lee of the point of Nesuc. Immediately we went ashore in search of water, but found only a dirty pool in which the water was so slat that we could scarcely drink it, but still it was an agreeable change from that we had on board.

We had time for a bath, and while preparing to take it saw two large sharks moving along the shore in water four or five feet deep, and so clear that their ugly eyes were visible. We hesitated, but, from the heat and confinement of the canoa, we were in real need; and stationing Albino on the prow to keep a look out, we accomplished our purpose. Afterward we rambled along the shore to pick up shells; but toward dark we were all hurrying back, flying before the natives, swarms of moschetoes, which pursued us with the same bloodthirsty spirit that animated the Indians along this coast when they pursued the Spaniards. We heaved upon our cable, hauled up our big stone, and dropped off to some distance from the shore, with horrible apprehensions for the night, but, fortunately, we escaped.

At daylight the next morning we were again under way, and, with a strong and favourable wind, steered from the coast for the island of Cozumel. Very soon, in the comparatively open sea, we felt the discomfort and even insecurity of our little vessel. The waves broke over us, wetting our luggage and ourselves, and interfering materially with Bernaldo's cooking. At about four o'clock in the afternoon we were upon the coast of Cozumel, and here for the first time we made a discovery, at the moment sufficiently annoying, viz., that our patron was not familiar with the coast of this island; it was bound with reefs; there were only certain places where it was practicable to run in, and he was afraid to make the attempt.

Our plan was to disembark at the rancho of Don Vicente Albino, and the patron did not know where it was. It was too late to look for it, and, sailing along till he saw a passage among the reefs, he laid the old canoa into it, and then threw out the big stone, but at some distance from the shore. On the outer reef was the wreck of a brig; her naked ribs were above the water, and the fate of her mariners no one knew.

The next morning, after some hours spent in groping about, we discovered the rancho of Don Vicente, distant about three miles. Here we encountered a strong current of perhaps four miles an hour; and, taking the wind close hauled, in a little while found that El Sol was not likely to have a very brilliant career that day. At length we went close in, furled sails, and betook ourselves to poles, by means of which, after two hours' hard work, we reached the little Bay of San Miguel, on which stood the rancho of Don Vicente. The clearing around it was the only one on the island, all the rest being thick woods. This bay had a sandy beach extending some distance to a rocky point, but even here the water was discoloured by sunken reefs. In the case of a norther it was an unsafe anchorage ground: El Sol would be driven upon the rocks, and the captain wished to leave us on shore, and go in search of a better harbour; but to this we objected, and for the present directed him to run her up close; when, standing upon the bow, and leaping with our setting poles, we landed upon the desolate island of Cozumel.

Above the line of the shore was a fine table of land, on which were several huts, built of poles, and thatched with palm leaves. One was large and commodious, divided into apartments, and contained rude benches and tables, as if prepared for our immediate occupation. Back of the house was an enclosure for a garden, overgrown, but with any quantity of tomatoes, ripe, wasting, and begging to be put into a turtle soup then in preparation on board the canoa.

This rancho was established by the pirate Molas, who, escaping from death in Merida, made his way hither. He succeeded in getting to him his wife and children and a few Indians, and for several years nothing was heard of him. In the mean time he laid the keel of a sloop, finished it with his own hands, carried it to Belize, and sold it; new subjects of excitement grew up, and, being in a measure forgotten, he again ventured to the mainland, and left the island to its solitude.

After him Don Vicente Albino undertook to establish upon it a rancho for the cultivation of cotton, which was broken up by the mutiny of his Indians and an attempt to murder him. When we met him at Yalahao he had just returned from his last visit, carrying away his property, and leaving five dogs tenants of the Island. After him came a stranger occupant than either, being no other than our old friend Mr. George Fisher, that "citizen of the world" introduced to the reader in the early part of these pages, who, since our separation in Merida, had consummated the history of his wandering life by becoming the purchaser of six leagues, or eighteen miles, of the island, had visited it himself with surveyors, set up his crosses along the shore, and was about undertaking a grand enterprise, that was to make the lonely island of Cozumel known to the commercial world.

Our act of taking possession was unusually exciting. It was an immense relief to escape from the confinement of the canoa. The situation commanded a view of the sea, and, barely distinguishable, in the distance was the coast of Yucatan. On the bank were large forest trees which had been spared in the clearing, and orange and cocoanut trees planted by Molas. The place had a sort of piratical aspect. In the hut were doors and green blinds from the cabin of some unlucky vessel, and reeving blocks, tar buckets, halliards, drinking gourds, fragments of rope, fishing nets, and two old hatches were scattered on the ground. Above all, the first object we discovered, which would have given a charm to a barren sand bank, was a well of pure and abundant water, which we fell upon at the moment of landing, and were almost like the Spanish soldier in the expedition of Cordova, who drank till he swelled and died. And, besides the relief of a pressing want, this well had a higher interest, for it assured us that our visit was not bootless. We saw in it, at the first glance, the work of the same builders with whose labours on the mainland we were now so familiar, being, like the subterranean chambers at Uxmal [a Mayan city on the Caribbean coast of the Yucatan mainland], dome shaped, but larger both at the mouth and in the interior.

This well was shaded by a large cocoanut. We hauled up under it one of the hatches, and, sitting around it on blocks, had served up the turtle which had been accomplishing its destiny on board the canoa. With our guns resting against the trees, long bears, and canoa costume, we were, perhaps, as piratical-seeming a trio as ever scuttled a ship at sea. In the afternoon we walked over the clearing, which was covered with a fine plantation of cotton, worth, as the patron said, several hundred dollars, with the pods open and blowing away, indicating that the rancho had been abandoned in haste, without regard to the preservation of property. Toward evening we strolled for a great distance along the shore, picking up shells, and at night we had a luxurious swing in our hammocks.

Christopher Columbus. From *Purchas His Pilgrimes,* Volume 2 (reprint ed., Glasgow, 1905).

Sir Francis Drake. From *Hakluyt's Voyages,* Volume 10 (reprint ed., Glasgow, 1904).

Sir John Hawkins. From *Hakluyt's Voyages*, Volume 9 (reprint ed., Glasgow, 1904).

Captain René Laudionniere. From *Hakluyt's Voyages*, Volume 9 (reprint ed., Glasgow, 1904).

Sir Walter Raleigh. From *Hakluyt's Voyages,* Volume 9 (reprint ed., Glasgow, 1904).

Caribbean Royal Palm. From Griffith Hughes' *The Natural History of Barbados* (London, 1750).

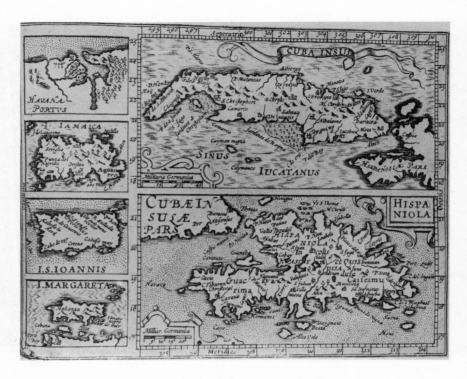

An early Spanish map from the Caribbean. From *Purchas His Pilgrimes*, Volume 14 (reprint ed., Glasgow, 1906).

A Cuna meeting house in Panama. From Lionel Wafer's *A New Voyage and Description of the Isthmus of America* (London, 1697).

The Parrot of Carolina (now extinct) was once found throughout Florida and the Carolinas. From Mark Catesby's *The Natural History of Carolina, Florida, and the Bahama Islands* (London, 1743).

The Caribbean Green Turtle. From Mark Catesby's *The Natural History of Carolina, Florida, and the Bahama Islands* (London, 1743).

Colonial Antigua. From Janet Schaw's *Journal of a Lady of Quality, 1774–1776*.

MORNING WALK, DOMINICA.

A morning walk on the island of Dominica. From James Anthony Froude's *The English in the West Indies* (New York, 1887).

A valley in the Blue Mountains of Jamaica. From James Anthony Froude's *The English in the West Indies* (New York, 1887).

A mountain trail, with arborescent ferns, on the island of Martinique. From Lafcadio Hearn's *Two Years in the French West Indies* (New York, 1902).

Mont Pelée on the island of Martinique. From Lafcadio Hearn's *Two Years in the French West Indies* (New York, 1902).

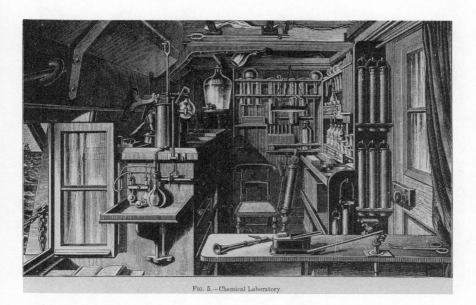

FIG. 5.—Chemical Laboratory.

Sir John Murray's laboratory on board the H.M.S. Challenger (1873–1876). From his *Report on the Scientific Results of the Voyage of H.M.S. Challenger* (Edinburgh, 1880–1895).

A Mayan Stellae on the Caribbean coast of Central America. From Frederick
Upham Adams' *Conquest of the Tropics* (Garden City, 1914).

A surveying crew in the coastal Caribbean jungle of Central America. From Frederick Upham Adams *Conquest of the Tropics* (Garden City, 1914).

Bananas gathered for rail transport to the Caribbean coast in Guatemala. From Frederick Upham Adams' *Conquest of the Tropics* (Garden City, 1914).

The opulent Jamaican home of an officer of the United Fruit Company. From Frederick Upham Adams' *Conquest of the Tropics* (Garden City, 1914).

Native residents of Jamaica. From Frederick Upham Adams' *Conquest of the Tropics* (Garden City, 1914).

Climax tropical rainforest in British Guiana. From William Beebe's *Jungle Peace* (New York, 1918).

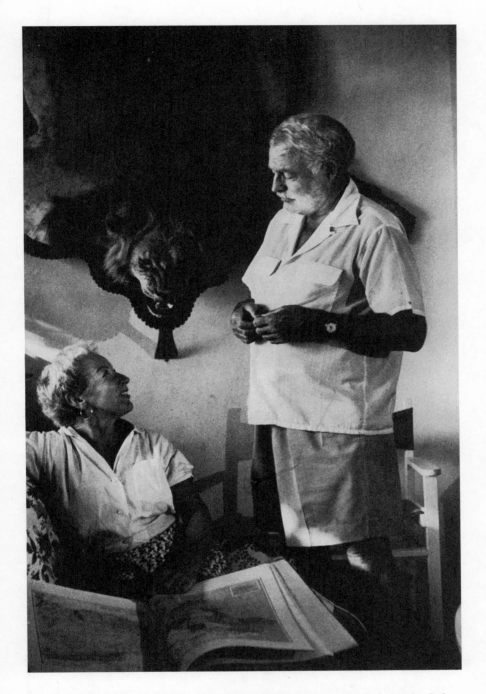

Ernest Hemingway and his fourth wife Mary at the author's home in Cuba. Reprinted with permission of the Ernest Hemingway Collection, John Fitzgerald Kennedy Library.

William Beebe's "wilderness laboratory" in the jungles of British Guiana near the Caribbean coast. From William Beebe's *Jungle Peace* (New York, 1918).

The coral reef on St. John Island in Virgin Islands National Park at low tide. Reprinted with permission of the National Park Service.

Angelfish and Finger Coral in Biscayne National Park (Florida). Reprinted with permission of the National Park Service.

Porkfish and Brain Coral in Virgin Islands National Park. Reprinted with permission of the National Park Service.

Sea Fan and Elkhorn Coral in Virgin Islands National Park. Reprinted with permission of the National Park Service.

28

The Grand Tour Up River

HARRIET BEECHER STOWE
(circa 1873)

*Harriet Beecher Stowe (1811–1896) was born in Litchfield,
Connecticut, the seventh child of Lyman Beecher, a prominent
Congregational pastor of his day. In 1824 Stowe was sent to a*
girl's seminary school that her twenty-three-year-old sister Catherine had established; there she studied Latin, French, Italian, history, literature, and theology.
The Beecher family moved to Cincinnati in 1832 and it was here in "The Queen
City of the West," employed as a teacher, that Harriet began to write her first
articles and to become involved in the abolitionist movement. She married a
struggling classics scholar, Calvin Ellis Stowe, in 1836, and subsequently bore
seven children. Calvin was appointed professor of classics at Bowdoin College in
1850, and it was in Maine that Harriet expanded one of her short stories into the
novel* Uncle Tom's Cabin, *which was published in 1852 and which, within one
year, had sold more than 300,000 copies. In 1867, at the age of fifty-six, Harriet
established herself on a small farm in Florida overlooking the St. Johns River; here
she raised oranges and wrote of her life in the subtropics. The memoir of her life on
the farm appeared in 1873 as* Palmetto Leaves, *and is an interesting piece of
nature writing. Her New England background is evident in references to the
writings of Ralph Waldo Emerson and Henry David Thoreau; she was probably
also familiar with the work of William Bartram and in places her prose resonates
with the* joie de vivre *of that great naturalist: "The swamp . . . is a perpetual
flower-garden, where Nature has raptures and frenzies of growth, and conducts
herself like a crazy, drunken, but beautiful* bacchante." *Like Bartram, she also
shows a tolerance of predators—water moccasins and alligators—that was in
advance of general thinking in her age.*

From *Palmetto-Leaves,* by Harriet Beecher Stowe (Boston: James R. Osgood and Company, 1873).

The St. John's is the grand water-highway through some of the most beautiful portions of Florida; and tourists, safely seated at ease on the decks of steamers, can penetrate into the mysteries and wonders of unbroken tropical forests. . . . When the magnolia-flowers were beginning to blossom [in May] we were ready, and took passage—a joyous party of eight or ten individuals—on the steamer "Darlington," commanded by Captain Broch, and, as is often asserted, by "Commodore Rose."

This latter, in this day of woman's rights is no mean example of female energy and vigor. She is stewardess of the boat, and magnifies her office. She is a colored woman, once a slave owned by Captain Broch, but emancipated, as the story goes, for her courage, and presence of mind, in saving his life in a steamboat disaster.

Rose is short and thick, weighing some two or three hundred, with a brown complexion, and a pleasing face and fine eyes. Her voice, like that of most colored women, is soft, and her manner of speaking pleasing. All this, however, relates to her demeanor when making herself agreable to passengers. In other circumstances, doubtless, she can speak louder, and with considerable more emphasis; and show, in short, those martial attributes which have won for her the appellation of the "Commodore." It is asserted that the whole charge of provisioning and running the boat, and all its internal arrangements, vests in Madam Rose; and that nobody can get ahead of her in a bargain, or resist her will in an arrangement. . . .

The St. John's River below Pilatka has few distinguishing features to mark it out from other great rivers. It is so wide, that the foliage of the shores cannot be definetly made out; and the tourist here, expecting his palm-trees and his magnolias and flowering-vines, is disappointed by sailing in what seems a never-ending great lake, where the shores are off in the distance too far to make out anything in particular. But, after leaving Pilatka, the river grows narrower, the overhanging banks approach nearer, and the foliage becomes more decidedly tropical in its character. . . .

It was the first part of May; and the forests were in that fulness of leafy perfection which they attain in the month of June at the North. But there is a peculiar, vivid brilliancy about the green of the new spring-leaves here, which we never saw elsewhere. It is a brilliancy like some of the new French greens, now so much in vogue, and reminding one of the metallic brightness of birds and insects. In the woods, the cypress is a singular and beautiful feature. It attains to a great age and immense size. The trunk and branches of an old cypress are smooth and white as ivory, while its light, feathery foilage is of the most dazzling golden-green; and rising, as it often does, amid clumps of dark varnished evergreens,—bay and magnolia and myrtle,—it has a singular and beautiful effect. The long swaying draperies of the gray moss interpose everywhere their wavering outlines and pearl tints amid the brightness and bloom of the forest, giving to its deep recesses the mystery of grottoes hung with fanciful vegetable stalactites.

The palmetto-tree appears in all stages,—from its earliest growth, when it looks like a fountain of great, green fan-leaves bursting from the earth, to its perfect shape, when, sixty or seventy feet in height, it rears its fan crown high in air. The oldest trees may be known by a perfectly smooth trunk; all traces of the scaly formation by which it has built itself up in ring after ring of leaves being obliterated. But younger trees, thirty or forty feet in height, often show a trunk which seems to present a regular criss-cross of basket-work,—the remaining scales from whence the old leaves have decayed and dropped away. These scaly trunks are often full of ferns, wild flowers, and vines, which hang in fantastic draperies down their sides, and form leafy and flowery pillars. The palmetto-hammocks, as they are called, are often miles in extent along the banks of the rivers. The tops of the palms rise up round in the distance as so many hay cocks, and seeming to rise one above another far as the eye can reach.

. . . It is the most wild, dream-like, enchanting sail conceivable. The river sometimes narrows so that the boat brushes under overhanging branches, and then widens into beautiful lakes dotted with wooded islands. Palmetto-hammocks, live-oak groves, cypress, pine, bay, and magnolia form an interchanging picture; vines hang festooned from tree to tree; wild flowers tempt the eye on the near banks; and one is constantly longing for the boat to delay here or there. . . . Every now and then the woods break away for a little space, and one sees orange and banana orchards, and houses evidently newly built. At many points the boat landed, and put off kegs of nails, hoes, ploughs, provisions, groceries. . . . One annoyance on board the boat was the constant and pertinacious firing kept up by that class of men who think that the chief end of man is to shoot something. Now, we can put up with good earnest hunting or fishing done for the purpose of procuring for man food, or even the fur and feathers that hit his fancy and taste.

But we detest indiscriminate and purposeless maiming and killing of happy animals, who have but one life to live, and for whom the agony of broken bones or torn flesh is a helpless, hopeless pain, unrelieved by any of the resources which enable us to endure. A parcel of hulking fellows sit on the deck of a boat, and pass through the sweetest paradise God ever made, without one idea of its loveliness, one gentle, sympathizing thought of the animal happiness with which the Creator has filled these recesses. All the way along is a constant fusillade upon every living thing that shows itself on the bank. Now a bird is hit, and hangs, head downward, with a broken wing; and a coarse laugh choruses the deed. Now an alligator is struck; and the applause is greater. We once saw a harmless young alligator, whose dying struggles, as he threw out his poor little black paws piteously like human hands, seemed to be vastly diverting to those cultivated individuals. They wanted nothing of him except to see how he would act when he was hit, dying agonies are so very amusing! . . . Killing for killing's sake belongs not even to the tiger. The tiger kills for food; man, for amusement.

29

St. Thomas, Virgin Islands and Bermuda

JOHN MURRAY
(circa 1873)

Sir John Murray (1841–1914) was among the fathers of modern marine biology and oceanography. Educated at the University of Edinburgh, Murray served as ship's surgeon on the whaler Jan Mayen *in 1868 and was subsequently appointed chief naturalist on the historic three and half year voyage of the H.M.S.* Challenger *(1873–1876). After returning to Scotland, he directed a research center in Edinburgh that became a worldwide meeting place for those studying marine biology and oceanography, both nascent sciences at the time. Murray was the editor of the monumental* Report on the Scientific Results of the Voyage of H.M.S. Challenger *(1880–1895), which ultimately filled fifty royal quarto volumes. His pioneering* Deep Sea Deposits *(1891) was a standard reference work for half a century, and his monograph* On the Structure and Origins of Coral Reefs and Islands *(1880) was as influential then as the writings of Darwin. It was Murray who prevailed upon the British Empire to annex Christmas Island in the Indian Ocean in 1887, and his biological paper* A Monograph of Christmas Island *(Royal Society, 1900) helped lay the groundwork for the modern science of island ecology. Murray was awarded numerous honorary degrees during his lifetime. He was made a fellow of the Royal Society in 1876 and was knighted in 1898.*

In this selection from the Challenger *report the author describes St. Thomas, a 32-square-mile island of volcanic origin in the Virgin Islands first colonized by Danish settlers in 1672. Most informative is Murray's observation that "only in a few remote parts of the island, and in small streaks of broken ground bordering the water-courses" did any of the original tropical forest exist, amply attesting to the ecological devastation that nearly always followed colonization. Also of interest in this respect are his comments vis-à-vis the feral goats, pigs, and birds that had in all likelihood by that time destroyed the fragile population of indigenous vertebrates. Finally, Murray's description of the lingering effects of hurricanes and tidal waves (he calls them "earthquake waves") on St. Thomas provides ample testimony of the power of nature in the Caribbean to abruptly change and challenge human life.*

Note: No relation to the editor.

From *The Voyage of the H.M.S. Challenger During the Years 1873–1876*, by John Murray (Edinburgh, 1885.)

St. Thomas, Virgin Islands

As the ship steamed towards the harbour at St. Thomas, Frigate Birds soared high overhead, with their long tail feathers stretched widely out. A number of brown Pelicans (*Pelecanus fuscus*) were flying at a moderate height near the shore, and every now and then dashing down with closed wings into the water on their prey like their close allies the Gannets. Often several of the birds dashed down together at the same instant.

The island of St. Thomas itself, as well as the outlying islets, is covered with a wild bush growth, which at first sight might perhaps be taken for indigenous vegetation, but is composed of plants that have overrun deserted sugar plantations. It is only in a few remote parts of the island, and in small streaks of broken ground bordering the water-courses, that any original forest exists. The whole of the available land in the island itself, and in all the adjoining islands, was planted with sugar cane until the emancipation of the slaves in 1833; since that time the ground has been allowed to run wild. . . .

The shore is covered with corals bleached white by the sun, and amongst these occur quantities of Calcareous Seaweeds (*Halimeda opuntia* and Halimeda *tridens*), branching masses composed of leaf-shaped joints of hard calcareous matter articulated together. These are all quite dry and bleached white, and hard and stiff, like corals. Seaweeds belonging to two very different groups of algae thus secrete a calcareous skeleton, *Halimeda* and its allies, belonging to the Siphonaceae—green coloured algae; and *Lithothamnion* and allied genera belonging to the Coral-linaceae, which are red coloured algae. These lime-secreting algae are of great importance from a geological point of view, as supplying a large part of the material of which calcareous reefs and sand rocks are built up. . . .

There is only one kind of Humming Bird at St. Thomas, but it is very common, and is constantly to be seen poised in the air in front of a blossom or darting across the roads. It is remarkable how closely Humming Birds resemble in their flight Sphinx Moths, such as our common Humming Bird Sphinx, so named from this resemblance. They make in their flight exactly the same rapid darts, sudden pauses, quick turns, and the same prolonged hovering over flowers. The most conspicuous land bird in the island is commonly called the "Black-witch" (*Crotophaga ani*). These birds are usually to be seen in flocks of three or four, in constant motion amongst the bushes, and screaming harshly when they apprehend danger. They behave very much like Magpies, but are somewhat smaller than the English Magpie and black all over. They belong structurally to the family of the Cuckoos (Cuculidae).

Two Snakes, one a species of *Typhlops* and the other apparently referable to the genus *Coronella,* were obtained, as also specimens of Lizards belonging to the genera *Anolis* and *Ameiva.* . . .

A species of White Ant (*Termes*) is very common. It makes large globular nests of a hard brown comb, as much as two feet in diameter, perched high up in the fork of a tree. From the bottom of the tree covered galleries about half an inch in breadth lead up on the surface of the bark to the nest, looking like long, narrow, brown streaks upon the tree trunk. The galleries usually follow a somewhat irregular course up the trunk to the nest, reminding one of the curious deviations which are always to be seen in footpaths, traced by people walking across fields, in their endeavours to go straight from one point to another. The galleries, or rather tubular ways, for they have bottoms to them, are made of the same tough brown substance as the nests, and are cemented firmly to the bark. Though they are so broad as to allow numerous Ants to pass and repass, they are only high enough for the Ants to walk under. When one of these galleries is broken, a number of soldier Termites come out and begin biting the marauder's hands, and though hardly making themselves felt, they are as brave as if they had a sting. A considerable length of the gallery has to be broken before any of the working Termites' beds are reached, as they retired from the scene of danger. A new species of Wasp (*Polistes madoci,* Kirby) was found.

An Agouti, a species of Rodent (*Dayprocta*), occurs in the island, and Mr. Wyman said that it was common in the gullies near his sugar plantation.

A shooting excursion to the opposite side of the island was organised in pursuit of wild goats, pigs, guinea fowl, and the domestic fowl which breed in the wild condition in various parts of the island, having sprung, in most instances, from stock which has escaped and been scattered during the hurricanes. The feral fowls are very wary, like their progenitors, the Indian Jungle-Fowl, and are not at all easy to shoot. The entire bag consisted of only one wild fowl. Flights of the brown Pelicans were met with passing over-head, flying one after another along the shore almost always exactly over the same spot on their way from one feeding ground to another. . . .

The stay at St. Thomas extended to eight days, which time was fully occupied, as far as the naval staff was concerned, in refitting and coaling the ship, in obtaining magnetic and other observations on shore, and in correcting the charts. The evidences of the destruction caused at St. Thomas by the hurricanes and occasional earthquake waves, more especially by that of 1867, were everywhere conspicuously apparent. Numbers of small houses were constructed partially with the bulkheads of wrecked ships; and even in 1873, six years after the last hurricane, there were a few wrecks still on the shore.

Bermuda

At, and in the neighbourhood of, this interesting group of islands, the Challenger remained from the 4th to the 23rd of April, and from the 28th May to the 13th June.

The group, with its outlying reefs, is in the form of an ellipse, the major axis of which lies in a N.E. and S.W. direction, and it is described generally as a coral atoll; but any one who has visited coral atolls in the China Sea, Pacific, or Indian Oceans, will be at once struck with some remarkable differences between these and Bermuda. The typical atoll consists of a low, more or less circular, strip of land enclosing a lagoon, into which there is usually a well-defined opening on the leeward side. In Bermuda the land is 260 feet in height at one point, and is massed to the southeast side of the atoll, with the exception of a small outlier known as the "North Rock," which is composed of the same "Aeolian" rocks as the mass of land to the southeast, and this indicates an extension of the land surface of the atoll in this direction at a former period. Although the outer reef is almost continuous, there is no well-defined lagoon as in a typical atoll. The whole of the northwest portion of the banks is crowded with coral flats and heads, with intervening lanes and spaces of coral sand, with a depth of usually 4 or 5 fathoms and nowhere more than 10 fathoms. The basins, known as Great Sound, Little Sound, and Castle Harbour, are almost completely enclosed by the Aeolian rocks, and have evidently been formed by the solvent action of the sea water on these rocks. Navigators have remarked upon the light blue colour of the water when compared with the deep blue of southern atolls. This arises most probably from the particles of calcareous matter suspended in the water whenever there is the slightest motion. Owing to the shallowness of the lagoon channels, the water becomes quite turbid when there is much wind, thus rendering the navigation of the narrows very difficult. The Aeolian rocks are found below the level of low water at many points of the islands.

A satisfactory of at least a local subsidence was given a few years ago. In preparing a bed for the great floating dock it was necessary to make an excavation in the Camber, extending to a depth of 50 feet below low water. First there came in the cutting, at a depth of 25 feet below the surface, a bed of calcareous mud, 5 feet thick, forming the floor of the basin; next, loose beds, 20 feet thick of what has been called "coral crust"—coral sand mixed with detached masses of *Diploria* and isolated examples of smaller corals and of many shells,—passing into "freestone,"—the coral sand cemented together but somewhat loosely coherent. Beneath this, at a depth of about 45 feet, there was a bed of a kind of peat, and vegetable soil containing stumps of cedar in a vertical position, and the remnants of other land vegetation, with the remains of *Helix bermudensis,* and of several birds; the bed of peat was ascertaining by boring to lie upon the ordinary hard "base-rock." . . .

Another important point to which attention was directed was the magnetic condition of the islands. Observations made by the Governor, General Lefroy, at his official residence, differed considerably from the Admiralty charts, and, consequently, instructions were received from the Hydrographer to ascertain whether those charts were in error or not. The observations made by the Expedition showed that the variation differed in various parts of the island as much as 6°, ranging from 4° W. to 10° W., the smallest amount being found at a small islet just under the lighthouse on Gibb's Hill, and the greatest at the point on the west side of Clarence Cove. The correct variation was found by swinging the ship on all points of the compass, and ascertaining its errors by azimuths of the sun, and the result so obtained agreed precisely with the Admiralty chart. It does not appear that before the visit of the Expedition this peculiarity of the Bermuda group was known, as the islands were said to consist entirely of calcareous rocks, derived from comminuted shells and corals, although Lieutenant Nelson, R.E., noticed on the island small pieces of oxide of iron of very questionable origin. It is, however, evident from these observations that some disturbing cause exists in the neighbourhood of the island which vitiates magnetic observations taken on shore. . . .

Bermuda and its outlying banks are thus situated on the summit of a large cone with a wide base, rising from the submerged plateau of the Atlantic, which is, in this region, three miles (2600 fathoms) beneath the surface of the sea. It is very probably an ancient volcano, now completely covered with a white shroud, composed of the skeletons and shells of organisms.

The late Sir C. Wyville Thompson was of opinion that the "red earth" which largely forms the soil of Bermuda had an organic origin, as well as the "red clay" which the Challenger discovered in all the greater depths of the ocean basins. He regarded the red earth and red clay as an ash left behind after the gradual removal of the lime by water charged with carbonic acid. This ash he regarded as a constituent part of the shells of Foraminifera, skeletons of Corals, and Molluscs. This theory does not seem to be in any way teneable. Analysis of carefully selected shells of Foraminifera, Heteropods, and Pteropods, did not show the slightest trace of alumina, and none has yet been discovered in coral skeletons. It is most probable that a large part of the clayey matter found in red clay and the red earth of Bermuda is derived from the disintegration of pumic, which is continually found floating on the surface of the sea. The Naturalists of the Challenger found it among the floating masses of Gulf Weed, and it is frequently picked up on the reefs of Bermuda and other Coral islands. The red earth contains a good many fragments of magnetite, augite, felspar, and glassy fragments, and when a large quantity of the rock of Bermuda is dissolved away with acid, a small number of fragments are also met with. These mineral particules most probably came originally from the pumise which had been cast up on the island for long ages (for it is known that these minerals are present in pumice), although possibly some of them may have come from the volcanic rock, which is believed to form the nucleus of the island.

The land surface of the islands is almost entirely composed of blown calcareous sand, more or less consolidated into hard rock. In several places, and especially at Tuckerstown and Elbow Bay, there exist considerable tracts covered with modern sand dunes, some of which are encroaching inland upon cultivated ground, and have overwhelmed at Elbow Bay a cottage, the chimney of which is now to be seen above the sand. The constant encroachment of the dunes is prevented by the growth upon them of several binding plants, amongst which a hard prickly grass (Cenchrus), with long, deeply penetrating root-fibres, is the most efficient. When these binding plants are artificially removed, the sand at once begins to shift.

The scenery of Bermuda is in some respects not unlike that of certain northern lake districts, for the numerous small islands which are dotted over the sounds and land-locked sheets of water are covered with vegetation down to the water's edge. The dark colour of the Juniper (*Juniperus bermudiana,* a species peculiar to these islands and the West Indies), called in the island "Cedar," the prevailing foliage, not unlike that of Pines in appearance, gives the landscape a northern aspect, and on cloudy days, the island, as viewed from the sea, looks cold and bleak. The extreme lowness of all the land, however, is characteristic and distinctive. Most conspicuous, next to the Juniper as a general feature in the vegetation, is probably the Oleander (*Nerium oleander*), which, having been introduced, flourishes everywhere. A large portion of the uncultivated land is covered with a dense growth of another introduced plant, *Lantana camera,* a most troublesome weed.

The most refreshing and beautiful vegetation in Bermuda is that growing in the marshes and caves. The marshes or peat bogs lie in the inland hollows between two ranges of hills, and are covered with a tall luxuriant growth of ferns, especially two species of *Osmunda* (*Osmunda cinnamomea* and *Osmunda regalis*). Some ferns are restricted to particular marshes; one salt marsh fern (*Acrostichum aureum*) grows densely to a height of 4 to 5 feet. Together with the ferns grows the Juniper, which thrives in the marshes, and a species of Palm (*Sabal blackburniana*), thus giving a pleasing variety to the foilage.

A very careful collection of the plants of the islands was made during the stay, and this, together with a most valuable series of specimens collected by General Lefroy after prolonged exertions extending over the whole period of his residence in the group, forms the basis of the treatise on the flora of the islands which forms one of the Botanical Reports of the Expedition. It is there shown that the group possesses far more vegetable forms peculiar to itself than had hitherto been suspected. It is probable that the occurrence of North American plants in the islands is connected with the fact that the islands are visited from time to time by immense numbers of migratory birds from that continent, especially during their great southern migration. Of these the American Golden Plover (*Charadrius marmoratus*) seems to visit Bermuda in the greatest numbers, but various other birds frequenting marshes— gallinules, rails, and snipes—arrive in no small quantities every year. These birds have possibly brought a good many plants to Bermuda, as seeds attached to their feet or feathers, or in their crops. Some of the most conspicuous of the present land birds of Bermuda, such as the "Red Bird," or Cardinal, have been introduced for ornamental effect.

The birds most interesting to the naturalist encountering them for the first time are the "Boatswain-birds" (*Phaethon flavirostris*). They are white, a little smaller than the commonest English Gull, and shaped more like a Sea-swallow or Tern, though allied to the Gannets and Cormorants; in the tail are two long narrow feathers of a reddish tint, which, as the bird flies, are kept extended behind, and give it a curious appearance. The birds breed, more or less gregariously, in holes in the rock formed by the weathering out of softer layers; it is easy to secure them in the hole by clapping a cap over its mouth, when both male and female can often be caught together. It is, however, quite a different matter to get hold of them for skinning: their bills are very sharp and strong, and they fight furiously, screaming all the while. Only one egg is laid, and it is of a dark red colour like that of the kestrel.

The corals of Bermuda may be seen growing to great advantage by the use of a water glass. The species are, as will be seen by the list below, as far as is yet known 25 in number, of which 23 are Anthozoan and 2 Hydrozoan; the latter (species of *Millepora*) are very abundant, and contribute largely to the reef formation. While some species, such as the great Brain Coral (*Diploria cerebriformis*), which is conspicuous at the bottom as a bright yellow mass, appear to prefer to grow where the water is lighted up by the sunshine, other species, such as *Millepora ramosa* and *Isophyllia dipsacea,* seem to thrive best in the shade. One species, *Agaricia fragilis,* occurs growing in colonies in great abundance in water from a foot to a fathom in depth, inside small caverns, and forms very thin and fragile plate-like laminae, which when bleached are almost the loveliest of corals.

30

La Pelée

LAFCADIO HEARN
(circa 1890)

Lafcadio Hearn (1850–1904) is not much remembered today, but in his time he was fairly well known as a newspaper journalist (The Cincinnati Enquirer; The New Orleans Times-Inquirer) *and a travel writer whose Caribbean and Japanese chronicles were well received. Hearn had doubtful beginnings as an American writer, for he was born to a Maltese mother and an Anglo-Irish father on the Greek island of Santa Maura (called in antiquity Leucadia), and after a dislocated childhood spent in Ireland, England, and France arrived as a penniless teenager in Cincinnati in 1869. Somehow he was working as a reporter for* The Cincinnati Enquirer *three years later. Hearn published sixteen books in his lifetime and from 1890 through 1904 lived in Japan, where he married a Japanese woman, Setsu Koizumi, and taught at the Imperial University and Waseda University. This selection, excerpted from his book of Caribbean sketches* Two Years in the French West Indies *(New York: Harper and Brothers, 1890) describes Hearn's ascent of Mont Pelée on the island of Martinique, a volcanic pinnacle that would erupt violently on May 8, 1902. Hearn's purple prose is vintage turn-of-the-century rhapsody; he paints the lush tropical scenery in a florid prose bordering on poetry.[1] Attaining the summit of Pelée, he is humbled by a vision of "Nature's eternal youth" and "the passionless permanence of that about us and beyond us." Hearn was finely attuned to the beauty of nature in a way that many of his predecessors were not, and in this respect anticipates the nature essayists of the twentieth century, who would also abandon the purely utilitarian approach for the more aesthetic.*

1. Most of the ellipses are Hearn's, and are indicative of his impressionistic style.

From *Two Years in the French West Indies,* by Lafcadio Hearn (New York: Harper and Brothers, 1890).

Sometimes, while looking at La Pelée, I have wondered if the enterprise of the great Japanese painter who made the Hundred Views of Fujiyama could not be imitated by some creole artist equally proud of his native hills, and fearless of the heat of the plains or the snakes of the slopes. A hundred views of Pelée might certainly be made: for the enormous mass is omnipresent to dwellers in the northern part of the island, and can be seen from the heights of the most southern mornes. It is visible from almost any part of St. Pierre,—which nestles in a fold of its rocky skirts. It overlooks all the island ranges, and overtops the mighty Pitons of Carbet by a thousand feet. . . .

Huge as the mountain looks from St. Pierre, the eye underestimates its bulk; and when you climb the mornes about the town, Labelle, d'Orange, or the much grander Parnasse, you are surprised to find how much vaster Pelée appears from these summits. Volcanic hills often seem higher, by reason of their steepness, than they really are; but Pelée deludes in another manner. From surrounding valleys it appears lower, and from adjacent mornes higher that it really is: the illusion in the former case being due to the singular slope of its contours, and the remarkable breadth of its base, occupying nearly all the northern end of the island; in the latter, to misconception of the comparative height of the eminence you have reached, which deceives by the precipitous pitch of its side . . . in bulk Pelée is grandiose: it spurs out across the island from the Caribbean to the Atlantic: the great chains of mornes about it are merely counter-forts; the Piton Pierrueux and the Piton Pain-a-Sucre (*Sugarloaf Peak*), and other elevations varying from 800 to 2100 feet, are its volcanic children. Nearly thirty rivers have their birth in its flanks,—besides many thermal springs, variously mineralized. As the culminant point of the island, Pelée is also the ruler of its meteorlogic life,—cloud-herder, lightning-forger, and rain-maker. During clear weather you can see it drawing to itself all the white vapors of the land,—robbing lesser eminences of their shoulder-wraps and head-coverings;—though the Pitons of Carbet (3700 feet) usually manage to retain about their middle a cloud-clout,—a *lantchô*. You will also see that the clouds run in a circle about Pelée,—gathering bulk as they turn by continual accessions from other points. If the crater be totally bare in the morning, and shows the broken edges very sharply against the blue, it is a sign of foul rather than of fair weather to come. . . . Is the great volcano dead? . . . Nobody knows. Less than forty years ago it rained ashes over all the roofs of St. Pierre;—within twenty years it has uttered mutterings. For the moment, it appears to sleep; and the clouds have dripped into the cup of its highest crater till it has become a lake, several hundred yards in circumference. The crater occupied by this lake—called L'Étang, or "the Pool"—has never been active within human memory. There are others,—difficult and dangerous to visit because opening on the side of a tremendous gorge; and it was one of these, no doubt, which has always been called *La Souffrière,* that rained ashes over the city in 1851. . . .

We enter the *grand-bois,*—the primitive forest,—the "high woods." As seen with a field-glass from St. Pierre, these woods present only the appearance of a band of moss belting the volcano, and following all its corrugations,— so densely do the leafy crests intermingle. But on actually entering them, you find yourself at once in green twilight, among lofty trunks uprising everywhere like huge pillars wrapped with vines;—and the interspaces between these bulks are all occupied by lianas and parasitic creepers,—some monstrous—veritable parasite trees,—ascending at all angles, or dropping straight down from the tallest crests to take root again. The effect in the dim light is that of innumerable black ropes and cables of varying thicknesses stretched taut from the soil to the tree-tops, and also from branch to branch, like rigging. There are rare and remarkable trees here,—acomats, courbarils, balatas, ceibas or fromagers, acajous, gommiers;—hundreds have been cut down by charcoalmakers; but the forest is still grand. It is to be regretted that the Government has placed no restriction upon the barbarous destruction of trees by the *charbonniers,* which is going on throughout the island. Many valuable woods are rapidly disappearing. The courbaril, yielding a fine-grained, heavy, chocolate-colored timber; the balata, giving a wood even heavier, denser, and darker; the acajou, producing a rich red wood, with a strong scent of cedar; the bois-de-fer; the bois d'Inde; the superb acomat,—all used to flourish by tens of thousands upon these volcanic slopes, whose productiveness is eighteen times greater than that of the richest European soil. All Martinique furniture used to be made of native woods; and the colored cabinet-makers still produce work which would probably astonish New York or London manufacturers. But today the island exports no more hard woods: it has even been found necessary to import much from neighboring islands;—and yet the destruction of forests still go on. The domestic fabrication of charcoal from forest-trees has been estimated at 1,400,000 hecto-litres per annum. Primitive forest still covers the island to the extent of 21.37 per cent; but to find precious woods now, one must climb heights like those of Pelée and Carbet, or penetrate into the mountains of the interior.

Most common formerly on these slopes were the gommiers, from which canoes of a single piece, forty-five feet long by seven wide, used to be made. There are plenty of gommiers still; but the difficulty of transporting them to the shore has latterly caused a demand for the gommiers of Dominica. The dimensions of canoes now made from these trees rarely exceed fifteen feet in length by eighteen inches in width: the art of making them is an inheritance from the ancient Caribs. First the trunk is shaped to the form of the canoe, and pointed at both ends; it is then hollowed out. The width of the hollow does not exceed six inches at the widest part; but the cavity is then filled with wet sand, which in the course of some weeks widens the excavation by its weight, and gives the boat perfect form. Finally gunwales of plank are fasted on; seats are put in—generally four;—and no boat is more durable nor more swift. . . .

Walking becomes more difficult;—there seems no termination to the grand-bois: always the same faint green light, the same rude natural stair-way of slippery roots,—half the time hidden by fern leaves and vines. Sharp ammoniacal scents are in the air; a dew, cold as ice-water, drenches our clothing. Unfamiliar insects make trilling noises in dark places; and now and then a series of soft clear notes ring out, almost like a thrush's whistle: the chant of a little tree-frog. The path becomes more and more overgrown; and but for the constant excursions of the cabbage-hunters, we should certainly have to cutlass every foot of the way through creepers and brambles. More and more amazing also is the interminable interweaving of roots: the whole forest is thus spun together—not underground so much as overground. These tropical trees do not strike deep, although able to climb steep slopes of porphyry and basalt: they send out great far-reaching webs of roots,—each such web interknotting with others all round it, and these in turn with further ones; while between their reticulations lianas ascend and descend: and a nameless multitude of shrubs as tough as india-rubber push up, together with mosses, grasses, and ferns. Square miles upon square miles of woods are thus interlocked and interbound into one mass solid enough to resist the pressure of a hurricane; and where there is no path already made, entrance into them can only be effected by the most dextrous cutlassing. . . .

At last we are rejoiced to observe that the trees are becoming smaller;—there are no more colossal trunks;—there are frequent glimpses of sky: the sun has risen well above the peaks, and sends occasional beams down through the leaves. Ten minutes, and we reach a clear space,—a wild savane, very steep, above which looms a higher belt of woods. Here we take another short rest. . . .

We enter the upper belt of woods—green twilight again. There are as many lianas as ever: but they are less massive in stem:—the trees, which are stunted, stand closer together;—and the web-work of roots is finer and more thickly spun. These are called the *petit-bois* (little woods), in contradistinction to the grands-bois, or high woods. Multitudes of balisiers, dwarf palms, aborescent ferns, wild guavas, mingle with the lower growths on either side of the path, which has narrowed to the breadth of a wheel-rut, and is nearly concealed by protruding grasses and fern leaves. Never does the sole of the foot press upon a surface large as itself,—always the slippery backs of roots crossing at all angles, like loop-traps, over sharp fragments of volcanic rock or pumice-stone. There are abrupt descents, sudden acclivities, mud-holes, and fissures;—one grasps at the ferns on both sides to keep from falling; and some ferns are spiked sometimes on the under surface, and tear the hands. But the barefooted guides stride on rapidly, erect as ever under their loads,—chopping off with their cutlasses any branches that hang too low. There are beautiful flowers here,—various unfamiliar species of lobelia;—pretty red and yellow blossoms belonging to plants which the creole physician calls *Bromeliaceae;* and a plant like the *Guy Lusacia* of Brazil, with violet-red petals. There is an indescribable multitude of ferns,— a very museum of ferns! The doctor, who is a great woodsman, says that he never makes a trip to the hills without finding some new kind of fern; and he had already a collection of several hundred.

The route is continually growing steeper, and makes a number of turns and windings: we reach another bit of savane, where we have to walk over black-pointed stones that resemble slag;—then more petits-bois, still more dwarfed, then another opening. The naked crest of the volcano appears like a peaked precipice, dark-red, with streaks of green, over a narrow but terrific chasm on the left: we are almost on a level with the crater, but must make a long circuit to reach it, through a wilderness of stunted timber and bush. The creoles call this undergrowth *razié:* it is really only a prolongation of the low jungle which carpets the high forests below, with this difference, there are fewer creepers and much more fern. Suddenly we reach a black gap in the path about thirty inches wide—half hidden by the tangle of leaves,—*La Fente.* It is a volcanic fissure which divides the whole ridge, and is said to have no bottom: for fear of a possible slip, the guides insist upon holding our hands while we cross it. Happily there are no more such clefts; but there are mud-holes, snags, roots, and loose rocks beyond counting. Least disagreeable are the *bourbiers,* in which you sink to your knees in black or gray slime. Then the path descends into open light again;—and we find ourselves at the Étang,—in the dead Crater of the three Palmistes. . . .

Regaining the bank, we prepare to ascend the Morne de la Croix. The circular path by which it is commonly reached is now under water; and we have to wade up to our waists. All the while clouds keep passing over us in great slow whirls. Some are white and half-transparent; others opaque and dark gray;—a dark cloud passing through a white one looks like a goblin. Gaining the opposite shore, we find a very rough path over splintered stone, ascending between the thickest fern-growths possible to imagine. The general tone of this fern is dark green; but there are paler cloudings of yellow and pin,—due to the varying age of the leaves, which are pressed into a cushion three or four feet high, and almost solid enough to sit upon. About two hundred and fifty yards from the crater edge, the path rises above this tangle, and zigzags up the morne, which now appears twice as lofty as from the lake, where we had a curiously foreshortened view of it. It then looked scarcely a hundred feet high; it is more than double that. The cone is green to the top with moss, low grasses, small fern, and creeping pretty plants, like violets, with big carmine flowers. The path is a black line: the rock laid bare by its looks as if burning to the core. We have now to use our hands in climbing; but the low thick ferns give a good hold. Out of breath, and drenched in perspiration, we reach the apex,—the highest point of the island. But we are curtained about with clouds,—moving in dense white and gray masses: we cannot see fifty feet away. . . .

The ground gives out a peculiar hollow sound when tapped, and is covered with a singular lichen,—all composed of round overlapping leaves about one-eighth of an inch in diameter, pale green, and tough as fish-scales. Here and there one sees a beautiful branching growth, like a mass of green coral: it is a gigantic moss. *Cabane-Jesus* ("bed of-Jesus") the patois name is: at Christmas-time, in all the churches, those decorated cribs in which the image of the Child-Saviour is laid are filled with it. The creeping crimson violet is also here. Fireflies with bronze-green bodies are crawling about;—I noticed also small frogs, large gray crickets, and a species of snail with a black shell. A solitary humming-bird passes, with a beautiful blue head, flaming like sapphire.

All at once the peak vibrates to a tremendous sound from somewhere below. . . . It is only a peal of thunder; but it startled at first, because the mountain rumbles and grumbles occasionally. . . . From the wilderness of ferns about the lake a sweet long low whistle comes—three times;—a *siffluer-de-montagne* has its nest there.

There is a rain-storm over the woods beneath us: clouds now hide everything but the point on which we rest; the crater of the Palmistes becomes invisible. But it is only for a little while that we are thus befogged: a wind comes, blows the clouds over us, lifts them up and folds them like a drapery, and slowly whirls them away northward. And for the first time the view is clear over the intervening gorge,—now spaned by the rocket-leap of a perfect rainbow.

Valleys and mornes, peaks and ravines,—succeeding each other swiftly as surge succeeds surge in a storm,—a weirdly tossed world, but beautiful as it is weird: all green the foreground, with all tints of green, shadowing off to billowy distances of purest blue. The sea-line remains invisible as ever: you know where it is only by the zone of pale light ringing the double sphericity of sky and ocean. And in this double blue void the island seems to hang suspended: far peaks seem to come up from nowhere, to rest on nothing—like forms of mirage. Useless to attempt photography;—distances take the same color as the sea. Vauclin's truncated mass is recognizable only by the shape of its indigo shadows. All is vague, vertiginous;—the land still seems to quiver with the prodigious forces that upheaved it. . . .

At the beginning, while gazing south, east, west, to the rim of the world, all laughed, shouted, interchanged the quick delight of new impressions: every face was radiant. . . . Now all look serious;—none speak. The first physical joy of finding oneself on this point in violet air, exalted above the hills, soon yields to other emotions inspired by the mighty vision and the colossal peace of the heights. Dominating all, I think, is the consciousness of the awful antiquity of what one is looking upon,—such a sensation, perhaps, as of old found utterance in that tremendous question of the Book of Job:—*"Was thou brought forth before the hills?"* . . . And the blue multitude of the peaks, the perpetual congregation of the mornes, seem to chorus in the vast resplendence,—telling of Nature's eternal youth, and the passionless permanence of that about us and beyond us and beneath,—until something like the fulness of a great grief begins to weigh at the heart. . . . For all this astonishment of beauty, all this majesty of light and form and color, will surely endure,—marvellous as now,—after we shall have lain down to sleep where no dreams come, and may never arise from the dust of our rest to look upon it.

31

The Tragedy of Pelée

GEORGE KENNAN
(circa 1902)

The 1902 eruption of Mt Pelée on Martinique ranks with those of Mt. Vesuvius and of Krakatoa as one of the most destructive volcanic events in history. In a matter of minutes all but one of the 30,000 inhabitants of St. Pierre were killed either by the 3,600° Fahrenheit shock wave or by the colossal barrage of airborne lava and pumice. George Kennan (no dates available) was a journalist member of the U. S. relief expedition that was dispatched immediately following news of the disaster. Kennan toured the ruins of St. Pierre, climbed Mt. Pelée, and interviewed eyewitnesses; his chronicle, The Tragedy of Pelée, a Narrative of Personal Experience and Observation in Martinique, *was published by the Outlook Company in New York later that year. This selection paints a vivid picture of the horror of the event and its aftermath, and is a sober reminder of the awesome power of nature, in the Caribbean and elsewhere. The black volcanic beach sands of Martinique attest to the fact that this great peak has erupted many times in the past, and will again in the future.*

From *The Tragedy of Pelée,* by George Kennan (New York: The Outlook Company, 1902).

The morning of May 8 dawned clear; but a column of vapor was rising to a great height above the main crater of Pelée, and ashes were falling all along the line of the coast from St. Pierre to Prêcheur. An occasional detonation could be heard in the direction of the mountain, but there was no other sign or forewarning of the impending catastrophe. Above eight o'clock, with a rending, roaring sound, a great cloud of black smoke appeared suddenly on the southwestern face of the volcano near its summit, and rushed swiftly down in the direction of St. Pierre as if it were smoke from the discharge of a colossal piece of artillery. There was no sharp, thunderous explosion when the cloud appeared, nor was it preceded or followed by an outburst of flame; but as it rolled like a great torrent of black fog down the mountain slope there was a continuous roar of half-blended staccato beats of varying intensity, something like the throbbing, pulsating roar of a Gatling-gun battery going into action. The time occupied by the descent of this volcanic tornado-cloud was not more, Mr. Clerc thinks, than two or three minutes; and if so, it moved with a velocity of between ninety and a hundred and thirty-five miles an hour. It struck the western end of Mont Parnasse about half a mile from the place where Mr. Clerc [Clerc related an eyewitness account to Kennan] was standing; swept directly over St. Pierre, wrecking and setting fire to the buildings as it passed, and then went diagonally out to sea, scorching the cocoanut [sic] palms and touching with an invisible torch a few inflammable houses at the extreme northern end of the village of Carbet.

It began almost immediately to grow dark—probably as a result of the mushrooming out of the immense, ash-laden column of vapor thrown heavenward from the main crater—and in ten or fifteen minutes the only light to be seen was a faint glow that came through the falling ashes from the burning ruins of St. Pierre. It was so dark that Mr. Clerc could make sure of the presence and safety of his wife and children only by groping for them and touching them with his hands. He could not see even the outlines of their figures. In twenty minutes or half an hour, a little light began to filter through the inky canopy of volcanic dust overhead, and it became possible to move about; but the landscape was still obscured by falling ashes mixed with rain; and Mount Pelée had wrapped itself from base to summit in a black mantle of vapor. Appalled by the frightful volcanic hurricane, the Egyptian darkness, the glow of the burning city, and the mystery of the whole terrible catastrophe, Mr. Clerc fled with his family and friends to a place of greater safety in the interior of the country. At the earliest opportunity he sent his wife and children to one of the neighboring islands—I think Guadeloupe—visited the ruins of St. Pierre, where many of his relatives and nearly all his dearest friends lay buried under thousands of tons of stones from shattered walls, and finally returned alone to his ash-powdered plantation at Vive.

. . . the most interesting person in Morne Rouge, at the time of our visit, was Auguste Ciparis, a negro criminal who lived through the destruction of St. Pierre in a dungeon of the city jail. We had heard of this man in Fort de France, and had been told that he was the sole survivor of the great catastrophe; but we had not been able to find anyone who had actually seen him, or who knew where he was, and we had finally come to regard him as the product of some newspaper man's imagination. Father Mary, however, assured us that he was a real person, and that he had been brought to Morne Rouge four days after the disaster by two negroes who had accidentally found him in the ruins of the city. . . . We found him in one of the bare, fly-infested rooms of an abandoned wooden dwelling-house on the main street which the cure had turned into a sort of lazaret. As there was no physician, surgeon, or pharmacy in the place, the unfortunate prisoner had had no treatment, and the air of the small, hot room was so heavy and foul with the offensive odor of his neglected burns that I could hardly force myself to breathe it. He was sitting stark naked, on the dirty striped mattress of a small wooden cot, with a bloody sheet thrown over his head like an Arab burnoose and gathered in about the loins. He had been more frightfully burned, I think, that any man I had ever seen. His face, strangely enough, had escaped injury, and his hair had not even been scorched; but there were terrible burns on his back and legs, and his badly swollen feet and hands were covered with yellow, offensive matter which had no resemblance whatever to human skin or flesh. The burns were apparently very deep—so deep that blood oozed from them—and to my unprofessional eye they looked as if they might have been made by hot steam.

When asked to describe all that happened at the time when he received these burns, Ciparis said that the cell he occupied in the St. Pierre prison was an underground dungeon, which had no other window than a grated aperture in the upper part of the door. On the morning of May 8, while he was waiting for breakfast, it suddenly grew very dark; and almost immediately afterward hot air, mixed with fine ashes, came in through the door-grating and burned him. He rushed and jumped in agony about the cell and cried for help; but there was no answer. He heard no noise, saw no fire, and smelled nothing except "what he thought was his own body burning." The intense heat lasted only a moment, and during that time he breathed as little as possible. There was no smoke in the cell and the hot air came in through the door-grating without any noticeable rush or blast. He had on, at that time, hat, shirt, and trouser, but no shoes. His clothing did not take fire, and yet his back was very severely burned under his shirt. The water in his cell did not get hot—or, at least, it was not hot when he first took a drink, after the catastrophe. . . . For a long time he groaned with pain, and cried at intervals, "Help! Save me!" but no one answered, and he did not hear a sound again until the following Sunday, nearly four days after the catastrophe [when he was rescued]. . . . He had been four days without food, and was consequently weak and faint; but after taking a drink of water he felt better, and was able, with some help and support from his rescuers, to walk six kilometers . . . to Morne Rouge.

Ciparis . . . answered all our questions simply and quietly, without making any attempt to exaggerate or to heighten the effect of his narrative by embroidering it with fanciful and marvelous details. He heard no explosions or detonations; saw no flames; smelled no sulphurous gas; and had no feeling of suffocation. He was simply burned by hot air and hot ashes which came into his cell through the door grating. . . . Thanks to Mr. Jaccaci, who sent to the Military Hospital in Fort de France for linseed oil, limewater, phenic acid, and aseptic bandages, the prisoner's burns, when we visited Morne Rouge the second time were properly cared for and dressed, and there seemed to be every probability that he would live.

. . . St. Pierre, before the catastrophe of May 8, was a picturesque, brightly colored French city, set down in a West Indian environment between a range of vine-draped, palm-fringed hills and the margin of a tranquil, indigo-blue sea. After the catastrophe, it was a wrecked, ruined city of the dead, wrapped in a gray winding-sheet of volcanic ashes.

The first impression that it made upon me when I landed on the wreck-strewn beach of the Place Bertin was one of loneliness, stillness, grayness, and almost unimaginable desolation. There was no color, no structural form, no traceable plan, and no sign whatever of recent life . . . one might have imagined that he was looking at the ruins of a big pueblo in an Arizona desert, which had been destroyed by a frightful earthquake a hundred years before. It was almost impossible to realize, or even to believe, that, within a month, this had been a bright, gay, beautiful city of thirty thousand inhabitants. . . . The building that stood highest . . . was the old cathedral. . . . The side walls had been thrown down . . . at the interior was a shapeless mass of ruins, in which lay, half-buried a large bell . . . what had once been a beautiful little park . . . had been turned into a flat expanse of dry volcanic mud, with the leafless and almost branchless trunks of the trees lying across it in parallel lines. . . . Away from the main streets there were only the foundations of walls and heaps of rounded stones to show where houses had been. . . . It was often impossible for me to determine whether I was in a street or in the midst of a ruined block of buildings. . . .

With regard to the effect of the blast upon the bodies of human beings [rescuers reported to me that] the bodies of the dead were generally distorted and had the color of burned coffee. Most of them lay in the streets, where they had been subjected to the heat of burning buildings . . . a very large number of bodies had burst at the abdomen; all spongy cellular tissues were greatly distended, and many skulls had parted at the sutures, without any indication of external injury . . . [which suggested] a sudden removal of atmospheric pressure, brought about in some way by the blast . . . [elsewhere] the colossal statue of the Virgin Mary, which weighed at least two or three tons, had been blown off its pedestal and carried to a distance of forty or fifty feet. Such effects could hardly have been produced by a blast of lower velocity than a hundred miles an hour. . . . We wandered over the ruins of the wrecked city for an hour and a half or two hours, and were then driven by a heavy rain to the shelter of the tug.

32

The Banana Plantations of Costa Rica

FREDERICK UPHAM ADAMS
(circa 1914)

Frederick Upham Adams (1859–1921) was a minor inventor and author of several books, including the documentary history Conquest of the Tropics, The Story of the Creative Enterprises Conducted by the United Fruit Company (*New York: Doubleday, Page and Company, 1914*). *As the influence of the former colonial powers—Britain, France, Spain—declined in the late nineteenth and early twentieth Century, a new kind of external entity exerted its power in the Caribbean: the international corporation. Wild nature was radically transformed in Guatemala, Nicaragua, Costa Rica, and elsewhere by the United Fruit Company, which, as Adams relates, employed tens of thousands on its fruit plantations. These "armies," as Adams calls them, deforested vast regions in order to plant bananas and other monoculture crops. The social and environmental effects of this activity have been profound.*

From *conquest of the Tropics, the Story of the Creative Enterprises Conducted by the United Fruit Company* (New York: Doubleday, Page and Company, 1914).

The banana plantations of the United Fruit Company in Costa Rica follow the valleys of three rivers which take their source in the mountains to the west and south. These rivers are named the Estrella, Banana, and Reventazon, the last emptying into the Caribbean a few miles north of Puerto Limon. More than 400 miles of railroad and tramways traverse these plantations and link them with the wharves at Puerto Limon. This railroad system also serves many independent growers of bananas who have contracts with the United Fruit Company. These independent growers are entitled to have their fruit collected and accepted twice a week, and in the "heavy" or rainy seasons they are entitled to four weekly cuttings and collections of their bananas. There are times, as I have explained, when this arrangement occasions heavy losses to the importer, who is compelled to accept large consignments for which there is no profitable market.

Scattered through this banana empire are a number of picturesque settlements, some of which have arrived at the dignity of towns, with churches, places of amusements, well-kept streets, electric lights and most of the accessories of advanced civilization. It seems strange to reflect that all of these towns, railroads, bridges, docks, steamships, and the bustling city of Puerto Limon itself are merely parts of a giant banana farm, and that this is only one of the farms in a series which dot the Caribbean coast from Guatemala to Santa Marta, Columbia.

Everywhere the observer sees the manifestations of a carefully designed machine calculated to yield the greatest possible result from a given application of endeavor. Here is an industrial army engaged in a constant battle with the forces of tropical nature. There is no telling when nature may strike an unexpected and dangerous blow. I crossed one railroad bridge whose predecessors had been swept away in floods thirty-one times, but it will take a record-breaking deluge to topple the huge steel structure which now spans this part of the Rio Reventazon. Corps of skilled engineers are constantly at work repairing defects and meeting new problems. Trained physicians keep watch and guard over the health of this army and hold in check any threatened invasion of contagious disease. The wireless telegraph flashes its instructions or warning out into all parts of the Caribbean, and keeps in close and constant communication with the Great White Fleet which bears to the north the fruits raised by the various divisions in this industrial army.

Sixty thousand trained men are working in the American tropics under the command of the skilled generals of the United Fruit Company, and to what end? To the end that the most perishable of tropical luxuries shall be produced so economically and handled so carefully and swiftly that it reaches the consumers of another clime in perfect condition and is offered for sale at prices lower than those charged for home-grown fruits! There is a task which would have daunted Hercules, but it is one within the easy power of the modern industrial miracle worker. Yet to me this mastery of time and space and flood and sea has all the spell of the romantic, and the subject should command the genius and melody of a poet rather than the halting comments of a worker in prose.

I shall never forget the first night I spent in Puerto Limon. I was on board the S.S. *Sixaola,* one of the ships of the Great White Fleet, and she lay at her dock . . . [with] four other ships. . . . Out in the bay the surf lazily caressed the shores of an island where once the pirate Morgan beached his ships and planned for new plunderings of defenseless coast towns. Kipling's lines to the "South Wind," in his poem to the English flag, suggested themselves:

Over a thousand islands lost in an idle main
Where the sea-egg flames on the coral and the long-backed breakers
    croon
Their endless ocean legends to the lazy, locked lagoon.

33

Folk-Tales of Andros Island, Bahamas

ELSIE CLEWS PARSONS
(circa 1918)

In 1918 the American Folklore Society published Folk-Tales of Andros Island, Bahamas (*New York: G. E. Stechert*), *a collection transcribed and edited by Elsie Clews Parsons (no dates available). At that time Andros Island was populated with around 7500 inhabitants of African-American descent; these settlers came from the Florida Everglades and the Mosquito coast of Nicaragua.[1] The stories have African, European, and Caribbean elements to them, and reflect a rich synthesis of cultural influences. "Forbidden Fruit," for example, suggests Eve's temptation at the Forbidden Tree in the Garden of Eden. "The Escape," on the other hand, which describes the escape of a sea turtle from captivity, probably derives in part from the experience of being liberated from slavery. "The Fish Lover" and "A Fish Turns into a Baby" assume a plasticity to nature—the easy transformation of life forms— that has a non-Western origin and is closer to the perspectives of nature found in West Africa and among the Amerindians. The value of these folk stories is that they challenge conventional perspectives on nature, and enable us to see nature freshly.*

1. Elsie Clews Parsons. *Folk-Tales of Andros Island, Bahamas* (New York: G. E. Stechert, 1918), ix.

From *Folk-Tales of Andros Island, Bahamas,* by Elsie Clews Parsons (New York: The American Folk-Lore Society, 1918).

The Fish Lover, *by Lizzie Richardson*

Dis was a young girl. 'Airy man come. Don' want him. May say, "You got to get married." Dis day gone to de water side an' commence to shed tears. See dis fish come. Say, "My deah, you love me?" Say, "Yes, darlin', I love you." Say, "You like to co'te me?"—"Yes, darlin', I like to co'te you." He (she) goin' home an' ketch one of de bes' fowl what he ma ha' an' kill it an' den he (she) goin' to de bay. He (she) sing,—

Ko - leay___ Ko - leay___ Sa - la - yan - du Ko
ko yo ma ta yea___ sa - la - yan - du.

After he ma didn't like de match, say "Moder, you don' like him. I love him." After he come to find out de man was a fish, hes broder come to de water side. Said, "Mamma, my sister co'tin' to a fish." Mamma say, "No, I don' believe it." Broder take his gun an' gwoin' to de water side, an' sing,—

> "Koleay Koleay Salayandu
> Ko ko yo ma ta yea salayandu."

De minute de fish come, den he shot it. He take de fish in to de moder. Say, "I tol' you dat sister was co'tin' to a fish, an' den you didn't believe me. I shoot it. Here it is." Dat story en.'

A Fish Turns Into A Baby, *by Marion Hurlbut*

Once it was a woman. She went in the market. She bought a fish. She come out; an' ven she behol' it, it was a baby. An' then she said, "Oh, what a pretty little baby!" An' she commenced to dance it, an' everybody come up an' prised de baby. She sing fer de baby,—

"Oh, dear! what is de matter?"

"Dear mother sen' me to buy a fish." An' when she come to fin' out, dear mother, it was a baby. It's finished.

Forbidden Fruit, by Lizzie Richardson

Dis man had a son, an' dis man travel far away, an' he beg his son not to touch dis fruit. "'Cause, if you touch dis fruit, I wouldn' be here, an' you be j'ined wid de sky." He say, "I gwine away for t'ree long months. Mind, don't pick it! If you eat it, you gwine up." An' he gwine away. After he eat it,—

Wa - lun-gan-ga ta ta tun-ga zu tun-ga zu tu, Wa - lun-gan-ga ta tay ta ta ta tu Ta-tay ta ta ta tu, Wo-lun-gan-ga Wo-lun - gan - ga ta ta tun - ga zu tun - ga zu tu.

He fader come. He knock one of de fruit on de tree root, an' de boy drop from de sky. He come alive. He pappa say, "Son, what pappa tell you?"—"All right, pappa, I would never do it again." Den he pa say, "I twine off to-morrow for seven long years; an' if you ever eat one of dem fruit, you be die." De boy gone right at it again. Him an' de tree gone right up to de sky. An' when de tree get away, stay dere! An' de fader been away six months, an' was no one to take de tree from dere, only de fader, cause he was obeah man. Den afterward, when de pa come an' take down de tree, he was a dead chil'. He ben up in de sky an' dry up.

The Escape, by Ann Wolfe

De' was a turtle dey catch. An' he tell 'em he wanted to get away. An' he was tricky. He tell 'em put him in a tub o' water an' he swim all roun'. He said de water was hot now. Carry him a leetle ways in de sea. Now, when dey carry him, he swin all roun'. He say, "People heah to see me?" Say, "Yes, make has', come back!" Say, "People beat a little for me."

Bon, bon, bon, bon, Cock-e-roach a-walk-in', Pa - le la la la la.

He swim off again. Say again, "People heah to see me?" People say, "Make has', ha' a good time to-night!" Den he went again an' didn' come back no mo'."

> Biddy biddy ban,
> My story en'.

Ask de cap'n de long-boat crew,
An he will tell you if dis story is true.

34

A Wilderness Laboratory

WILLIAM BEEBE
(circa 1918)

William Beebe (1877–1962) began his scientific career in 1899 as the curator of ornithology at the New York Zoological Gardens. After 1919 he served as director of the Department of Tropical Research at the New York Zoological Society (Bronx Zoo). In 1934 Beebe descended in a bathysphere to a depth of 3028 feet off Bermuda, which was a world record at that time. Beebe led numerous expeditions around the globe, from Borneo to British Guiana. He was a popular lecturer and helped, with his friend and peer Theodore Roosevelt, to disseminate the discoveries of natural history to the masses. Beebe authored over a dozen books, including a fine anthology of nature writing The Book of Naturalists: An Anthology of the Best Natural History *(New York: Alfred A. Knopf, 1944) and* Jungle Peace *(New York: Henry Holt, 1918), which chronicles his establishment of the Tropical Research Station in British Guiana. In this passage from* Jungle Peace *Beebe describes his long walks through the jungle with Theodore Roosevelt ("I know of no earthly pleasure more to be desired") and the interior of the wilderness laboratory ("The vampire bats never allowed us to become bored"). Although Beebe's perspective was limited by his ethnocentrism and by his intensely scientific focus, to be contrasted with the more worldly outlook of Edward O. Wilson in his selection on Surinam, Beebe was nevertheless wholly committed to understanding and preserving the wilderness.*

From *Jungle Peace,* by William Beebe (New York: Henry Holt and Company, 1918).

When the idea of a tropical research station occurred to me, the first person with whom I discussed the matter was Colonel Roosevelt. In all of my scientific undertakings under the auspices of the New York Zoological Society, I have found his attitude always one of whole-souled sympathy, checked and practicalized by trenchant criticism and advice. For Colonel Roosevelt, besides his other abilities and interests, is one of the best of our American naturalists. To a solid foundation of scientific knowledge, gained direct from literature, he adds one of the widest and keenest of experiences in the field. His published work is always based on a utilization of the two sources, and is characterized by a commendable restraint and the leaven of a philosophy which combines an unalterable adhesion to facts, with moderation of theory and an unhesitating use of the three words which should be ready for instant use in the vocabulary of every honest scientist, "I don't know."

My object in founding the research station was to destroy the bogie of danger and difficulty supposed to attend all tropical investigation, and to show that scientists from north temperate regions could accomplish keen, intensive, protracted scientific work in tropical jungles without injury to health or detriment to the facility of mental activity, and at extremely moderate expense. This will open to direct personal investigation, regions which, more than any others, promise dynamic results from evolutional study, and will supplement the work of museums with correlated researches upon living and freshly killed organisms. This was a "progressive" doctrine which Colonel Roosevelt endorsed with enthusiasm, and after we had brought semblance of a comfortable American home to great, rambling Kalacoon, we were able to welcome Colonel and Mrs. Roosevelt as the first visitors to the accomplishment of the project which, months before, we had so enthusiastically discussed at Oyster Bay.

The jungles of South America were no novelty to Colonel Roosevelt, but to be able to traverse them over smooth, easy trails, in a comfortable temperature and with no annoyance of flies or mosquitoes, was an experience which none of had enjoyed before. To Mrs. Roosevelt it was all new—the huge, buttressed trunks, the maze of lianas in tangles, loops and spirals, the sudden burst of pink or lavender blossoms in a sunlit spot, and the piercingly sweet, liquid notes of the goldbird, "like the bird of Siegfried," as she aptly said. . . .

Most memorable to me were the long walks which Colonel Roosevelt and I took on the Kaburi Trail, that narrow path which is the only entrance by land to all the great hinterland lying between the Essequibo and Mazruni Rivers. Majestically the massive trees rose on either side, so that while our contracted aisle was as lofty as the nave of a cathedral, yet it was densely shaded by the interlocking foliage high overhead. Our progress was thus through a glorified tunnel; we traveled molewise with only here and there a glimpse of the sky. Every walk was filled to the brim for me with that infinitely satisfying joy, derived from frank, sympathetic communion with an enthusiastic, true friend. I know of no earthly pleasure more to be desired. Perhaps this is because friends are so rare with whom one can be wholly natural, with one's guard completely down, unafraid of a misunderstanding—an omnimental communion.

It was with dismay, at the end of one long walk, that I realized we had forgotten to search for the tropical creatures for which we had presumably set out. We had kept the jungle birds and animals well at distance by a constant flow of human speech—argumentative, eulogistic, condemnatory—of literary and field and museum doings of the scientific world. . . .

Close to where we walked on those first days, we were later to find our best hunting. During the next few months all the more interesting animals of this part of South America were shot or their presence noticed; jaguars, tapirs, deer, pecaries, howling monkeys, vampires [vampire bats], agoutis, jaguarondis, otters, sloths, and armadillos. Host of birds, almost half the entire number of species found in the Colony, made their home hereabouts, macaws, bellbirds, curasows, trumpeters, toucans, the great harpy eagle and the tiniest of iridescent hummingbirds.

Within a week our great front room, full thirty by sixty feet, with sixteen large windows, was a laboratory in appearance and odor. Hundreds of jars and vials, vivaria and insectaries, microscopes, guns, and cameras, with all their details and mysterious inner workings, left no table vacant. With book-shelves up, there remained only the walls, which little by little became mosaics of maps, diagrams, sketches, drying skins, Indian weapons, birds' nests and shot-holes. Whiffs of formaline, chloroform, and xylol, together with the odors of occasional mislaid or neglected specimens, left no doubt as to the character of the room. We found that the tradewind [from the Caribbean Sea] came from the front, and also that we had much to discuss after the lamps were put out; so we turned the couches into their rightful functions of cots, and the three of us slept here and there in the great room.

The vampire bats never allowed us to become bored. There were no mosquitoes or flies, so we used no nets; but for months we burned a lantern. Low around our heads swept the soft wings of the little creatures, while the bat enthusiast now and then fired his auxiliary pistol. Later we found that a score of them roosted behind a broken clapboard, and, by spreading a seine below and around this, we were able to capture and examine the entire colony at will. Tarantulas were common, but not in the least offensive, and we learned to know where to look for a big black fellow and a small gray one who kept the room free from cockroaches. One or two scorpions were caught indoors, but the three centipedes which appeared occasionally were those which had been brought in and were always escaping from a defective vivarium. There were no other dangers or inconveniences, if we can apply such terms to these comparatively harmless creatures.

This was the background of our labors, our laboratory as our English visitors called it: cool in the daytime, cold at night, where one could work as well in the north, and where a morning's tramp usually furnished material sufficient for a week of research. . . .

35

Letter to Maxwell Perkins

ERNEST HEMINGWAY
(circa 1935)

No anthology of Caribbean nature writing would be complete without a selection by Ernest Hemingway (1899–1961), who lived in Key West, Florida, and Havana, Cuba, on a nearly permanent basis after 1928. Most of Hemingway's major short stories—including such works as "The Snows of Kilimanjaro" and "The Short Happy Life of Francis Macomber"—and all of his extended prose works after The Sun Also Rises *(Scribner's, 1926) were written either in Key West or Havana. This list of longer works of fiction and nonfiction includes* A Farewell to Arms, *part of* For Whom the Bell Tolls, Across the River and into the Trees, *part of* To Have and Have Not, The Old Man and the Sea, A Moveable Feast, Islands in the Stream, The Garden of Eden, The Green Hills of Africa, The Dangerous Summer, *and* Death in the Afternoon.

In 1934—during the depths of the Great Depression—Hemingway had the Pilar, *a custom-designed fishing cruiser, built at a cost of $7500. Hemingway was an avid big-game fisherman and often roamed the coast of Cuba and the Gulf Stream in pursuit of his favorite species, the Atlantic blue marlin. In recognition of his love for Cuba, Hemingway donated his Nobel Prize gold medallion to the Virgen de Cobre, Cuba's national saint. When he died in 1961, his home in Cuba—Finca Vigia—was made into a Cuban national museum. Much of his personal library of 7400 books, his favorite safari rifle (the Mannlicher carbine), and many of his big-game trophies are still found in Finca Vigia, which is carefully preserved just as he left it. The* Pilar *was brought up from the sea and now rests permanently outside his home.*

In this letter to Maxwell Perkins—Hemingway's editor at Charles Scribner's in New York—the author writes eloquently of the natural and human toll of the famous 1935 Matecumbe hurricane, a killer storm that packed two-hundred-mile-an-hour winds and seventeen-foot tidal surges and devastated the Florida Keys. Hemingway is particularly critical of the Roosevelt Administration, which failed to evacuate the World War I veterans of the Civilian Conservation Corps who were constructing the highway between Miami and Key West. His description of the devastation that followed the hurricane, including the hundreds killed, is as powerful as anything he ever wrote.

From *Ernest Hemingway: Selected Letters 1917–1961,* edited by Carolos Baker (New York: Scribner's, 1981).

Dear Max:

I was glad to have your letter and would have answered sooner except for the hurricane which came the same night I received it. We got only the outside edge. It was due for midnight and I went to bed at ten to get a couple of hours sleep if possible having made everything as safe as possible with the boat. Went with the barometer on a chair by the bed and a flashlight to use when the lights should go. At midnight the barometer had fallen to 29.50 and the wind was coming very high and in gusts of great strength tearing down trees, branches etc. Car drowned out and got down to boat afoot and stood by until 5 a.m. when the wind shifting into the west we knew the storm had crossed to the north and was going away. All the next day the winds were too high to get out and there was no communication with the kys. Telephone, cable and telegraph all down, too rough for boats to live [sic]. The next day we got across [to Lower Matecumbe Key] and found things in a terrible shape. Imagine you have read it in the papers but nothing could give an idea of the destruction. Between 700 and 1000 dead. Many, today, still unburied. The foliage absolutely stripped as though by fire for forty miles and the land looking like the abandoned bed of a river. Not a building of any sort standing. Over thirty miles of railway washed and blown away. We were the first in to Camp Five of the veterans who were working on the Highway construction. Out of 187 only 8 survived. Saw more dead than I'd seen in one place since the lower Piave in June of 1918.

The veterans in those camps were practically murdered. The Florida East Coast had a train ready for nearly twenty four hours to take them off the Keys. The people in charge are said to have wired Washington for orders. Washington wired Miami Weather Bureau which is said to have replied there was no danger and it would be a useless expense. The train did not start until the storm started. It never got within thirty miles of the two lower camps. The people in charge of the veterans and the weather bureau can split the responsibility between them.

What I know and can swear to is this; that while the storm was at its height on Matecumbe and most of the people already dead the Miami bureau sent a warning of winds of gale strength on the keys from Key Largo to Key West and of Hurricane intensity in the Florida straights [straits] below Key West. They lost the storm completely and did not use the most rudimentary good sense in figuring its progress.

Long Key fishing camp is completely destroyed and so are all the settlements on Matecumbe both upper and lower. There is over thirty miles of the R.R. completely gone and there will probably never be another train in to

Key West. Highway is not as badly damaged as the R.R. but would take six months to repair. The R.R. may make a bluff that they will rebuild in order to sell the govt their right of way for the highway. Anyway Key West will be isolated for at least six months except for boat service and plane from Miami.

The Marine Corps plane that is flying some of the 1st class mail just brought two sets of page proof going up to page 130 [*To Have and Have Not*]. Do you want me to send this back before the other comes?

To get back to your letter.

But first I wish I could have had with me the bloody poop that has been having his publishers put out publicity matter that he has been staying in Miami because he needs a hurricane in the book he is writing and that it looked as though he wasn't going to have one and him so disappointed.

Max, you can't imagine it, two women, naked, tossed up into trees by the water, swollen and stinking, their breasts as big as balloons, flies between their legs. Then, by figuring, you locate where it is and recognize them as the two very nice girls who ran a sandwich place and filling-station three miles from the ferry. We located sixty nine bodies where no one had been able to get in. Indian Key absolutely swept clean, not a blade of grass, and over the high center of it were scattered live conchs that came in with the sea, craw fish, and dead morays. The whole bottom of the sea blew over it. I would like to have had that little literary bastard that wanted his hurricane along to rub his nose in some of it. Harry Hopkins [presidential advisor] and Roosevelt who sent those poor bonus march guys down there to get rid of them got rid of them all right. Now they say they should all be buried in Arlington and no bodies to be burned or buried on the spot which meant trying to carry stuff that came apart blown so tight that they burst when you lifted them, rotten, running, putrid, decomposed, absolutely impossible to embalm, carry them out six, eight miles to a boat, on the boat for ten to twenty more to put them into boxes and the whole thing stinking to make you vomit—enroute to arlington. Most of the protests against burning or burying came from the Miami undertakers that get 100 dollars apiece per veteran. Plain pine boxes called coffins at $50 apiece. They could have been quicklimed right in where they are found, identification made from their pay disks and papers and crosses put up. Later dig up the bones and ship them.

Joe Lowe the original of the Rummy in that story of mine One Trip Across [1934] was drowned at the Ferry Slip.

Had just finished a damn good long story and was on another when this started with the warning on saturday night. They had all day Sunday and all day monday to get those vets out and never did it. If they had taken half the precautions with them that we took with our boat not a one would have been lost.

Feel too lousy now to write. Out rained on, sleeping on the deck of the run boat, nothing to drink through all that business so ought to remember it, but damned if I want it for my novel. We made five trips with provisions for survivors to different places and nothing but dead men to eat the grub.

(September 7, 1935)

36

The Nature of the Everglades

MARJORY STONEMAN DOUGLAS
(circa 1947)

*Marjory Stoneman Douglas (1899–   ) is as synonymous
with Everglades National Park as Margaret Murie is with
Teton National Park. Douglas' book* The Everglades: River of
Grass *(St. Simons: Mockingbird) appeared in 1947, the same year that President
Truman signed the bill authorizing formation of the national park. She was an
influential activist in the movement to create Everglades National Park, and* The
Everglades *helped to increase national awareness of this newly formed refuge.
Today the Everglades is one of the most threatened national parks in the world, as
the precious water upon which its unique ecosystem depends is increasingly
diverted to water lawns and citrus groves in eastern Dade County around Miami.
The Florida panther is among the most critically endangered mammals on the
planet. In this passage Douglas describes some of the fascinating plant associations that characterize life in this "river of grass," from the isolated hammocks of
Caribbean pine and palmetto to the larger hardwood forests with many of the
species found in the West Indies.*

From *The Everglades: River of Grass,* by Marjory Stoneman Douglas (St. Simons Island,
Georgia: Mockingbird Books, 1947, 1974).

The saw grass and the water made the Everglades both simple and unique. Yet bordering and encroaching on that simplicity, fighting for foothold on its coasts and islands, a diversity of life lives upon the rock that holds it. The saw grass in its essential harshness supports little else. It repelled man. But on the rock the crowding forms made life abundant, so that between the two the chronicle is balanced.

One begins with the plants.

If the saw grass here is four thousand years old, many other of these plant associations may have been here almost as long.

In the time of which I write, toward the end of the past century when everything was as it had been, the southern vague watery rim of Okeechobee was bordered by a strange jungle. The crusted wave foam was washed down among windrows of dead reeds and branches and rotting fish. In that decay a wide band of jungle trees sprang up.

Southwest it was all custard apple, a subtropic, rough-barked, inconspicuous tree, with small pointed leaves and soft fruits. It grew fiercely, crowded on roots that became gnarled trunks or trunks twisted and arched into bracing roots in the drag of the water. The spilth and decay of the custard apple, the guano of crowds of birds that fed on them, whitening the leaves, built up in the watery sunlessness below them an area of rich black peat, denser than muck, two or three miles wide and six or eight feet deep. The earliest Americans on the lake called this area "the custard apple bottoms." It was edged with tall leather ferns and Boston ferns and knotted with vines, which no man could get through without axes or dunamite. Lake water crept darkly below.

The southeast was edged with a less tropical jungle, scrub willow with its light-green pointed leaves and yellow catkins and the ropy brown bark of elderberries, bearing out of their lacy plates of white blossoms the purple-black fruit about which the blue jays and the mockingbirds, the great black-glinting Florida crows, the grackles and the red-winged blackbirds in their thousands set up a flapping and creaking and crowing and ker-eeing. Bees and bright flies and yellow butterflies hovered when the blossoms were sweet. Under their shadows ground rattlers moved sluggishly. Winds carried to them from the reedy lake clouds of feeble white insects lake people call "chizzle winks," which breed and die in myriads in a short few days.

These were the willow-and-elder bottoms, which fought shrewdly with the saw grass for every rocky space. The dark-brown peaty muck they left went east up the lake edge between the sand ridges and the saw-grass arms.

Over all this thick jungle region climbed and hung down in moving green curtains the heart-shaped leaves of moon-vines. In the luminous unseen dark of the night the moon-flowers opened acres after acres of flat white blossoms, cloud white, foam white, and still. Northward, lake water moved darkly under the tiny pointed reflections of the stars. Below the region the moonflowers and the moon made their own, with no man's eye to see them, moved the enormous darkness without light of the saw-grass river.

East along the curving Everglades borders and west by the farther coast stood everywhere in their endless ranks the great companies of the pines. Where they grew the rock was highest—"high pine land," people called it. Their ranks went off across an open slough in a feathery cliff, a rampart of trunks red-brown in the setting sun, bearing tops like a long streamer of green smoke. Their warm piny breaths blew in the sun along the salt winds. They covered here, as they did everywhere in Florida, interminable miles.

Some southern longleaf, "common yellow pine," with its taller trunk and bushier branches is scattered south from the Caloosahatchee and down the east coast to the New River. But below there, wherever it could find foothold in high rock, and up behind the western mangrove to what is now Gordon Pass, which is the area of West Indian vegetation, grows the Caribbean pine. It stands everywhere about the borders of the Caribbean. It is called slash pine. But in Dade County from the first it was called Dade County pine.

Its trunks are set thick with rust and brown and grayish bark patches, which resist fire. The patterns of its skimpy branches people find strange, or beautiful. Dying alone, as they often do away from their great companies, killed by lightning or the borer that instantly finds injured bark, these pines stand dead a long time, rigid gray or silver, their gestures frozen. The young fluffy pines start up everywhere about them, bearing long pale candles in the new light of spring.

With the Caribbean pines, as they do with other pines of the South, always grow the palmettos. These are saw palmettos, silver-green, blue-green, or in dry times magnificent tawny-gold across vast open savannas. Their spiky fans cover all the ground beneath the pine trees, on unseen spiny trunks. If they are burned, with a great oily popping and seething, only the blackened trunks are left, writhing like heavy snakes.

The small brown Florida deer step neatly at the edge of pine forests like these. The brown wildcats know them. The clear light falls mottled through the branches faintly green over endless fan points. Inconspicuous wild flowers grow in the wiry grass between palmettos, faint blue chicory, or yellow tea bush, or the tiny wild poinsettias with their small brush strokes of scarlet. The quail pipe and their new-hatched young run like mice with their small cheeping, at the edge of such pineland, and the brown marsh rabbit with small ears and no apparent tail nibbles some bit of leaf.

A diamondback rattlesnake may push out here slowly after such a rabbit or the cotton mice, or lie after shedding his flaky old skin to sun the brilliant dark lozenge marks on his almost yellowish new scales, slow to coil or rattle unless angered. Then in a blur he draws back in quick angles that wide-jawed head with the high nose balanced over the coils, his slitted eyes fixed and following his object, the forked tongue flicking through the closed jaws, tasting the disturbed air. His raised tail shakes the dry rattle of its horny bells. His strength, his anger, engorges that thick muscular body, ruffles his barky scales. If he strikes it is at one-third of his length. The jaws open back so that the long fangs strike forward and deep. His recovery is quicker than the eye can see. Or he lifts tall that kingly head before he lowers it in retreat, holding himself grandly, with the same dignity that has made him the king among all these beasts.

All the woodpeckers in south Florida yank and hitch and cluck and rap their way up these great patched pine trunks, all with red heads, the downy, the hairy, the red-bellied, and that diabolical creature with a red and white and black head like a medieval battle-ax, the pileated, which the early settlers called so truly "the Lord God Almight." But in those early days the even more impressive ivory-billed, which we shall never see again, startled these pine-woods with his masterly riveting.

Even in the middle of the saw-grass river, where an out-crop of old rock is the only evidence of preglacial times, the pines grow tall to show where the rock lies. The buzzards and the black vultures, their ragged wing tips like brush strokes of India ink, sail and sail and rise on the upcurrents and soar in their pure flight, turning about some old roost they have always kept and returned to year after year. Their piercing glances watch for the glint of flies' wings over carrion they crave, the most valuable birds in the world. Or from the muddy water holes about the pineland the brown-black water moccasins slide their wet ridged scales. Startled, they coil to retract those open, white-lined jaws, like a queer white flower to anything peering down. Death is there too.

Where the pines are thin, the Indians found their first sources of life. There grow foot-tall, ferny green cycads, plants older than this rock, with yellow and orange cones for flowers and great thick roots. This is the "coontie" of the oldest Indian legend. Its root is grated and squeezed and sifted to flour to make the thick watery gruel "sofkee," which was always the basis of the Indians' diet here. The Indians' legend came partly from the Spanish fathers. They say that once there was a great famine here in Florida. The Indians prayed to the Master of Breath, who sent down His Son, God's Little Boy, to walk about at the edge of the pinelands and the Glades. And wherever He walked, there in His heel marks grew the coontie, for the Indians to eat and reverence.

Sometimes it is called compte. The early white men learned of it and grated it to make starch and knew it as arrowroot. By the pinelands north of the Miami River, the Indians camped often, so that their women could gather it in what was called the Coontie grounds. . . .

But if, on these rocky outcrops, the pines and the palmettoes were destroyed, by lightning or the old fires of Indians, another great tree took its place and gradually changed, with its own associated forms, the whole nature of the place. This was the live oak, the first of the hardwoods. They made the first hammocks at the edge of rivers or on the driest Everglades islands. . . .

The live oaks, like dim giants crowded and choked by a thrusting forest of younger hardwoods, made that great Miami hammock, the largest tropical jungle on the North American mainland, which spread south of the Miami River like a dark cloud along that crumbling, spring-fed ledge of rock. Here where the leaf-screened light falls only in moving hoary ruins of live oaks are clouded by vines and resurrection ferns, their roots deep in the rotting limestone shelves among wet potholes green-shadowed with the richest fern life in the world—maidenhair and Boston ferns and brackens and ferns innumerable. At night the mosquitoes shrill in the inky blackness prickled with fireflies.

About the live oaks is waged the central drama of all this jungle, the silent, fighting, creeping struggle for sunlight of the strangler fig. It is one of those great trees people call rubber trees or Banyans. They are all *Ficus,* but the strangler is *Ficus aurea.* A strangler seed dropped by a bird in a cranny of oak bark will sprout and send down fine brown root hairs that dangle and lengthen until they touch the ground. There they grip and thicken and become buttresses. Over the small hard oak leaves the thick dark-green oily strangler's leaves lift and shut out the sun. Its long columnar trunks and octopus roots wrap as if they were melted and poured about the parent trunk, flowing upward and downward in wooden nets and baskets and flutings and enlacings, until later the strangler will stand like a cathedral about a fragment of tree it has killed, crowning leaves and vast branches supported by columns and vaultings and pilings of its bowery roots.

The stranglers are only the most evident and dramatic of all these crowding tropical jungle trees; smooth red-brown gumbo limbos, ilex, eugenias, satinwoods, mastic, cherry laurel, paradise trees, the poisonous manchineel, the poison-wood, the Florida boxwood and hundreds more which the hurricanes brought over from Cuba and the West Indies.

This was the jungle that people thought the Everglades resembled. Birds flit through it only rarely. The little striped skunk leaves its trail. The brilliant coral snake burries its deadly black nose in its loam. The false coral, the harlequin, with its yellow nose, is hardly less hidden. Spiders stretch their exquisite traps for pale insects. Small brown scorpions move on the rotting logs. And far up among the tufted air plants the small native orchids are as brown and pale yellow and faint white as the light they seek.

Everywhere among these branches moves imperceptibly one of the loveliest life forms of these coasts—the pale-ivory, pale-coral, pale-yellow and pale-rose, whorled and etched and banded shell of the *Liguus,* the tree snails. Their pointed shell bubbles are found chiefly on smooth-barked trees in the dry hammocks, but every Everglades island-hammock has its own varieties, subspecies developed in countless lifetimes in a single unique area, varying with an infinity of delicate differences. They came from the tropics. They are a world in themselves. . . .

But here especially the strangest of the butterflies quivers silently in the bands of sun in the green light of leaves, the only one of its tropical kind on this mainland. It is the *Heliconius,* named for the sun, barred black and pale yellow as the light and shade, wavering always in companies, which no bird will touch. The *Heliconius* drowse of nights in colonies, delicately crowded and hanging on a single small tree. When bright moon light reaches them they have been seen to wake and drift about, filling a leafy glade with their quivering moon-colored half-sleep.

About the rivers of the west, north of the tropic vegetation line, grows the water oak. The water oaks grow taller and more regular than the live oaks. Their longer pointed leaves drop off the bare boughs in a brief winter and put on their new light green long before the rusty live oaks renew themselves, in that misty river country. Both crowd down to the glossy water and make landscapes like old dim pictures where the deer came down delicately and the cows stand, to drink among their own reflections.

In the great Miami hammock, along the banks of almost every river, bordering the salt marshes, scattered in the thinner pineland, making their own shapely and recognizable island-hammocks within the Everglades river, everywhere, actually, except in the densest growth of the saw grass itself, stands the Sabal palmetto. To distinguish it from the low shrubby saw palmetto, it is called the cabbage palm. With its gray-green fans glittering like metal in the brilliance, its round top bearing also branches of queer blossoms and hard dark berries, the cabbage palm grows singly or in dramatic clumps over stout round trunks. The basketwork of old fan hilts is broken off below as the trunk grows tall and smooth. Ferns and vines and air plants and lizards and spiders live in that basketwork. They are often engulfed by strangler figs. They bristle on the banks of fresh-water rivers among the oaks. They make dense islands in the saw-grass river.

They are a northern growth, unrelated to the tropical palms, to the coconut palms that rise above the outer beaches and are set everywhere in cities, or the great royal palms that tower along the Everglades keys and in a few magnificent hammocks of their own toward the west coast. The Spaniards introduced the coconuts to Panama from the Philippines, the royals are native West Indians. Their nuts were blown over from Cuba and germinated in the rain-washed debris of some tropical cyclone. Other delicate palms, like the silver palm of the lower mainland, came the same way.

Then there is the enduring cypress. There are many cypresses in the world but the Everglades region has two: the short, often dwarf, pond cypress and the tall freshwater river cypress. It is the river cypress that is tall, to 125 feet, silver gray, columnar, almost pyramidal on its broad fluted base, whose curiously short branches lose their leaves in winter and stand ghostly and gaunt among the hanging Spanish moss and red-tongued air plants. Spring draws out from the ancient wood the tiny scratched lines of its thready leaves, the palest yellow-green darkening to emerald. It is a fine timber tree. White and green, over brown water, against an amazing blue and white sky, it is most strangely beautiful.

The cypress that grows in muddy water has that curious accompaniment, the rootlike extension into the air, like dead stumps, called cypress knees, which are thought to aerate the mudbound roots. The dry-land cypress does not need them. It grows up rivers of both coasts and about the lake. But in its greatest area, a vast dramatic association of river cypress and pond cypress marks the west bank of the saw-grass river, and forms the Big Cypress Swamp.

The Big Cypress extends south from the Devil's Garden, a wilderness of pine and scrubby stuff and bushes, near that dome of land in the angle of the Caloosahatchee and the lake, south in great fingers which reach to the headwaters of the Turner River, as far down as the salt water and the mangrove. The rock below it is uneven and ridgy, all hollows and higher places. It is called "swamp" because in the rains the water stands in it and does not run off. It is not moving water, like the saw-grass Glades. It was called "the Big Cypress" because it covered so great an area.

The river cypresses stand there in wintertime in great gray-scratched heads, like small hills, towering above the dense and lower pond, or dwarf, cypress between, thinly set in the wetter hollows of wire grass, starred with white spider lilies and sedges and, in drier places, milkwort in saffron-headed swaths. Red-shouldered hawks cruise the low cypress and the marshlands, marsh hawks balance and tip, showing white rump marks, and far over at the edge of a thicket a deer feeds, and flicks his white-edged tail before he lifts his head and stares.

From high in a plane at that time of year the Big Cypress seems an undulating misted surface full of peaks and gray valleys changing to feathering green. East of it, sharply defined as river from its banks, move the vast reaches of saw grass.

The brown deer, the pale-colored lithe beautiful panthers that feed on them, the tuft-eared wildcats with their high-angled hind legs, the opossum and the rats and the rabbits have lived in and around it and the Devil's Garden and the higher pinelands to the west since this world began. The quail pipe and call through the open spaces. The great barred owls hoot far off in the nights and the chuck-will'w-widows on the edge of the pines aspirate their long whistling echoing cries. The bronze turkeys, the most intelligent of all the birds or beasts, feed in the watery places and roost early in the thick cypress tops, far from the prowlers below. And the black Florida bear, which sleeps even here his short winter sleep, goes rooting and grumbling and shoving through the underbrush, ripping up logs for grubs and tearing at berries, scorning no mice.

The bears move to the beaches and, like the panthers, dig for turtle eggs. They catch crabs and chew them solemnly and eat birds' eggs if they find them, and ripe beach plums. The panthers prey most on the range hogs of the settlers, and so they are hunted with dogs, and fight viciously, killing many before they leap into trees and, snarling, never to be tamed, are shot.

Here in the cypress pools—but for that matter, everywhere in the watery Glades, from lake to sea—lives the Glades' first citizen, the otter. Like the birds, he is everywhere. The oily fur of his long lithe body is ready for heat or cold, so long as it is wet. His webbed hands are more cunning than the racoon's. His broad jolly muzzle explores everything, tests everything, knows everything. His quickness is a snake's lightning quickness. He has a snake's suppleness and recovery, but not the snake's timidity. His heart is stout and nothing stops him.

The otter has been seen to swim and flirt and turn among a crowd of thrashing alligators, from whose clumsy attack he has only to dive and flash away. He knows how to enjoy life in the sun better than all the rest of all the creatures. He is gay. He is crammed with lively spirit. He makes a mud slide down a bank, and teaches his cubs to fling themselves down it and romp and tumble and swim upside down in the frothing water. He is fond of his female and plays with a ball and has fun. His ready grinning curiosity and friendliness betray him to the hunter and trapper. This is his home.

On the scanty dwarf cypress the gray Ward's heron stands rigid. The big black-and-white wood ibis, like a stork, which flies so high and so far in such grave and orderly squadrons, slides downward on hollow wing and lights with a great flapping and balancing that makes the tree look silly under its teetering grip as it stares down its great curved beak for a frog there below. It is as though all the life of the Everglades region, every form of beast or bird or gnat or garfish in the pools, or the invisible life that pulses in the scum on the pools, was concentrated in the Big Cypress.

The dwarf cypress has its area, perhaps the most fantastic of all, far toward Cape Sable, south of the live-oak jungle that was called Paradise Key, where the royal palms stood high overhead like bursting beacons seen across the sloughs. Men have said they have seen panthers here, not tan, but inky black. There southward, under the even more brilliant light, as if already the clouds reflected the glare from the sea beyond, the small cypress, four or five feet tall, stands in the rock itself, barely etched with green. These trees seem centuries old, and they are very old indeed, in spirit of fire and hurricane. Even in full leaf their green is scant. There are moccasins around their roots out of the standing clear water and high, high over, a bald eagle lazily lifting or an osprey beating up from the fishing flats. . . .

So, fringing the salt marshes or the higher saw-grass meadows of the southeast, where the deer make their paths, there begins in earnest the dark mangrove wilderness. It is a world as monotonous, as unique, as the saw grass. It looks as if there was nothing here but mangroves and mud stinking with vegetable rot and saltreek and the moving sea water.

Mangroves exist in many places in the tropics. But this area is the most magnificent mangrove forest, and the greatest, in the American hemisphere.

Two kinds of mangroves dominate this association, the black and the red. It begins on the last peat with tall hammocks and forests of buttonwoods, called "white mangrove," not a true mangrove at all but *Conocarpus*. Then in the first level of the high tide stands deep-rooted the black mangrove, the *Avicennia nitida,* not tall, but thick, which often sends from its submerged roots up through two or three feet of mud and water the curious pneumatophores, like thousands of sharp bristling sticks, most difficult to wade through. They are breathing organs. The dark-green leaves above them often exude salt crystals. The roots stain the water brown with strong tannin.

Beyond that, marching out into the tides low or high, and rooted deep below them in marl over the rock, goes the great *Rhizophora,* the red mangrove, on its thousands of acres of entwined, buttressed and bracing gray arches. The huge trunks, often seven feet in circumference, stand as high as eight feet here, one hundred in the drier spots. Their canopy of green obliterates the sky. In the shadowy light over that world of arches over water all is clear gloom.

Entering wave ridges are beaten down, here. The foam washes in all the flotsam of the sea, the accumulated drift of the shallows. The thick leaves turn yellow continually and continually fall. The decay rises among those arches and the younger growths slowly march seaward across it, holding and building the land.

From the high branches long hairy ropes swing and hang down to reach the water and branch into roots. Some have few fruits. Some are heavy with long seeds like small thin torpedoes, which fall and stick in the mud under low tide and grow. But more commonly they float and are carried endlessly on sea currents that bring them upright and alive, ready to root, on other far mangroveless tropic shores.

Where these mangroves came from, to this young mud over the older rock, cannot be guessed. They may be one of the great parent forests from which seeds have been carried as far as the South Pacific. Nobody knows.

The mangrove here is at least as old as the Everglades, of which it marks the end.

37

The World of the Reef Flats

RACHEL CARSON
(circa 1955)

Rachel Carson (1907–1964) followed in the environmental activist tradition of Bob Marshall and Aldo Leopold, both of whom were, like Carson, employed as biologists by the U. S. Government for significant periods. Carson's special contribution to the movement came in the publication of her influential book The Silent Spring (*Boston: Houghton Mifflin, 1962*), *which linked the use of DDT and other pesticides to the widespread destruction of the environment. As a result of this best-selling book, President John F. Kennedy launched a governmental investigation that led to the banning of DDT and other dangerous pesticides in the United States, although American companies continue to export them to countries where they are not yet outlawed. A marine biologist by profession, Rachel Carson was educated at the Pennsylvania College for Women, Johns Hopkins University, and the Marine Biological Laboratory at Woods Hole, Massachusetts. In addition to working for the U. S. Fish and Wildlife Service, Carson taught at the University of Maryland and at Johns Hopkins University. In this passage from* The Edge of the Sea (*Boston: Houghton Mifflin, 1955*), *Rachel Carson writes about the echinoderms of the coral reef flats in south Florida. In this and other highly successful nature books, Rachel Carson paved the way for other popularizers and defenders of the seas. The life and work of Rachel Carson attest to the extraordinary power that a book can have in terms of constructively influencing public opinion* and *public policy.*

From *The Edge of the Sea,* by Rachel Carson (Boston: Houghton Mifflin, 1962).

The world of the reef flats is inhabited by echinoderms of every sort: starfishes, brittle stars, sea urchins, sand dollars, and holothurians all are at home on the coral rock, in the shifting coral sands, among the gorgonian sea gardens and the grass-carpeted bottoms. All are important in the economy of the marine world—as links in the living chains by which materials are taken from the sea, passed from one to another, returned to the sea, borrowed again. Some are important also in the geologic processes of earth building and earth destruction—the processes by which rock is worn away and ground to sand, by which the sediments that carpet the sea floor are accumulated, shifted, sorted, and distributed. And at death their hard skeletons contribute calcium for the needs of other animals or for the building of the reefs.

Out on the reefs the long-spined black sea urchin excavates cavities along the base of the coral wall; each sinks into its depression and turns its spines outward, so that a swimmer moving along the reef sees forests of black quills. This urchin also wanders in over the reef flats, where it nestles close to the base of a loggerhead sponge, or sometimes, apparently finding no need of concealment, rests in open, sand-floored areas.

A full-grown black urchin may have a body or test nearly 4 inches in diameter, with spines 12 to 15 inches long. This is one of the comparatively few shore animals that are poisonous to the touch, and the effect of contact with one of the slender, hollow spines is said to be like that of a hornet sting, or may even be more serious for a child or an especially susceptible adult. Apparently the mucous coating of the spines bears the irritant or poison.

This urchin is extraordinary in the degree of its awareness of the surroundings. A hand extended over it will cause all the spines to swivel about on their mountings, pointing menacingly at the intruding object. If the hand is moved from side to side the spines swing about, following it. According to Professor Norman Millott of the University College of the West Indies, nerve receptors scattered widely over the body receive the message conveyed by a change in the intensity of light, responding most sharply to suddenly decreased light as a shadowy portent of danger. To this extent, then, the urchin may actually "see" moving objects passing nearby.

Linked in some mysterious way with one of the great rhythms of nature, this sea urchin spawns at the time of the full moon. The eggs and sperm are shed into the water once in each lunar month during the summer season, on the nights of strongest moonlight. Whatever the stimulus to which all the individuals of the species respond, it assures that prodigal and simultaneous release of reproductive cells that nature often demands for the perpetuation of a species.

Off some of the Keys, in shallow water, lives the so-called slate-pencil urchin, named for its short stout spines. This is an urchin of solitary habit, single individuals sheltering under or among the reef rocks near the low-tide level. It seems a sluggish creature of dull perceptions, unaware of the presence of an intruder, and making no effort to cling by means of its tube feet when it is picked up. It belongs to the only family of modern echinoderms that also existed in Paleozoic time; the recent members of the group show little change from the form of ancestors that lived hundreds of millions of years ago.

Another urchin with short and slender spines and color variations ranging from deep violet to green, rose, or white, sometimes occurs abundantly on sandy bottoms carpeted with turtle grass, camouflaging itself with bits of grass and shell and coral fragments held in its tube feet. Like many other urchins, it performs a geologic function. Nibbling away at shells and coral rock with its white teeth, it chips off fragments that are then passed through the grinding mill of its digestive tract; these organic fragments, trimmed, ground, and polished within the urchins, contribute to the sands of tropical beaches.

And the tribes of the starfish and the brittle stars are everywhere represented on these coral flats. The great sea star, Oreaster, stout and powerful of body, perhaps lives more abundantly a little offshore, where whole constellations of them gather on the white sand. But solitary specimens wander inshore, seeking especially the grassy areas.

A small reddish-brown starfish, Linkia, has the strange habit of breaking off an arm, which then grows a cluster of four new arms that are temporarily in a "comet" form. Sometimes the animal breaks across the central disc; regeneration may result in six- or seven-rayed animals. These divisions seem to be a method of reproduction practised by the young, for adult animals cease to fragment and produce eggs.

About the bases of gorgonians, under and inside of sponges, under movable rocks and down in little, eroded caverns in the coral rock live the brittle stars. With their long and flexible arms, each composed of a series of "vertebrae" shaped like hourglasses, they are capable of sinuous and graceful motion. Sometimes they stand on the tips of two arms and sway in the motion of the water currents, bending the other arms in movements as graceful as those of a ballet dancer. They creep over the substratum by throwing two of their arms forward and pulling up the body or disc and the remaining arms. The brittle stars feed on minute mollusks and worms and other small animals. In turn, they are eaten by many fish and other predators, and sometimes fall victim to certain parasites. A small green alga may live in the skin of the brittle star; there it dissolves the calcareous plates, so that the arms may break apart. Or a curious little degenerate copepod may live as a parasite within the gonads, destroying them and rendering the animal sterile.

My first meeting with a live West Indian basket stars was something I shall never forget. I was wading off Ohio Key in water little more than knee deep when I found it among some seaweeds, gently drifting on the tide. Its upper surface was the color of a young fawn, with lighter shades beneath. The searching, exploring, testing branchlets at the tips of the arms reminded me of the delicate tendrils by which a growing vine seeks out places to which it may attach itself. For many minutes I stood beside it, lost to all but its extraordinary and somehow fragile beauty. I had no wish to "collect" it; to disturb such a being would have seemed a desecration. Finally the rising tide and the need to visit other parts of the flat before they become too deeply flooded drove me on, and when I returned the basket star had disappeared.

The basket starfish or basket fish is related to the brittle stars and serpent stars but displays remarkable differences of structure: each of the five arms diverges into branching V's, which branch again, and then again and again until a maze of curling tendrils forms the periphery of the animal. Indulging their taste for the dramatic, early naturalists named the basket stars for those monsters of Greek mythology, the Gorgons, who wore snakes in place of hair and whose hideous aspect was supposed to turn men to stone; so the family comprising these bizarre echinoderms is known as the Gorgonocephalidae. To some imaginations their appearance may be "snaky-locked," but the effect is one of beauty, grace, and elegance.

All the way from the Arctic to the West Indies basket stars of one species or another live in coastal waters, and many go down to lightless sea bottoms nearly a mile beneath the surface. They may walk about over the ocean floor, moving delicately on the tips of their arms. As Alexander Agassiz long ago described it, the animal stands "as it were on tiptoe, so that the ramifications of the arms form a kind of trellis-work allaround it, reaching to the ground, while the disk forms a roof." Or again they may cling to gorgonians or other fixed sea growths and reach out into the water. The branching arms serve as a fine-meshed net to ensnare small sea creatures. On some grounds the basket stars are not only abundant but associate in herds of many individuals as though for a common purpose. Then the arms of neighboring animals become entwined in a continuous living net to capture all the small fry of the sea who venture, or are helplessly carried, within reach of the millions of grasping tendrils.

38

Trinidad

V. S. NAIPAUL
(circa 1962)

V. S. (Vidiadhar Surajprasad) Naipaul (1932–   ) was born on the island of Trinidad to Hindu parents. He was educated at the University of Oxford (1950–1954) and, since 1957, has published some nineteen books, including The Middle Passage *(London: Andre Deutsch, 1957) and* The Loss of El Dorado *(New York: Alfred Knopf, 1970), both nonfiction works relating to the Caribbean. Naipaul is known for his frank portraits of post-colonial society in the West Indies. In this selection from* The Middle Passage, *a travel book that covers Trinidad, British Guiana, Surinam, Martinique, and Jamaica, Naipaul writes eloquently of pastoral nature on his native island of Trinidad, and finds beauty in the common coconut tree, the sugarcane fields, and the cocoa woods. The same author who has written elsewhere in* The Middle Passage *that "for many years afterwards in England, falling asleep in bedsitters with the electric fire on, I had been awakened by the nightmare that I was back in tropical Trinidad"[1] finds here some momentary solace. Such is the power of nature to restore our wonder, and assuage our anguish.*

1. *The Middle Passage* (London: Andre Deutsch, 1957), 41.

From *The Middle Passage,* by V. S. Naipaul (Penguin, 1962).

In the country it was quieter except when a loudspeaker van, volume raised to a fiendish pitch, ran slowly about the roads advertising an Indian film. I often went to the country, and not only for the silence. It seemed to me that I was seeing the landscape for the first time. I had hated the sun and the unchanging seasons. I had believed that the foliage had no variety and could never understand how the word "tropical" held romance for so many. Now I was taken by the common coconut tree, the cliché of the Caribbean. I discovered, what every child in Trinidad knows, that if you stand under the tree and look up, the tapering chrome ribs of the branches are like the spokes of a perfectly circular wheel. I had forgotten the largeness of the leaves and the variety of their shapes: the digitated breadfruit leaf, the heart-shaped wild tannia, the curving razor-shaped banana frond which sunlight rendered almost transparent. To ride past a coconut plantation was to see a rapidly changing criss-cross of slender curved trunks, a greyish-white in a green gloom.

I had never liked the sugarcane fields. Flat, treeless and hot, they stood for everything I had hated about the tropics and the West Indies. "Cane is Bitter" is the title of a story by Samuel Selvon and might well be the epigraph of a history of the Caribbean. It is a brutal plant, tall and grass-like, with rough, razor-edged blades. I knew it was the basis of the economy, but I preferred trees and shade. Now, in the uneven land of Central and South Trinidad, I saw that even sugarcane can be beautiful. On the plains just before crop-time, you drive through it, walls of grass on either side; but in rolling country you can look down on a hillside covered with tall sugarcane in arrow: steel-blue plumes dancing above a grey-green carpet, grey-green because each long blade curves back on itself, revealing its paler underside.

The cocoa woods were another thing. They were like the woods of fairy tales, dark and shadowed and cool. The cocoa-pods, hanging by thick short stems, were like wax fruit in brilliant green and yellow and red and crimson and purple. Once, on a late afternoon drive to Tamana, I found the fields flooded. Out of the flat yellow water, which gurgled in the darkness, the black trunks of the stunted trees rose.

After each journey I returned to Port of Spain past Shanty Town, the mangrove swamp, the orange mist of the burning rubbish dump, the goats, the expectant corbeaux, all against a sunset that reddened the glassy water of the Gulf.

Everyone has to learn to see the West Indies tropics for himself. The landscape has never been recorded, and to go to the Trinidad Art Society exhibition is to see how little local painters help. The expatriates contribute a few watercolours, the Trinidadians a lot of local colour. "Tropical Fruit" is the title of one painting, a title which would have some meaning in the Temperate Zone. Another, startlingly, is "Native Hut." There are the usual picturesque native characters and native customs, the vision that of the tourist, at whom most of these native paintings seem to be aimed. The beach scenes are done with colours straight out of the tube, with no effort to capture the depth of sky, the brilliancy of light, the insubstantiality of colour in the tropics. The more gifted painters have ceased to record the landscape: the patterns of the leaves are too beguiling. In art, as in almost everything else, Trinidad has in one step moved from primitivism to modernism.

39

Beachcombing in the Virgin Islands

PAUL BROOKS
(circa 1964)

Paul Brooks (no dates available) was for many years editor-in-chief at Houghton Mifflin Company in Boston. He is the author of The House of Life: Rachel Carson at Work *(Boston: Houghton Mifflin, 1972),* Speaking for Nature: How Literary Naturalists from Henry Thoreau to Rachel Carson Have Shaped America *(Boston: Houghton Mifflin, 1980), and* Roadless Area *(New York: Alfred A. Knopf, 1964). Brooks is also the recipient of the John Burroughs Award for Nature Writing. In this selection from "Beachcombing in the Virgin Islands," an essay in his collection* Roadless Area, *Paul Brooks describes the thrill of seeing a coral reef for the first time. Here the author finds fish in "every shape that can swim," and "color comparable to that of the butterflies and moths," and great tarpon "cruising . . . like battleships." Truly, as Brooks states, there is little on Earth that can compare with the extraordinary profusion of life that is found in the coral reefs of the Caribbean. In a few pages nature writer David Rains Wallace, writing of this same coral reef a quarter of a century after Paul Brooks, finds disturbing evidence of man's slow undoing of the wild magnificence that is Virgin Islands National Park.*

From *Roadless Areas,* by Paul Brooks (Knopf, 1964).

. . . A dark area of the bay bordering the rocky part of the shore had been pointed out as a coral reef. Approaching as closely as we could on foot, we put on the flippers and masks (an initial feeling of claustrophobia quickly vanishes) and swam toward it. What we expected to see I don't know. What we saw was a new world, in a new dimension.

The first sight of a coral reef is one of life's memorable firsts. Intellectually you have known that this underwater world exists. Friends back from winter vacations have spoken glowingly about it, and you have "oh'd" and "ah'd" in polite response to their excitement. You have read about it in books and seen it (on a far grander scale than you will ever experience) in professional color movies of the life of the deep. Yet none of this prepares you for the moment when you first look through that magic glass, belly-down in the warm, gin-clear water. You feel "like some watcher of the skies/When a new planet swims into his ken"—except that this time you are doing the swimming.

The shapes, the color, the motion—all are strange, yet eerily suggestive of scenery on the earth's surface. Pinnacles and flat-topped mesas rise above the level sands of the shallows; farther offshore, canyons plunge into darkness. But the sharp shadows of a terrestrial landscape are lacking: everything is bathed in a soft, diffused light. Coral, though composed of millions of minute animals, is plantlike in its growth. The variety of patterns is bewildering: trees with thick trunks and proliferating branches, others composed of segments that suggest the giant Joshuas of the desert; round grooved boulders of "brain coral," and delicate branching "staghorn coral"; gently waving sea fans, wispy tresses, broad rubbery umbrellas. This weird miniature forest, however, is not the cool green of the woods on land; it is a subtle blend of the warm colors of the palette: red-browns, ochers, subdued pinks and purples. And its beauty is but a background for the incredibly gaudy fish that swim in and out among the branches.

The fish, singly and in schools, are what first catch the eye and hold it in a sort of suspension of disbelief. Here is every shape that can swim: fish slender as a pencil or round as a dish; smoothly streamlined or blunt-nosed and square; triangles and teardrops and flying wings; fish that seem to be all head and others that seem to be swimming backwards owing to the great "eye" painted to their tails, like the eye on the hind wing of a Polyphemus moth. Here, indeed, is color comparable to that of the butterflies and moths: bold combinations of bright purple and yellow, of yellow and black; bodies of coppery red and aure-blue bodies with yellow tails; color in broad vertical bands, in spots, in stripes, or softly blended like the pattern of light from a stained-glass window. And this magic world is ever in motion, some fish "grazing" on the minute algae that grow on the coral, others darting in and out of the caves in the coral rock where they are completely hidden from sight (a tiny fish will drive off an intruder twice his size, like a kingbird harrying a crow), still others cruising slowly along; singly or in schools, indifferent to the clumsy Gulliver sloshing about in their sky. The whole community sways rhythmically to and fro with the slow pulsation of the waves; you see but scarcely feel the motion, for you are drifting with it—drifting over the world of Matthew Arnold's "Forsaken Merman":

> Sand-strewn caverns, cool and deep,
> Where the winds are all asleep;
> Where the spent lights quiver and gleam,
> Where the salt weed sways in the stream,
> Where the sea-beasts, ranged all round,
> Feed in the ooze of their pasture ground.

Friendly beasts, most of them. In the shallows, you have only to watch for the sea urchins, clusters of long, black, poisonous hatpins fixed to the coral rock. Barracuda frequent these waters, but the experts do not consider them dangerous unless (as seems unlikely) you go swimming about with bleeding wounds. Sharks may come close inshore after dark. We swam happily several times in the moonlight till we learned that the natives—who should know—do their swimming by day, when there is no chance of a myopic shark mistaking the calf of a leg for a wounded fish. We saw neither sharks nor barracuda; this did not disappoint us in the least. The largest beasts—and everything looms larger under water—were the tarpon, steel-gray giants cruising slowly among the reef fish, like battleships amid a fleet of bright-colored sailing dinghies. One evening at dusk, feeding only a few yards from shore, they roiled up the water in a terrifying display of power, as schools of jack—a sizable fish in themselves—leapt into the air before them.

40

Sea Turtles of the Caribbean

ARCHIE CARR
(circa 1967)

Few scientists have been so successful in their conservation efforts as Archie Carr (1909–1986), a Florida biologist who devoted his life to the preservation of the endangered sea turtles of the Caribbean. With grants from the National Science Foundation and other agencies and organizations, Carr and his colleagues worked to restore sea turtles to beaches throughout the islands of the West Indies, as well as to Caribbean beaches on the Central American mainland. Carr also pioneered in the tracking of sea turtles in their migratory patterns; since 1955 over 20,000 turtles have been tagged at the site of his most intense research—Tortugero beach in Costa Rica. Since Carr's death the Caribbean Conservation Corporation which he founded has continued its effort to preserve sea turtles in the region. In this passage Dr. Carr describes Operation Green Turtle, a project designed to "re-establish green turtle rookeries in places known to have once been nesting grounds." Carr's life and writings are an inspiration, and demonstrate the power that one person, and particularly the words that he or she writes, can have on the world.

From *So Excellent a Fishe, A Natural History of Sea Turtles* (New York: Scribner's, 1967).

The green turtle was an important factor in the colonization of the Americas. It was herbivorous, abundant, and edible—even when prepared by cooks not aware that it can be made a gourmet's dish. It lived all about the tropical littoral and grazed in schools on turtle grass pastures that now are mostly vacant. It nested in numbers in places where no turtles ever come ashore today, or come only one on a mile in a year. The British Navy counted on green turtle to extend its cruising in the New World. The Spanish took on turtle for the voyage back home to Cadiz. A green turtle was as big as a heifer, easy to catch, and easy to keep alive on its back in a space no greater than itself. It was an ideal food resource, and it went into the cooking pots of the salt-water peasantry and tureens of the flagships alike. It fed a host of people and to some of them it became a dish of almost ceremonial stature. In England the green turtle came to be known as the London Alderman's Turtle, because an Alderman's Banquet was considered grossly incomplete if it failed to begin with clear green turtle soup.

The one flaw in the green turtle resource was that the females came ashore to lay their eggs. At breeding time, when survival is in most delicate balance, all sea turtles leave the familiar safety of the sea, where they have grown to a size that makes them almost immune to predation, and lumber ashore and expose themselves and their offspring to the hazards of the land. A green turtle on shore is almost defenseless. She weighs on the average nearly three hundred pounds but seems almost wholly unable to use her bulk and strength in active self-defense. She is awkward of gait, myopic of vision, and single-track of mind. Once the nesting has started, she will go on doggedly through the hour-long ceremony with a pack of dogs digging out her nest beneath her, or with drunken Indians drumming on her back. It is as if she were sure that this last legacy to her race must be left, whatever her own fate might be.

So long as the dangers of this time on land remained natural ones—Indians, jaguars, and pumas for the old turtles; gulls, vultures, coatis, and the like for the eggs and young—the populations held their own. But then the Europeans came to the Caribbean, with ships to victual and slaves to feed. Through the centuries the turtle beaches were raided. Eggs were dried in strings like wrinkled beads, the old turtles were turned on their backs and either barbecued on the beach or hauled away on the decks of schooners. It is not possible to say how widely the green turtle nested in primitive times, but there were certainly several big rookeries in the western Caribbean, and probably many. Today there is only Turtle Bogue.

That was the reason I chose Tortuguero as the place for a research camp and tagging operations; and why, later on, the Caribbean Conservation

Corporation established the hatchery for its restoration project there. The Bogue is simply the only place there is. Elsewhere along the shore green turtles nest singly or in small bands. There are even a few records of green turtles nesting in Florida during the past decade. But everywhere except at Tortuguero, the nesting is so spotty and intermittent that no worthwhile tagging can be done, and the hatchlings and eggs for restoration programs are not available in the necessary numbers.

The only other place in the Caribbean where there is a real green turtle rookery is Aves Island, a barely exposed bank in the Leeward Islands a hundred miles off Monserrat. This feeble expanse of land seems to be the Tortuguero of the eastern Caribbean—the only place anywhere in the whole West Indian archipelago where there are big nesting aggregations. But Aves is a weak foothold. Besides being small, distant, and surrounded by tumultuous seas the island appears to have decreased in all its dimensions since it first was measured during the past century. It is apparently disappearing under the sea. We went out there one July in a boat equipped with all kinds of navigation aids, we almost missed the landfall after a rough night's run from Monserrat. We found the island by only a hairbreadth when the captain in the crow's nest sighted birds and breakers far abeam. How the nesting turtles find Aves each July is not known. I will say more of that mystery in later chapters.

Every year a half dozen sailboats go out from Dominica to look for Aves, hoping to bring back loads of turtles. Few of them ever find the island. It is clear that only the remote and inaccessible location of the sinking islet has saved a breeding colony of green turtles for the eastern Caribbean.

So Tortuguero is the last stronghold for *Chelonia* in half the Caribbean Sea. The colony has held out at the Bogue because of the isolation of the place. It is cut off from the hinterland by swamp and rain forest. To boats it offers no anchorage offshore and a dangerous bar to cross where the river enters the sea. In its own way Tortuguero is almost as hard to get to as Aves Island is. But even so, when I first went there the whole nesting beach was being worked intensively by turtle hunters. During those years, almost the only turtles that were able to nest and get back into the sea were those that came up in howling squalls that kept the *veladores* storm-bound in their coco-thatch huts.

The situation is a little better today. Several years ago the Ministry of Agriculture in San Jose declared the first three miles of the nesting beach a reserve for our research and tagging project. With the advent of the Caribbean Conservation Corporation, the protection was extended to five miles. Now, happily, the turning of nesting turtles and taking of eggs is legally proscribed on the whole Caribbean coast of Costa Rica. With this solid protection, and with the efforts to restore turtles to other former nesting sites in the Caribbean, the position of the green turtle seems less melancholy than it was ten years ago.

The aim of *Operation Green Turtle* is to re-establish green turtle rookeries in places known to have been nesting grounds. Batches of Tortuguero hatchlings are released, with the hope they will grow to maturity imprinted by the smell, or taste, or feel of the place where they entered the sea and will be instinctively drawn back there at breeding time, as the salmon is drawn to its hatching place. They might simply go back to Tortuguero, of course. It is also possible that the odds against hatchling survival are so vast that our mere thousands of planted turtles are hopelessly swamped by the array of environmental hazards they face. The program has been under way five seasons, and more than a hundred thousand hatchlings have been released at twenty-two different localities. There has been no solid sign that the primary objective is being fulfilled, that turtles are coming up to nest where hatchlings were put into the sea. But green turtles may have to be six years old before they begin to nest, and it may still be some time before it is clear whether new nesting colonies are being established.

Meanwhile there have been important side benefits from the program. In some of the introduction sites the little turtles appear to be staying on and establishing resident populations, instead of setting out in the expected long-range developmental travel. Hurricanes washed away the oldest of these planted colonies, but others seem to be taking hold. Another happy trend, which may simply reflect the protection that our presence and activities have brought to the Tortuguero nesting colony, is an increase in the number of distant returns in the tagging program. The first protection ever given the Tortuguero colony came in 1955, long enough ago for the increased hatchling yield of the beach to have become breeding green turtles. It seems likely that this may account for the spilling-out of Tortuguero turtles into more distant resident range. It is certainly this factor that has brought an apparent increase in nesting at the Bogue itself. I believe more turtles are coming now to Tortuguero than came in the early years.

I know more people are. The first big influx came when the hardiest core of The Brotherhood of the Green Turtle and the Caribbean Conservation Corporation held a meeting at the camp. With a little airplane from Expreso Aereo Vanolli, we laboriously airlifted in twelve people complete with beer, ice, and air mattresses.

Ben and Mrs. Phipps were there, and Josh Powers and his son Thomas and, Jim Oliver and Chuck Bogert came down from The American Museum of Natural History. It was Jim, now Director of the Museum, who later made the arrangements with Dr. Galler and the Office of Naval Research that resulted in the *Albatross* coming to the Bogue. Hugh Popenoe and Ray Crist were there from the University of Florida, and the NBC newsman John Hlavacek showed up, just out of Castro's jail in Havana. There was a very good-looking girl from Jamaica named Elizabeth Sears. She had a toe in a plaster cast. I forget why she came or what was wrong with her toe. Gus Pascarella was there taking pictures and Billy Cruz, who is now Costa Rican representative of the Caribbean Conservation Corporation, came down from San Jose to "know the place," as they say in Spanish. It seemed queer his having to know Tortuguero, when he had told me all about it twelve years before. Nowadays Billy knows Tortuguero like the back of his hand.

To me, remembering Tortuguero in earlier years, that gathering was as bizarre as a conclave of pygmies would have been. The Bogue would always be to me a place of solitude, of quiet waiting for rain to stop or turtles to get there, or for the Vanolli plane to come. I remember standing outside the camp and listening to the gringo voices laughing under the electric light, and thinking back to other nights with only the wind to hear.

Not that the Bogue was always quiet, even in the old years. The Big Drunks of the Miskito Indians on Saturday nights were pretty exciting. So were the soldiers who came in once from somewhere to investigate a rumored invasion, and got separated and made a terrific noise shooting at each other in the woods across the river. One night a tapir wandered into the sawmill compound and stayed there all night knocking over stacks of boards. The next morning when they started up the sawmill engine the tapir ran about the settlement in a frenzy with a boy popping at him with the only twenty-two rifle in the town. The tapir finally charged down the riverbank and ran off across the bottom, as they are able to do. So things have happened in the lonesome little place.

But the high point of all my Tortuguero time came when the members of The Brotherhood of the Green Turtle filed solemnly out to the beach, each carrying his personal turtle tag inscribed by a jeweler in San Jose with the distinguished name of the owner. Each man clamped his tag to a flipper held steady by Harry Hirth and Leo Martinez; and then we set the turtles free to bear names like Phipps, Powers, and Oliver to the ends of the Caribbean and beyond. The dignity with which Harry and Leo supervised those rites was a stirring thing to see. And a proper culmination of the ceremony was that a year and a half later Jim Oliver's tag was sent back by a Nicaraguan fisherman who caught the turtle in the Miskito Cays two hundred miles away.

That was the year of the biggest change at the Bogue. The next year the big two-engine Navy Grumman came roaring in. It dropped a smoke bomb, to show what cross-wind the sea breeze might be making on the river. It circled over the ocean, glided back into the narrow alley between the wooded banks, threw the river into the air for a thousand yards, and settled into the water before our dock. All the village came out to watch the incongruous fury of the coming of the *Albatross*. When it stopped, dugouts paddled out and brought the crew ashore. We all introduced ourselves and the men looked the camp over and got the lay of the land. We showed them the hatchery a hundred yards up the beach, and the tank house where the accumulating hatch of baby turtles was kept. We talked a while about the schedule for the turtle flights, and then we headed for Sibella's.

For all our years at the turtle camp we had been fed by Sibella Martinez. Sibella is a Columbian Creole whose father brought her to Tortuguero forty years ago. Our camp is located a third of a mile down the beach from her house, but we cover the distance with admirable regularity. This time, part of the crowd went in canoes and some of us walked. I was with the group that walked. As we approached the confusion of leaf-covered buildings, which Sibella's home has grown into during three decades, we could see the others landing at the dock. Jo Conner was there from the University of Florida, and my wife, Margie, and Kip Ross, a photographer from Washington, and half of the crew of the *Albatross*. As the two parties converged on Sibella's backyard-door a white horse, half-hidden under two towering sacks of coconuts, came threading its way among us. The horse was followed by a bearded gnome of a Nicaraguan who was helping Sibella's brother, Sam Martinez, dry his copra. Two dogs barked in a perfunctory way. A black pig that lay across the path in a patch of sunshine grunted at the thought of moving to let us pass, but never moved. A foot-long basilisk lizard ran up a palm trunk, stopped in a splash of sunlight and clung there, gleaming green and crested like a tiny dinosaur out of a comic strip, or out of the Mesozoic.

Seeing the basilisk there so green and bizarre on the palm tree made me think to look again at the people who had gathered to partake of Sibella's hospitality. It was an imposing clientele, with the Navy fliers all in their Kodachrome suits. You might wonder how Sibella would take such an invasion coming only half-announced that morning by a neighbor's children carrying our message. But the year before, Sibella had fed sixteen members of The Brotherhood of the Green Turtle, and never batted an eye. She has only the vacillating yield of the sawmill commissary to draw from, pieced-out by sporadic windfalls of bush meat that successful hunters share around or by supplies walked in from Colorado bar sixteen miles away; but she seems immune to the shock of not knowing how many people there will be to feed.

We went inside. After the usual flurry of people on the verge of being about to eat, we all got seated on the benches at the long table with the oilcloth cover. Sibella came in, and everybody got up again.

"Sibella," I said, "this is the U. S. Navy."

"Yes, Mister Carr," she said, and then to the Navy men, for some reason in Spanish, she said, *"Mucho gusto,"* and we all sat down again.

With a practised eye I took stock of the victuals Sibella this time had conjured up. Beans, rice, unsweetened lemonade, and bread were there as always. These were rock bottom for even the hard times when the sawmill went broke and its commissary closed, and they were the groundwork of all her fancier meals too. The bread was neither the crusty marvel the Cubans make nor the repulsive bakers' bread of the United States. It was and always is at Sibella's strong bread with body, topography, flavor, and nourishment. It is bread such as many women used to make; and what has happened to it, and to the character of people who accept the repellent bread prevalent in North America today, I am not able to imagine. Anyway, with that bread of Sibella's and nothing else, you would leave the table fed.

This time there was plenty besides. There was turtle, for instance, in two conditions. There were stewed fins, which are my favorite turtle dish and likely to become the favorite of any man not offended by the gelatinous matrix in which the fins arrive; and there was also fricasseed turtle meat adroitly spiced. These were more or less staples of the season. More festive was a splendid pot of tepiscuintle. The tepiscuintle is a rodent related to the guinea pig, only bigger and better to eat. This one was braised. Another dish contained what proved to be the stewed remains of a giant rooster I had known in life; and there was also an oddly made but savory preparation of tarpon. Plain jumping tarpon from the pass, with the meat minced away from the myosepta. You may think tarpon is not good to eat, but that is only before you have tried Sibella's.

It was a bit of a company meal. Some days get to be all the same, as I said, with only beans and rice and bread. But even so, it was and always is a surprise what Sibella could do with the old black wood stove that has staggered about her kitchen for a dozen years, and with no supermarket anywhere around.

When everyone had been fed we went back to camp. The plane captain and two of the crew that year were the kind of men who get uneasy if they are not doing something useful. They got to work fixing the pup and generator and other things around the place; and pretty soon everything was working for the first time that season. After a while night came and we went out to watch the turtles nesting.

There are five kinds—five genera—of sea turtles in the world. There are the loggerheads (*Caretta*), the ridleys (*Lepidochelys*), the hawkbills (*Eretomochelys*), the green turtles (*Chelonia*), and the leatherbacks (*Dermochelus*). Of these only the last three nest at Tortuguero, and only the green turtle goes there in great numbers. Almost any night from July through September a walker on the Bogue beach will come upon a green turtle.

Everybody ought to see a turtle nesting. It is an impressive thing to see, the pilgrimage of a sea creature back to the land its ancestors left a hundred million years ago. The nesting rites begin, for the watcher, at least, when the turtle strands in the surf. That part is hard to watch, those minutes when she comes up with the breakers and stays there for a while, rising with a wave then bumping back softly on the sand, making up her mind. She blinks and peers, turns her nose down and presses it onto the wave-washed bottom, then looks up and all around and blinks some more. She is clearly making a decision. What her criteria are, nobody knows, and as I say, this coming to land is next to impossible to watch. The turtle is wild and skittish when she first touches shore, and even the light of a match struck far up the beach may send her back to the sea.

But I have seen a turtle landing a few times—or snatches of landings. In strong moonlight you can make the turtle out—or, eerily, on the rare pitch-dark night when the surf breaks phosphorescent like rolling fire. If on such a night a turtle by luck comes out near where you are being very still, you can see her stop with the backwash foaming flame around her, push her head this way and that with a darting motion less like the slow movement you expect of a green turtle than like a lizard or snake, then lower her head and nose the hard, wet beach as if to smell for telltale signs of generations of ancestors there before her. At this stage, anything but steady quiet on shore will scare her back to sea, maybe to come out again fifty yards up the beach, maybe not to return till another night. You have to do a lot of walking and waiting to see the coming of a turtle out of the water. I have never seen a good photograph or movie of it. We have had a lot of able photographers down at Tortuguero, but none has caught this first step in the arrival of a water reptile coming once in two or three years to dig the hostile land.

But once she has gone up into the dry feel of the windblown sand and begun to dig, if a turtle is really of a mind to lay, she can be watched, as I said, by gangs of people waving flashlights in her face, and will go on through her set maneuvers oblivious to any amount of hullabaloo. Having found the proper place to stop, generally at the edge of the first vegetation or beside the rise of a dune or log, the turtle makes trial swipes at the sand with her long front swimming flippers. From that point on she seems to sink gradually into a behavioral groove in which finally she becomes oblivious to all distraction. I remember a photographer trying to get a series of flashlight pictures of a turtle nesting, back before everybody started using electronic flash guns. The climate had somehow got into the man's flash bulbs, and for half an hour he kept shooting away with every other bulb exploding like a little grenade, throwing glass about and driving the rest of us back into the dark. But all the time the turtle went on methodically digging the big pit she rests in while she lays, then delicately she shaped the urn of the nest hole and laid a hundred-odd eggs in it. She filled the nest, covered the pit, and concealed the site with sand thrown about by her long front fins, and them made her way slowly back to the sea. Never once did she show any sign that she cared about popping bulbs or flying glass.

The incubation period of the green turtle is about sixty days. The first year of *Operation Green Turtle* we had asked Roosevelt Roads to schedule the arrival of his airplane for a date we figured would be a little way into the hatching season. Just before the airplane got to camp, turtles began to hatch by hundreds. We soon had three thousand of them in the holding tanks, and more coming faster every night. It was time to be off on the big airlift. Before the tanks got overcrowded we were away on the first flight, to Cartagena, Columbia, by way of the Canal Zone. The next flight was to Nicaragua and British Honduras. After that we left again on an island-hopping journey up through the Windward and Leeward islands. Finally we took a load of turtles and equipment from the dismantled camp directly from Tortuguero to Miami. Before it was all over we had spread 18,500 green turtle hatchlings among sixteen different places in the Caribbean, in the Bahamas, and on the southeastern coast of Florida.

Since that first incongruous coming of the *Albatross* to Tortuguero there have been four more successive years of *Operation Green Turtle*. According to our original calculations the first turtles flown out five years ago should now be maturing and ready to go somewhere to nest. But maybe we figured badly with the scant growth data available. It now seems pretty sure that *Chelonia* takes longer to grow up than we reckoned at the start. Possibly, also, the odds against hatchling survival are so high that planting mere hundreds of them to pioneer in a new site is a move foredoomed to failure by the law of probabilities. It is even possible that the whole fundamental assumption that green turtles that mature after being displaced as hatchlings will return to the place you take them is wrong. An instinctive drive may take them back to their ancestral shore instead; or possibly they just scatter about wherever the currents drop them off, and answer their breeding urge on any shore that seems attractive.

Or, maybe they are really out there, those that live on out of the first thousands, ready to come ashore in the places where we released them, and to return in numbers great enough to allow the sexes to find each other and leave behind the seeds of new green turtle colonies. Nobody knows what to expect, really.

But one thing is sure: as an offbeat venture in public relations *Operation Green Turtle* is already a success. In a dozen Caribbean cities the flights have brought out friendliness in folk whose views on the United States range from the mildly jaundiced to the very bitter. It is mostly cheerful people who show up at the airports and gather around each season's *Albatross*. And their good will is not confined to green turtles and the amiable crews of the airplanes that deliver them. It is bound to spill over a little to gringos as a breed, and to extend itself to the whole outlandish conception of preserving live natural resources of any kind. Good will not turtle soup, but it is an asset all the same. The *Albatrosses* have planted more than the baby turtles they have brought.

41

Natural History

DEREK WALCOTT
(circa 1976)

Derek Walcott (1930–   ) is probably the best known Caribbean poet writing today. Walcott was born on St. Lucia in the British West Indies and graduated in 1953 with a Bachelor of Arts degree from the University of the West Indies in Jamaica. He has lived and taught widely in the Caribbean, England, and the United States. In this poem "Natural History," from his collection Sea Grapes *(New York: Farrar, Straus and Giroux, 1976) Walcott provides his readers with four startling images from nature in the Caribbean. They are meant to challenge perspective, and to cause man, "the walking fish," who is struggling to evolve from one state to another, to ask and answer the questions upon which his survival, and by inference that of all life, depends.*

From *Sea Grapes,* by Derek Walcott (New York: Farrar, Straus and Giroux, 1976).

1

The Walking Fish

There was a shape across the bay,
stunned on the sand.
It was like a huge fish, or a man
like a huge fish.

It did not move. I could not look away.
It was here I began.
The waves

scudded over my back;
where they snagged they formed scales
scalloped at the edges. My ducts
subside now. Bellows.

For years
my sky has been water;
I have paddled under the bubbles
of phosphorescent moons,

my eyes
glazed by a film
that set into gelatinous scales,
their quick salt itch drying.

The scallops
harden, the nostrils shrivel,
splayed, the webbed fingers burrow
into this sand.

I'll wait
Waves, waves wash over my back.
The tears prickle quickly out of my eye.

I'll wait
for a geological epoch.
My biggest thrill is a blink—
one blink every geological epoch.

The waves now
have receded into the far, faint
caves of my ears. I shed glazed
fins like sea-fans, dragon-serrated.

This beach
is just like the other where I was born.
I feel green and black with a chain-mail
of silver, then a fine net of pores

through which the sea breathes,
through which the Atlantic remembers,
through which in flutes the five oceans whistle.

Lumber once, then
stop. Dragons no longer fly,
the groaning mastodon's gone down

in the brea of muck,
the tiger's sabres turned coral,
the pterodactyl shrunk to a bat,

but I name
this foothold, with a grateful croak,
earth. I can arch my back

I can squat,
I can paddle my forefins,
fingers of grass in the sand
and grass in my fingers—

Lurch up.
Earth falls away. Up.
The horizon drops past my belly.

Dunes, there,
behind the dunes, others,
my kind, other gutturals waiting,

learning
their unsteady walk.
There is nothing in that ocean
above the horizon,

in that sea,
where the great white fish swam,
everything has changed

or has changed us.
Or, as I
paddle this air, breathe this new sea, am I
still swimming through one gigantic eye?

II

Frogs

Moonlight, and the sun-dials of frogs sadden the lawn.
Tires will grind them like head-lamp marbled crabs, like splayed
Biafran children, and tomorrow's sun
reprint them till they take on
the monochrome of asphalt,
the tabloid, iron tones of death. History
is natural—famine, genocide,
as natural as moonlight
and man is great who rises at this cost;
like the Bikini turtles, who, after the holocaust,
swam deeper into sand, their history reversed
from nature, or the mad birds
that burrowed into earth, while ocean,
a god once, rages, at a loss for words.

III

Turtles

To have misplaced your instinct for the sea,
to blunder with each cataracted eye
staring past panic, or panic so bland,
the gripping, slipping paddles row through sand
changed by man's will to ocean.
The mutant turtles teach adaptability
to man, the walking fish,
who with his forefins used to pray upright,
before the bomb's fountaining: "Let there be light!"

IV

Butterflies

They fall in ribbons down the paths of ocean,
the foam-pale butterflies, but the flowers are salt.
They prove the charms of rapine, that the emotion
called beauty has earned this result.

 **42**

Bernhardsdorp

EDWARD O. WILSON
(circa 1984)

Edward O. Wilson (1929–) is Baird Professor of Science at Harvard University. His books include Sociobiology: The New Synthesis *(Cambridge: Harvard University Press, 1975),* On Human Nature *(Cambridge: Harvard University Press, 1979), and* Biophilia *(Cambridge: Harvard University Press, 1984). Wilson has also co-authored with Bert Hölldobler a massive 732-page study of ants, a species he has studied intensively in Surinam [*The Ants *(Cambridge: Harvard University Press, 1990)]. His book* On Human Nature *was awarded the Pulitzer Prize for general nonfiction in 1979. There is an excellent transcript of a discussion Wilson had with the nature writer Barry Lopez on the subject of natural history writing in* Writing Natural History: Dialogues with Authors, *which was edited by Edward Leuders and published by the University of Utah Press in 1989. In that book Wilson states that as science and the humanities increasingly converge in nature writing we may be seeing the genre "emerging into its twenty-first century form."*[1] *In this selection from* Biophilia, *Wilson synthesizes science writing, travel writing, and personal memoir into a new sort of nature writing that transcends and expands the genre. Of particular note in this book is the strong political position Wilson takes* vis-à-vis *the government of Surinam and its treatment of the people and natural resources of the land. The Roman Stoics believed that the laws of nature should govern the laws of man, and one cannot help but think that nature writing in the next century will follow this Wilson line and become more political as time and human events progress.*

1. Edward Leuders, Editor. *Writing Natural History: Dialogues with Authors* (Salt Lake City: University of Utah Press, 1989), 13.

From *Biophilia,* by Edward O. Wilson (Cambridge: Harvard University Press, 1984).

At Bernhardsdorp on an otherwise ordinary tropical morning, the sunlight bore down harshly, the air was still and humid, and life appeared withdrawn and waiting. A single thunderhead lay on the horizon, its immense anvil shape diminished by distance, an intimation of the rainy season still two or three weeks away. A footpath tunneled through the trees and lianas, pointing toward the Saramacca River and far beyond, to the Orinoco and Amazon basins. The woodland around the village struggled up from the crystalline sands of the Zanderij formation. It was a miniature archipelago of glades and creekside forest enclosed by savanna—grassland with scattered trees and high bushes. To the south it expanded to become a continuous lacework fragmenting the savanna and transforming it in turn into an archipelago. Then, as if conjured upward by some unseen force, the woodland rose by stages into the triple-canopied rain forest, the principal habitat of South America's awesome ecological heartland.

In the village a woman walked slowly around an iron cooking pot, stirring the fire beneath with a soot-blackened machete. Plump and barefoot, about thirty years old, she wore two long pigtails and a new cotton dress in rose floral print. From politeness, or perhaps just shyness, she gave no outward sign of recognition. I was an apparition, out of place and irrelevant, about to pass on down the footpath and out of her circle of required attention. At her feet a small child traced meanders in the dirt with a stick. The village round them was a cluster of no more than ten one-room dwellings. The walls were made of palm leaves woven into a herring-bone pattern in which dark bolts zigzagged upward and to the onlooker's right across flesh-colored squares. The design was the sole indigenous artifact on display. Bernhardsdorp was too close to Paramaribo, Surinam's capital, with its flood of cheap manufactured products to keep the look of a real Arawak village. In culture as in name, it had yielded to the colonial Dutch.

A tame peccary watched me with beady concentration from beneath the shadowed eaves of a house. With my own, taxonomist's eye I registered the defining traits of the collared species, *Dicotyles tajacu:* head too large for the piglike body, fur coarse and brindled, neck circled by a pale thin stripe, snout tapered, ears erect, tail reduced to a nub. Poised on stiff little dancer's legs, the young male seemed perpetually fierce and ready to charge yet frozen in place, like the metal boar on an ancient Gallic standard.

A note: Pigs, and presumably their close relatives the peccaries, are among the most intelligent of animals. Some biologists believe them to be brighter than dogs, roughly the rivals of elephants and porpoises. They form herds of ten to twenty members, restlessly patrolling territories of about a square mile. In certain ways they behave more like wolves and dogs than social ungulates. They recognize one another as individuals, sleep with their fur touching, and bark back and forth when on the move. The adults are organized into dominance orders in which the females are ascendant over males, the reverse of the usual mammalian arrangements. They attack in groups if cornered, their scapular fur bristling outward like porcupine quills, and can slash to the bone with sharp canine teeth. Yet individuals are easily tamed if captured as infants and their repertory stunted by the impoverishing constraints of human care.

So I felt uneasy—perhaps the word is embarrassed—in the presence of a captive individual. This young adult was a perfect anatomical specimen with only the rudiments of social behavior. But he was much more: a powerful presence, programed at birth to respond through learning steps in exactly the collared-peccary way and no other to the immemorial environment from which he had been stolen, now a mute speaker trapped inside the unnatural clearing, like a messenger to me from an unexplored world.

I stayed in the village only a few minutes. I had come to study ants and other social insects living in Surinam. No trivial task: over a hundred species of ants and termites are found within a square mile of average South American tropical forests. When all the animals in a randomly selected patch of woodland are collected together and weighed, from tapirs and parrots down to the smallest insects and roundworms, one third of the weight is found to consist of ants and termites. If you close your eyes and lay your hand on a tree trunk almost anywhere in the tropics until you feel something touch it, more times than not the crawler will be an ant. Kick open a rotting log and termites pour out. Drop a crumb of bread on the ground and within minutes ants of one kind or another drag it down a nest hole. Foraging ants are the chief predators of insects and other small animals in the tropical forest, and termites are the key animal decomposers of wood. Between them they form the conduit for a large part of the energy flowing through the forest. Sunlights to leaf to caterpillar to ant to anteater to jaguar to maggot to humus to termite to dissipated heat: such are the links that compose the great energy network around Surinam's villages.

I carried the standard equipment of a field biologist: camera; canvas satchel containing forceps, trowel, ax, mosquito repellent, jars, vials of alcohol, and notebook; a twenty-power hand lens swinging with a reassuring tug around the neck; partly fogged eyeglasses sliding down the nose and khaki shirt plastered to the back with sweat. My attention was on the forest; it has been there all my life. I can work up some appreciation for the travel stories of Paul Theroux and other urbanophile authors who treat human settlements as virtually the whole world and the intervening natural habitats as troublesome barriers. But everywhere I have gone—South America, Australia, New Guinea, Asia—I have thought exactly the opposite. Jungles and grasslands are the logical destinations, and towns and farmland the labyrinths that people have imposed between them sometime in the past. I cherish the green enclaves accidentally left behind.

Once on a tour of Old Jerusalem, standing near the elevated site of Solomon's Throne, I looked down across the Jericho Road to the dark olive trees of Gethsemane and wondered which native Palestinian plants and animals might still be found in the shade underneath. Thinking of "Go to the ant, thou sluggard; consider her ways," I knelt on the cobblestones to watch harvester ants carry seeds down holes to their subterranean granaries, the same food-gathering activity that had impressed the Old Testament writer, and possibly the same species at the very same place. As I walked with my host back past the Temple Mount toward the Muslim Quarter, I made inner calculations of the number of ant species found within the city walls. There was a perfect logic to such eccentricity: the million-year history of Jerusalem is at least as compelling as its past three thousand years.

At Bernhardsdorp I imagined richness and order as an intensity of light. The woman, child, and peccary turned into incandescent points. Around them the village became a black disk, relatively devoid of life, its artifacts adding next to nothing. The woodland beyond was a luminous bank, sparked here and there by the moving lights of birds, mammals, and larger insects.

I walked into the forest, struck as always by the coolness of the shade beneath tropical vegetation, and continued until I came to a small glade that opened onto the sandy path. I narrowed the world down to the span of a few meters. Again I tried to compose the mental set—call it the naturalist's trance, the hunter's trance—by which biologists locate more elusive organisms. I imagined that this place and all its treasures were mine alone and might be so forever in memory—if the bulldozer came.

In a twist my mind came free and I was aware of the hard workings of the natural world beyond the periphery of ordinary attention, where passions lose their meaning and history is in another dimension, without people, and great events pass without record or judgement. I was a transient of no consequence in this familiar yet deeply alien world that I had come to love. The uncounted products of evolution were gathered there for purposes having nothing to do with me; their long Cenozoic was enciphered into a genetic code I could not understand. The effect was strangely calming. Breathing and heartbeat diminished, concentration intensified. It seemed to me that something extraordinary in the forest was very close to where I stood, moving to the surface and discovery.

I focused on a few centimeters of ground and vegetation. I willed animals to materialize, and they came erratically into view. Metallic-blue mosquitoes floated down from the canopy in search of a bare patch of skin, cockroaches with variegated wings perched butterfly-like on sunlit leaves, black carpenter ants sheathed in recumbent golden hairs filed in haste through moss on a rotting log. I turned my head slightly and all of them vanished. Together they composed only an infinitesimal fraction of the life actually present. The woods were a biological maelstrom of which only the surface could be scanned by the naked eye. Within my circle of vision, millions of unseen organisms died each second. Their destruction was swift and silent; no bodies thrashed about, no blood leaked into the ground. The microscopic bodies were broken apart in clean biochemical chops by predators and scavengers, then assimilated to create millions of new organisms, each second.

Ecologists speak of "chaotic regimes" that rise from orderly processes and give rise to others in turn during the passage of life from lower to higher levels of organization. The forest was a tangled bank tumbling down to the grassland's border. Inside it was a living sea through which I moved like a diver groping across a littered floor. But I knew that all around me bits and pieces, the individual organisms and their populations, were working with extreme precision. A few of the species were locked together in forms of symbiosis so intricate that to pull out one would bring others spiraling to extinction. Such is the consequence of adaptation by coevolution, the reciprocal genetic change of species that interact with each other through many life cycles. Eliminate just one kind of tree out of hundreds in such a forest, and some of its pollinators, leafeaters, and woodborers will disappear with it, then various of their parasites and key predators, and perhaps a species of bat or bird that depends on its fruit—and when will the reverberations end? Perhaps not until a larger part of the diversity of the forest collapses like an arch crumbling as the keystone is pulled away. More likely the effects will remain local, ending with a minor shift in the overall pattern of abundance among the numerous surviving species. In either case the effects are beyond the power of present-day ecologists to predict. It is enough to work on the assumption that all of the details matter in the end, in some unknown but vital way.

After the sun's energy is captured by the green plants, it flows through chains of organisms dendritically, like blood spreading from the arteries into networks of microscopic capillaries. It is in such capillaries, in the life cycles of thousands of individual species, that life's important work is done. Thus nothing in the whole system makes sense until the natural history of the constituent species becomes known. The study of every kind of organism matters, everywhere in the world. That conviction leads the field biologist to places like Surinam and the outer limits of evolution, of which this case is exemplary:

> The three-toed sloth feeds on leaves high in the canopy of the lowland forests through large portions of South and Central America. Within its fur live tiny moths, the species *Cryptoses choloepi,* found nowhere else on earth. When a sloth descends to the forest floor to defecate (once a week), female moths leave the fur briefly to deposit their eggs on the fresh dung. The emerging caterpillars build nests of silk and start to feed. Three weeks later they complete their development by turning into adult moths, and then fly up into the canopy in search of sloths. By living directly on the bodies of the sloths, the adult *Cryptoses* assure their offspring first crack at the nutrient-rich excrement and a competitive advantage over the myriad of other coprophages.

At Bernhardsdorp the sun passed behind a small cloud and the woodland darkened. For a moment all that marvelous environment was leveled and subdued. The sun came out again and shattered the vegetative surfaces into light-based niches. They included intensely lighted leaf tops and the tops of miniature canyons cutting vertically through tree bark to create shadowed depths two or three centimeters below. The light filtered down from above as it does in the sea, giving out permanently in the lowermost recesses of buttressed tree trunks and penetralia of the soil and rotting leaves. As the light's intensity rose and fell with the transit of the sun, silverfish, beetles, spiders, bark lice, and other creatures were summoned from their sanctuaries and retreated back in alternation. They responded according to receptor thresholds built into their eyes and brains, filtering devices that differ from one kind of animal to another. By such inborn controls the species imposed a kind of prudent self-discipline. They unconsciously halted their population growth before squeezing out competitors, and others did the same. No altruism was needed to achieve this balance, only specialization. Coexistence was an incidental by-product of the Darwinian advantage that accrued from the avoidance of competition. During the long span of evolution the species divided the environment among themselves, so that now each tenuously preempted certain of the capillaries of energy flow. Through repeated genetic changes they sidestepped competitors and built elaborate defenses against the host of predator species that relentlessly tracked them through matching genetic countermoves. The result was a splendid array of specialists, including moths that live in the fur of three-toed sloths.

Now to the very heart of wonder. Because species diversity was created prior to humanity, and because we evolved within it, we have never fathomed its limits. As a consequence, the living world is the natural domain of the most restless and paradoxical part of the human spirit. Our sense of wonder grows exponentially: the greater the knowledge, the deeper the mystery and the more we seek knowledge to create new mystery. This catalytic reaction, seemingly an inborn human trait, draws us perpetually forward in a search for new places and new life. Nature is to be mastered, but (we hope) never completely. A quiet passion burns, not for total control for the sensation of constant advance.

At Bernhardsdorp I tried to convert this notion into form that would satisfy a private need. My mind maneuvered through an unending world suited to the naturalist. I looked in reverie down the path through the savanna woodland and imagined walking to the Saramacca River and beyond, over the horizon, into a timeless reconnaissance through virgin forests to the land of magical names, Yekiwana, Jivaro, Siriono, Tapirape, Siona-Secoya, Yumana, back and forth, never to run out of fresh jungle paths and glades.

The same archetypal image has been shared in variations by others, and most vividly during the colonization of the New World. It comes through clearly as the receding valleys and frontier trails of nineteenth-century landscape art in the paintings of Albert Bierstadt, Frederick Edwin Church, Thomas Cole, and their contemporaries during the crossing of the American West and the innermost reaches of South America.

In Bierstadt's *Sunset in Yosemite Valley* (L868), you look down a slope that eases onto the level valley floor, where a river flows quietly away through waist-high grass, thickets, and scattered trees. The sun is near the horizon. Its dying light, washing the surface in reddish gold, has begun to yield to blackish green shadows along the near side of the valley. A cloud bank has lowered to just beneath the tops of the sheer rock walls. More protective than threatening, it has transformed the valley into a tunnel opening out through the far end into a sweep of land. The world beyond is obscured by the blaze of the setting sun into which we are forced to gaze in order to see that far. The valley, empty of people, is safe: no fences, no paths, no owners. In a few minutes we could walk to the river, make camp, and afterward explore away from the banks at leisure. The ground in sight is human-sized, measured literally by foot strides and strange new plants and animals large enough to be studied at twenty paces. The dreamlike quality of the painting rolls time forward: what might the morning bring? History is still young, and human imagination has not yet been chained by precise geographic knowledge. Whenever we wish, we can strike out through the valley to the unknown terrain beyond, to a borderland of still conceivable prodigies—bottomless vales and boundless floods, in Edgar Allen Poe's excited imagery, "and chasms, and caves and Tital woods with forms that no man can discover." The American frontier called up the old emotions that had pulled human populations like a living sheet over the world during the ice ages. The still unfallen western world, as Melville wrote of the symbolizing White Steed in *Moby Dick,* revived the glories of those primeval times when Adam walked majestic as a god."

Then a tragedy: this image is almost gone. Although perhaps as old as man, it has faded during our own lifetime. The wildernesses of the world have shriveled into timber leases and threatened nature reserves. Their parlous state presents us with a dilemma, which the historian Leo Marx has called the machine in the garden. The natural world is the refuge of the spirit, remote, static, richer even than human imagination. But we cannot exist in this paradise without the machine that tears it apart. We are killing the thing we love, our Eden, progenitrix, and sibyl. Human beings are not captive peccaries, natural creatures torn from a sylvan niche and imprisoned within a world of artifacts. The noble savage, a biological impossibility, never existed. The human relation to nature is vastly more subtle and ambivalent, probably for this reason. Over thousands of generations the mind evolved within a ripening culture, creating itself out of symbols and tools, and genetic advantage accrued from planned modifications of the environment. The unique operations of the brain are the result of natural selection operating through the filter of culture. They have suspended us between the two antipodal ideals of nature and machine, forest and city, the natural and the artifactual, relentlessly seeking, in the words of the geographer Yi-Fu Tuan, an equilibrium not of this world.

So at Bernhardsdorp my own thoughts were inconstant. They skipped south off to the Saramacca and on deep into the Amazon basin, the least spoiled garden on Earth, and then swiftly back north to Paramaribo and New York, greatest of machines. The machines had taken me there, and if I ever seriously thought of confronting nature without the conveniences of civilization, reality soon regained my whole attention. The living sea is full of miniature horrors designed to reduce visiting biologists to their constituent amino acids in quick time. Arboviruses visit the careless intruder with a dismaying variety of chills and diarrhea. Breakbone fever swells the joints to agonizing tightness. Skin ulcers spread remorselessly outward from thorn scratches on the ankle. Triatoma assassin bugs suck blood from the sleeper's face during the night and leave behind fatal microorganisms of Chagas' disease—surely history's most unfair exhange. Leishmaniasis, schistosomiasis, malignant tertian malaria, filariasis, echinococcosis, onchocerciasis, yellow fever, amoebic dysentery, bleeding botfly cysts . . . evolution has devised a hundred ways to macerate livers and turn blood into a parasite's broth. So the romantic voyager swallows chloraquin, gratefully accepts gamma globulin shots, sleeps under mosquito netting, and remembers to put on rubber boots before wading in freshwater streams. He hopes that enough fuel was put into the Land Rover that morning, and he hurries back to camp in time for a hot meal at dusk.

The impossible dilemma caused no problem for ancentral men. For millions of years human beings simply went at nature with everything they had, scrounging food and fighting off predators across a known world of a few square miles. Life was short, fate terrifying, and reproduction an urgent priority: children, if freely conceived, just about replaced the family members who seemed to be dying all the time. The population flickered around equilibrium, and sometimes whole bands became extinct. Nature was something out there—nameless and limitless, a force to beat against, cajole, and exploit.

If the machine gave no quarter, it was also too weak to break the wilderness. But no matter: the ambiguity of the opposing ideals was a superb strategy for survival, just so long as the people who used it stayed sufficiently ignorant. It enhanced the genetic evolution of the brain and generated more and better culture. The world began to yield, first to the agriculturists and then to technicians, merchants, and circumnavigators. Humanity accelerated toward the machine antipode, heedless of the natural desire of the mind to keep the opposite as well. Now we are near the end. The inner voice murmurs *You went too far,* and disturbed the world, and gave away too much for your control of Nature. Perhaps Hobbes's definition is correct, and this will be the hell we earned for realizing truth too late. But I demur in all this. I suggest otherwise: the same knowledge that brought the dilemma to its climax contains the solution. Think of scooping up a handful of soil and leaf litter and spreading it out on a white ground cloth, in the manner of the field biologist, for close examination. This unprepossessing lump contains more order and richness of structure, and particularity of history, than the entire surfaces of all the other (lifeless) planets. It is a miniature wilderness that can take almost forever to explore.

I walked on through the woodland at Bernhardsdorp to see what the day had to offer. In a decaying log I found a species of ant previously known only from the midnight zone of a cave in Trinidad. With the aid of my hand lens I identified it from its unique combination of teeth, spines, and body sculpture. A month before I had hiked across five miles of foothills in central Trinidad to find it in the original underground habitat. Now suddenly here it was again, nesting and foraging in the open. Scratch from the list what had been considered the only "true" cave ant in the world—possessed of works pale yellow, nearly eyeless, and sluggish in movement. Scratch the scientific name *Spelaeomyrmex,* meaning literally cave ant, as a separate taxonomic entity. I knew that it would have to be classified elsewhere, into a larger and more conventional genus called *Erebomyrma,* ant of Hades. A small quick victory, to be reported later in a technical journal that specializes on such topics and is read by perhaps a dozen fellow myrmecologists. I turned to watch some huge-eyed ants with the formidable name *Gigantiops destructor.* When I gave one of the foraging workers a freshly killed termite, it ran off in a straight line across the forest floor. Thirty feet away it vanished into a small hollow tree branch that was partly covered by decaying leaves. Inside the central cavity I found a dozen workers and their mother queen—one of the first colonies of this unusual insect ever recorded. All in all, the excursion had been more productive than average. Like a prospector obsessed with ore samples, hoping for gold, I gathered a few more promising specimens in vials of ethyl alcohol and headed home, through the village and out onto the paved road leading north to Paramaribo.

Later I set the day in my memory with its parts preserved for retrieval and closer inspection. Mundane events acquired the raiment of symbolism, and this is what I concluded from them: That the naturalist's journey has only begun and for all intents and purposes will go on forever. That it is possible to spend a lifetime in a magellanic voyage around the trunk of a single tree. That as the exploration is pressed, it will engage more of the things close to the human heart and spirit. And if this much is true, it seems possible that the naturalist's vision is only a specialized product of a biophilic instinct shared by all, that it can be elaborated to benefit more and more people. Humanity is exalted not because we are so far above other living creatures, but because knowing them well elevates the very concept of life.

43

The Silent Manatee

ROGER CARAS
(circa 1985)

After serving in the Army during the Korean War, Roger Caras (1928–) returned to the United States and graduated with a Bachelor of Arts degree in Cinema from the University of Southern California. Since that time Caras has worked in film and television; he is currently a special environmental correspondent for ABC-TV News, where he reports regularly on the evening news and prepares documentary specials on wildlife and conservation issues. His book Monarch of Deadman Bay: The Life and Death of a Kodiak Bear *(Boston: Little Brown, 1969) won the John Burroughs Award for Nature Writing and he has also been awarded the Joseph Wood Krutch Medal (1977) and Israel's Oryx Award for Wildlife Conservation (1984). Roger Caras is the Ernest Thompson Seton of his age; no other nature writer approaches Caras in his ability to portray the lives of animals from their own perspective. In this selection from* The Endless Migrations *(New York: E. P. Dutton, 1985) Caras describes a cow and calf manatee as they drift south along the Florida coast toward warmer water. Their's is a life increasingly imperiled by development throughout the Caribbean region.*

From *The Endless Migrations,* by Roger Caras (New York: Dutton, 1985).

Far, far to the south of any range ever known by a polar bear, another marine mammal of great bulk follows a course dictated by its need for food and warm water. From the southernmost stretch of the South Carolina coast, down the east coast of the Floridian peninsula, around its tip and up the west coast, then west to Texas, when the weather and the water are warm enough, the manatee is to be found. A slow, calm, quiet animal, it must surface to breathe, which it does with a particularly pleasing and relaxed, sighing sound. A vegetarian, it harms nothing, competes with no one, but is often threatened by chance and carelessness and the changes wrought by the advent of time. Long ago its ancestors, perhaps related to the animals from which our cows arose, gave up the land for warm seas. Since accomplishing that adjustment, the biology of the manatee has been reluctant to make any other.

The adult manatee sensed the first signs of discomfort. It had spent the summer in a shallow lagoon fed by fresh-water springs inland from Florida's northeast coast. Years before, a ship channel had been gouged out of the river bottom, and it was this channel that manatee had followed in from the coast. It had no trouble adjusting for salty, then brackish, then sweet fresh water. It maneuvered its massive thirteen-foot bulk easily and slowly and nibbled at water weeds by pulling the water hyacinth down from below. It hung in the water and two or three times every five to seven minutes pushed its nostrils up through the barrier into the air above.

But now there was discomfort. A cold front had brought the winter temperature down to 60 degrees, and that was the threshold of peril. Fourteen degrees lower and the water would become a deathtrap. Despite its bulk the manatee had little tolerance. It survived in a world of narrow margins. At 46 degrees above zero the manatee would die. Aware of this in some primitive way, it began moving out of the shallow lagoon, sighing softly to bring its calf to its side. They began moving toward the coast. Once they reached salt water they would turn south, slip around the tip of the Floridian peninsula, and seek warmer waters in the Gulf. That was their own means of survival—slow-motion flight before cold eddies and currents. That is how they had been programmed by their time in the sea as refugees from competition on land.

Hour by hour the taste of salt in the water increased and the thugging, crumping sounds of boats became more frequent. The pair stayed close to the river bank and nosed through the shallow water, through the water weeds, as each mechanical monster violated their quiet world, their submerged world of peace. Intrusive sound is vulgar and harsh, and the manatees recoiled from it almost as if they knew that to be true.

On one occasion an immense oceangoing tug churned up the channel as it pushed a huge barge of bulk cargo ahead of it. The blades of the tug's screw were large enough to chop a manatee in half, but the animals kept clear and pushed into the salty front that lay ahead, seeking both warmth and peace.

Then, on the fourth day, the ocean opened up before them. They worked their way out through the river's estuary, staying to shallow water to avoid the thunderous noise of the shipping and lighter power craft that pulsed in from all directions. They turned south, and then, suddenly, the water began to warm rapidly. A few hundred yards farther the temperature rose more than 20 degrees and they floated into an area where over a hundred of their kind hung in contentment, with their single-lobed flukes lower than their heads. They had arrived at an outspill from a power plant, and hot water continuously poured into the seas, creating a serendipitous manatee refuge. And there were no powerboats, no shipping, just warmth free of intrusion.

It was an artificial lagoon ideal for manatee, ideal but for one factor. Beyond the heated bay the temperature of the seawater continued to drop. Cold water was held back by the constant outflow of the power plant, but the temperature beyond rapidly dropped to some 50 degrees as a northern front began moving a cold current ahead of it. Finally the water beyond the lagoon reached 45 degrees. It was now an invisible barrier as strong as steel fencing holding the manatees to their sanctuary. The cold water could not penetrate the ten-acre space; the sluice flow was too steady, too heavy for that. There was another factor, however. Within two weeks the plant was scheduled to be shut down for long-term repairs and, in part, conversion. The manatees could all die. They could be inundated when the sluices stopped and the cold water moved in on them like a giant club—this unless the temperature of the water beyond the outspill area rose sharply before their sanctuary dissolved.

Far out to sea, undulating toward the north, where it would eventually swing east, was the Gulf Stream. It was warm enough to keep most of the British Isles and even Iceland temperate, more temperate than New York City even though that city is on the same latitude as Madrid. The Gulf Stream is a capricious current and is at times forced seaward by cold masses moving down the coast of the Carolinas, Georgia, and Florida. Then, again, it will swing in toward land, and that is what happened a week after the manatee cow and her calf found the haven of the power station discharge area. The cold wave passed and lost itself in the Caribbean, and the Gulf Stream arced inward as the coastal waters began to warm. By the time the power station began closing down, as the discharge slowed to a trickle, the water beyond the artificial bay was warm enough for the manatee to move south along the coast toward the string of islands known as the Keys. The barrier was down, and the first to move were those closest to the mouth of the bay. They slipped out and turned south automatically. Soon others followed, and within two days no more than a dozen manatees remained in the inlet. In time they would leave as well.

The cow and her calf pushed south toward Miami Beach, Key Biscayne, and the other islands beyond. Almost at random they wandered into shallow rivers and canals, hung close to shore, and fed on the succulent underwater vegetation. They fed mostly at night, but their soft sighing at the surface could be heard at any hour. If a particularly noisy powerboat came screaming through a canal close to where they hung suspended they dropped toward the muddy bottom. They could stay submerged for fifteen minutes without distress, but before sixteen minutes had passed they had to breathe again. Normally they breathed at five-minute intervals, but that was when there was no apparent danger nearby. They lived their lives in slow motion and simply retired from anything existing at any other pace.

The two animals stayed close together, usually touching, as they drifted under bridges and passed private docks and the gaping mouths of marinas, from which their foes the powerboats spewed forth. They brushed against buoys and markers, making them bob in the water and nod almost politely as old friends passed by below unseen. Gulls and ducks and other water riders looked down, only mildly interested, as the hulks moved beneath them. Wading birds—egrets, herons, and their kin—some migrating visitors from much farther north, stopped stalking frogs and crayfish and other prey long enough to acknowledge the passage with a call of *kraaaaankkk* of *cawaw* or other sounds more shrill.

Mother and daughter pushed on toward warmth and food, keeping to themselves and the water's edge. Canals suited them well, for they were dredged and had sharp corners below rather than rapidly ascending shores like a natural lake or stream. Very often they went for two or even three days without feeding, for the same dredging that gave them a safe bottom contour often destroyed plant life. But there was food enough, and the temperature held, and at intervals the two travelers emerged into salty water and pushed along the coast again. They drifted back and forth between rivers, canals, and small lakes and the sea. When they reached the first Keys south of the peninsula's tip, they passed seaward of them and, south of Tavernier, moved through the cut toward the west and emerged into the Florida Bay part of the Gulf of Mexico. Barely clear of the Keys, they began moving north, passing just offshore, west of the islands whose eastern shores they had passed a week before. And again they reached peninsular Florida, and their journey northward continued. They chose at random from canals, ponds, small rivers, and the ocean off the beach.

Once they had passed Sanibel Island they moved close to shore, passing between Pine and Lacosta islands. For several days they fed in a tangled river system and then came back to the Gulf again south of Englewood, near Gasparilla Island. Every day was marked with hazard, as their trip south had been, for boats shrieked by, swung around mangrove islands, and bore down on them at speeds surpassing anything they could attain. Their only defense was to sink, and they did that at the first pulse of an intruding craft. By sinking and by holding as close as possible to every shore, every bank, they avoided the wrenching impact that had already killed more than a dozen of the manatees that had taken refuge at the foot of the east coast power plant weeks before. The calf observed her mother and learned of hazard by experiencing it with her.

Now she did not wait for her parent to react. She had learned the great secret of manatee survival, and at the first warning sound she sank on her own, although her mother was never far behind.

At one point they passed close to a group of six blue sharks, not one less than ten feet long. But the sharks had just fed on offal dumped from a fleet of fishing craft and were too lazy to attack. The manatees moved as close to shore as the bottom grade would allow and there was no engagement. Had there been, it would have been fatal for at least the calf and perhaps the mother as well. Following the near encounter with the sharks the manatees moved into a river and hung there for several days. Small crocodile, rare in Florida but still to be found in some areas, ignored them, as did the more frequently encountered alligators. Most were far too small to attempt a prize of their size. And then they reached the northern edge of the Gulf, where both Florida and the coast of North America swing to the west. Their course too was toward the west, Alabama and Louisiana, which lay far ahead. The water was warm, and the epic journey of the somnambulant manatees would succeed another time.

As each mile unfolds before a migrating animal the potential for new hazards is laid bare. Not only are the worlds through which they pass ever-changing sequences but the fact of their passage, of their passing from one uncertain environment to another, compounds the chances for surprise and intrusion. The manatee's world, particularly, since it is so inherently serene, is open to the shock of invasion and collision. Temperature, the mechanics of the human world, other animals, natural obstacles, all are potential enemies.

One last dangerous encounter awaited the mother manatee and her calf before they reached the peace of their warm wintering grounds. A shrimp trawler laced out its nets across the opening between two small islands. Beyond was a harbor almost completely enclosed by land, and in certain weather conditions clouds of shrimp moved in from offshore and pulsed through the sea like a gray-pink tide. A drag here could gather up tons of the small animals and dump them, squirming, onto the deck for quick sorting by machine and freezing once the boat brought them to the water-edge processing plant only a score of miles away.

The manatees could hear the shrimper and feel the vibrations in the water as the now alarmed mass of shrimp ran before the net. But the manatees could not understand what was happening or from which direction the real hazard came. The net was moving toward them and bore with it the potential to entangle them and pull them under and hold them there longer than their lungs could endure. A netted manatee drowns as readily as any land animal would. Manatees do not eat shrimp, but they moved toward them and then through the cloud, for the greater menace seemed to be coming at them from another direction. They swam directly toward the net, and then, as it so often will, the sea offered a surprise ending. Just as the net was about to engulf the manatees in an incredible mass of confused and tumbling shrimp, the bottom of the net hooked onto the ribs of a broken boat that had died there in a hurricane years earlier. For fifty feet of its two-mile length the net was pulled below the surface and held there, with twelve feet of clear free water above it, before its bottom rocked the skeletal boat and broke free its floats to carry it back into position. In those few minutes a river of shrimp flowed over the top edge of the net into the free water beyond, and the manatee mother and calf flowed with them, flopped across, and dipped down toward the bottom and pumped their flukes until the net and its capacity to kill were well behind them. Without ever comprehending the danger they had faced, they escaped it and moved on toward the west.

When cold fronts stopped moving down into the northern areas of Florida with their accompanying effects on water temperature, the manatees would sense that they had to retrace their journey. They would move east, then south, then east and north again. Theirs too was a rhythm, and their return to the east and north was an act of unconscious faith. All migratory animals must act on faith, for they die if what they have learned to expect by genetic memory fails them. They cannot call ahead, there is no all-clear signal, just timing and faith. It is a faith on which the universe is built.

44

The Passing Wisdom of Birds

BARRY LOPEZ
(circa 1985)

*Barry Lopez (1945–   ) is one of his country's most distin-
guished nature writers. In 1978 he received the John Burroughs Medal for Nature Writing for* Of Wolves and Men
*(New York: Charles Scribner's and Sons) and in 1986 he was awarded the
American Book Award for* Arctic Dreams *(New York: Charles Scribner's and
Sons). When not around the globe exploring and writing, Lopez makes his home in
a small Oregon town. In this selection from his essay collection* Crossing Open
Ground *(New York: Charles Scribner's and Sons, 1988), Lopez takes Cortés'
burning of the Aztec aviary as a point of departure for a larger discussion of the
relationship between humankind and nature. What is needed, Lopez states is "a
more equitable set of relationships" and a perspective bent not on conquest and
subjugation but rather on harmony and equilibrium. Lopez believes we have much
to learn from the alternative perspectives on nature represented by the cultures we
have displaced in the Caribbean, in the Mexican highlands, and elsewhere in the
Western Hemisphere and in the world.*

From *Crossing Open Ground,* by Barry Lopez (New York: Scribner's, 1988).

On the eighth of November, 1519, Hernando Cortés and four hundred Spanish soldiers marched self-consciously out of the city of Iztapalapa, Mexico, and started across the great Iztapalapan Causeway separating the lakes of Xochimilco and Chalco. They had been received the afternoon before in Iztapalapa as demi-gods; but they stared now in disbelief at what lay before them. Reflecting brilliantly on the vast plain of dark water like a landscape of sunlit chalk, its lines sharp as cut stone in the dustless air at 7200 feet, was the Aztec Byzantium—Tenochtitlán. Mexico City.

It is impossible to know what was in the facile, highly charged mind of Cortés that morning, anticipating his first meeting with the reluctant Montezuma; but Bernal Diaz, who was present, tells us what was on the minds of the soldiers. They asked each other was it *real*—gleaming Iztapalapa behind them, the smooth causeway beneath their feet, imposing Tenochtitlán ahead? The Spanish had been in the New World for twenty-seven years, but what they discovered in the Valley of Mexico that fall "had never been heard of or seen before, nor even dreamed about" in their world. What astounded them was not, solely, the extent and sophistication of the engineering that divided and encompassed the lakes surrounding Tenochtitlán; nor the evidence that a separate culture, utterly different from their own, pursued a complex life in this huge city. It was the depth and pervasiveness of the natural beauty before their senses.

The day before, they had strolled the spotless streets of Iztapalapa through plots of full-blossomed flowers, arranged in patterns and in colors pleasing to the eye; through irrigated fruit orchards; and into still groves of aromatic trees, like cedar. They sat in the shade of bright cotton awnings in quiet stone patios and marveled at the robustness and the well-rended orderliness of the vegetable gardens around them. Roses glowed against the lime-washed walls of the houses like garnets and alexandrites. In the hour before sunset, the cool, fragrant air was filled with the whirr and flutter of birds, and lit with birdsong.

That had been Iztapalapa. Mexico City, they thought, even as their leader dismounted that morning with solemn deliberation from that magical creature, the horse, to meet an advancing Montezuma ornately caparisoned in gold and silver and bird feathers—Mexico City, they thought as they approached, could only outdo Iztapalapa. And it did. With Montezuma's tentative welcome they were free to wander in its various precincts. Mexico City confirmed the image of a people gardening with meticulous care and with exquisite attention to line and detail at the edge of nature.

It is clear from Diaz's historical account that the soldiers were stunned by the physical beauty of Tenochtitlán. Venice came to their minds in comparison, because of its canals; but Venice was not as intensely fresh, as well lit as Mexico City. And there was not to be found in Venice, or in Salamanca or Paris for that matter, anything like the great aviaries where thousands of birds—white egrets, energetic wrens and thrushes, fierce accipiters, brilliantly colored parrots—were housed and tended. They were as captivating, as fabulous, as the displays of flowers: vermilion flycatchers, copper-tailed trogons, green jays, blue-throated hummingbirds, and summer tanagers. Great blue herons, brooding condors.

And throughout the city wild birds nested.

Even Cortés, intensely preoccupied with politics, with guiding a diplomacy of conquest in the region, noticed the birds. He was struck, too, by the affinity of the Mexican people for their gardens and for the measured and intricate flow of water through their city. He took time to write Charles V in Spain, describing it all.

Cortés's men, says Diaz, never seemed to tire of the arboretums, gardens, and aviaries in the months following their entry into the city. By June 1520, however, Cortés's psychological manipulation of Montezuma and a concomitant arrogance, greed, and disrespect on the part of the Spanish military force had become too much for the Mexicans, and they drove them out. Cortés, relentless and vengeful, returned to the Valley of Mexico eleven months later with a larger army and laid siege to the city. Canal by canal, garden by garden, home by home, he destroyed what he had described to Charles V as "the most beautiful city in the world." On June 16, in a move calculated to humiliate and frighten the Mexican people, Cortés set fire to the aviaries.

The grotesqueness and unmitigated violence of Cortés's act has come back to me repeatedly in reading of early European encounters with the landscape of the New World, like a kind of darkness. The siege of Mexico City was fought barbarously on both sides; and the breathtaking parks and beautiful gardens of Mexico City, of course, stood hard by temples in which human life was regularly offered up to Aztec gods, by priests whose hair was matted with human gore and blood. No human culture has ever existed apart from its dark side. But what Cortés did, even under conditions of war, flies wildly in the face of a desire to find a dignified and honorable relationship with nature. It is an ambitious and vague longing, but one that has been with us for centuries, I think, and which today is a voice heard clearly from many different quarters—political science, anthropology, biology, philosophy. The desire is that, our colonial conquests of the human and natural world finally at an end, we will find our way back to a more equitable set of relationships with all we have subjugated. I say back because the early cultures from which Western civilization evolved, such as the Magdalenian phase of Cro-Magnon culture in Europe, apparently had a less contentious arrangement with nature before the development of agriculture in northern Mesopotamia, and the rise of cities.

The image of Cortés burning the aviaries is not simply for me an image of a kind of destructive madness that lies at the heart of imperialistic conquest; it is also a symbol of a long-term failure of Western civilization to recognize the intrinsic worth of the American landscape, and its potential value to human societies that have since come to be at odds with the natural world. While English, French, and Spanish explorers were cruising the eastern shores of America, dreaming of feudal fiefdoms, gold, and political advantage, the continent itself was, already, occupied in a complex way by more than five hundred different cultures, each of which regarded itself as living in some kind of enlightened intimacy with the land. A chance to rediscover the original wisdom inherent in the myriad sorts of human relationships possible with the nonhuman world, of course, was not of concern to us in the sixteenth century, as it is now, particularly to geographers, philosophers, historians, and ecologists. It would not in fact become clear for centuries that the metaphysics we had thrown out thousands of years before was still intact in tribal America. America offered us the opportunity to deliberate with historical perspective, to see if we wished to reclaim that metaphysics.

The need to reexamine our experience in the New World is, increasingly, a practical need. Contemporary American culture, founded on the original material wealth of the continent, on its timber, ores, and furs, has become a culture that devours the earth. Minerals, fresh water, darkness, tribal peoples, everything the planet produces we now consume in prodigious amounts. There are at least two schools of thought on how to rectify this high rate of consumption, which most Western thinkers agree is unsustainable and likely wrongheaded if not disastrous. First, there are technical approaches. No matter how sophisticated or innovative these may be, however, they finally seem only clever or artful adjustments, not solutions. Secondly, we can consider a change in attitude toward nature, adopting a fundamentally different way of thinking about it than we have previously had, perhaps ever had as human beings. The insights of aboriginal peoples are of inestimable value here in rethinking our relationships with the natural world (i.e., in figuring out how to get ourselves back *into* it); but the solution to our plight, I think, is likely to be something no other cutlure has ever thought of something over which !Kung, Inuit, Navajo, Walbiri, and other traditions we have turned to for wisdom in the twentieth century will marvel at as well.

The question before us is how do we find a viable natural philosophy, one that places us again within the elements of our natural history. The answer, I believe, lies with wild animals.

II

Over the past ten years it has been my privilege to spend time in the field in North America with biologists studying several different kinds of animals, including wolves, polar bears, mountain lions, seals, and whales. Of all that could be said about this exercise, about people watching animals, I would like to restrict myself to but one or two things. First, although such studies are scientific they are conducted by human beings whose individual speculations may take them out beyond the bounds of scientific inquiry. The animals they scrutinize may draw them back into an older, more intimate and less rational association with the local landscape. In this frame of mind, they may privately begin to question the methodology of Western science, especially its purported objectivity and its troublesome lack of heart. It may seem to them incapable of addressing questions they intuit are crucial. Even as they perceive its flaws, however, scientists continue to offer such studies as a dependable source of reliable information—and they are. Science's flaws as a tool of inquiry are relatively minor, and it is further saved by its strengths.

Science's strength lies with its rigor and objectivity, and it is undoubtedly as rigorous as any system available to us. Even with its flaws (its failure, for example, to address disorderly or idiosyncratic behavior) field biology is as strong and reliable in its way as the collective wisdom of a hunting people actively involved with the land. The highest order of field work being done in biology today, then, from an elucidation of the way polar bears hunt ringed seals to working out the ecology of night-flying moths pollinating agaves in the Mojave Desert, forms part of the foundation for a modern realignment with the natural world. (The other parts of the foundation would include work done by anthropologists among hunter-gatherer people and studies by natural geographers; philosophical work in the tradition of Aldo Leopold and Rachel Carson; and the nearly indispensable element of personal experience.)

I often search out scientific reports to read; many are based on years of research and have been patiently thought through. Despite my regard, however, I read with caution, for I cannot rid myself of the thought that, even though it is the best theoretical approach we have, the process is not perfect. I have participated in some of this type of work and know that innocent mistakes are occasionally made in the data. I understand how influential a misleading coincidence can become in the overall collection of data; how unconsciously the human mind can follow a teasing parallel. I am cautious, too, for even more fundamental reasons. It is hard to say exactly what any animal is *doing*. It is impossible to know when or where an event in an animal's life begins or ends. And our human senses confine us to realms that may contain only a small part of the information produced in an event. Something critical could be missing and we would not know. And as far as the experiments themselves are concerned, although we can design and carry out thousands of them, no animal can ever be described as the sum of these experiments. And, finally, though it is possible to write precisely about something, this does not automatically mean one is accurate.

The scientific approach is flawed, therefore, by its imposition of a subjective framework around animal behavior; but it only fails, really, because it is incomplete. We would be rash, using this approach exclusively, to claim to understand any one animal, let alone the environment in which that animal is evolving. Two remedies to this dilemma of the partially perceived animal suggest themselves. One, obviously, is to turn to the long-term field observations of non-Western cultural traditions. These non-Aristotelian, non-Cartesian, non-Baconian views of wild animals are stimulating, challenging, and, like a good bibliography, heuristic, pointing one toward discovery. (They are also problematic in that, for example, they do not take sufficiently into account the full range of behavior of migratory animals and they have a highly nonlinear [though ultimately, possibly, more correct] understanding of population biology.)

A second, much less practiced remedy is to cultivate within ourselves a sense of mystery—to see that the possibilities for an expression of life in any environment, or in any single animal, are larger than we can predict or understand, and that this is all right. Biology should borrow here from quantum physics, which accepts the premise that, under certain circumstances, the observer can be deceived. Quantum physics, with its ambiguous particles and ten-dimensional universes, is a branch of science that has in fact returned us to a state of awe with nature, without threatening our intellectual capacity to analyze complex events.

If it is true that modern people desire a new relationship with the natural world, one that is not condescending, manipulative, and purely utilitarian; and if the foundation upon which the relationship is to be built is as I suggest—a natural history growing largely out of science and the insights of native peoples—then a staggering task lies before us.

The initial steps to be taken seem obvious. First, we must identify and protect those regions where landscapes largely undisturbed by human technology remain intact. Within these ecosystems lie blueprints for the different patterns of life that have matured outside the pervasive influence of myriad Western technologies (though no place on earth has escaped their influence entirely). We can contemplate and study endlessly the natural associations here, and draw from these smaller universes a sophisticated wisdom about process and event, and about evolution. Second, we need to subscribe a great public support to the discipline of field biology. Third, we need to seek an introduction to the reservoirs of intelligence that native cultures have preserved in both oral tradition and in their personal experience with the land, the highly complex detail of a way of life not yet torn entirely from the fabric of nature.

We must, too, look out after the repositories of our own long-term cultural wisdom more keenly. Our libraries, which preserve the best of what we have to say about ourselves and nature, are under seige in an age of cost-benefit analysis. We need to immerse ourselves thoughtfully, too, in what is being written and produced on tape and film, so that we become able to distinguish again between truthful expression and mere entertainment. We need to do this not only for our own sake but so that our children, who too often have only the half-eclipsed lives of zoo animals or the contrived dramas of television wildlife adventure before them, will know that this heritage is disappearing and what we are apt to lose with it.

What disappears with a debasement of wild landscapes is more than genetic diversity, more than a homeland for Henry Beston's "other nations," more, to be perfectly selfish, than a source of future medical cures for human illness or a chance for personal revitalization on a wilderness trip. We stand to lose the focus of our ideals. We stand to lose our sense of dignity, of compassion, even our sense of what we call God. The philosophy of nature we set aside eight thousand years ago in the Fertile Crescent we can, I think, locate again and greatly refine in North America. The New World is a landscape still overwhelming in the vigor of its animals and plants, resonant with mystery. It encourages, still, an enlightened response toward indigenous cultures that differ from our own, whether Aztecan, Lakotan, lupine, avian, or invertebrate. By broadening our sense of the intrinsic worth of life and by cultivating respect for other ways of moving toward perfection, we may find a sense of resolution we have been looking for, I think, for centuries.

Two practical steps occur to me. Each by itself is so small I hesitate to set forth; but to say nothing would be cowardly, and both appear to me to be reasonable, a beginning. They also acknowledge an obvious impediment: to bridge the chasm between a colonial attitude toward the land and a more filial relationship with it takes time. The task has always been, and must be, carried into the next generation.

The first thought I would offer is that each university and college in the country establish the position of university naturalist, a position to be held by a student in his or her senior year and passed on at the end of the year to another student. The university naturalist would be responsible for establishing and maintaining a natural history of the campus, would confer with architects and grounds keepers, escort guests, and otherwise look out after the nonhuman elements of the campus, their relationships to human beings, and the preservation of this knowledge. Though the position itself might be honorary and unsalaried, the student would receive substantial academic credit for his or her work and would be provided with a budget to conduct research, maintain a library, and produce an occasional paper. Dependent on his or her gifts and personality, the university naturalist might elect to teach a course or to speak at some point during the academic year. In concert with the university archivist an university historian naturalist would seek to protect the relationships-in-time that define a culture's growth and ideals.

A second suggestion is more difficult to implement, but no less important than a system of university naturalists. In recent years several American and British publishers have developed plans to reprint in an extended series classic works of natural history. These plans should be pursued; the list of books should include not only works of contemporary natural history but early works by such people as Thomas Nuttal and William Bartram, so that the project has historical depth. It should also include books by nonscientists who have immersed themselves "beyond reason" in the world occupied by animals and who have emerged with stunning reports, such as J. A. Baker's *The Peregrine*. And books that offer us a resounding and affecting vision of the landscape, such as John Van Dyke's *The Desert*. It should also include the writings of anthropologists who have worked, or are working, with the native peoples of North America to define an indigenous natural history, such as Richard Nelson's *Make Prayers to the Raven*. And a special effort should be made to unearth those voices that once spoke eloquently for parts of the country the natural history of which is now too often overlooked, or overshadowed, by a focus on western or northern North American ecosystems: the pine barrens of New Jersey, the Connecticut River Valley, the White Mountains of New Hampshire, the remnant hardwood forests of Indiana and Ohio, the Outer Banks, the relictual prairies of Texas, and the mangrove swamps and piney woods of Georgia.

Such a collection, it seems to me, should be assembled with several thoughts in mind. It should be inexpensive so that the books can fall easily into the hands of young people. It should document the extraordinary variety of natural ecosystems in North America, and reflect the great range of dignified and legitimate human response to them. And it should make clear that human beings belong in these landscapes, that they too, are a part of the earth's natural history.

III

The image I carry of Cortés setting fire to the aviaries in New Mexico City that June day in 1521 is an image I cannot rid myself of. It stands, in my mind, for a fundamental lapse of wisdom in the European conquest of America, an underlying trouble in which political conquest, personal greed, revenge, and national pride outweigh what is innocent, beautiful, serene, and defenseless— the birds. The incineration of these creatures 450 years ago is not something that can be rectified today. Indeed, one could argue, the same oblivious irreverence is still with us, among those who would ravage and poison the earth to sustain the economic growth of Western societies. But Cortés's act can be transcended. It is possible to fix in the mind that heedless violence, the hysterical cries of the birds, the stench of death, to look it square in the face and say that there is more to us than this, this will not forever distinguish us among the other cultures. It is possible to imagine that on the far side of the Renaissance and the Enlightenment we can recover the threads of an earlier wisdom.

Again I think of the animals, because of the myriad ways in which they have helped us since we first regarded each other differently. They offered us early models of rectitude and determination in adversity, which we put into stories. The grace of a moving animal, in some ineluctable way, kindles still in us a sense of imitation. They continue to produce for us a sense of the Other: to encounter a truly wild animal on its own ground is to know the defeat of thought, to feel reason overpowered. The animals have fed us; and the cultures of the great hunters particularly—the bears, the dogs, and the cats—have provided the central metaphors by which we have taken satisfaction in our ways and explained ourselves to strangers.

Cortés's soldiers, on their walks through the gleaming gardens of Teo-nochtitlán, would have been as struck by the flight paths of songbirds as we are today. In neither a horizontal nor a vertical dimension do these pathways match the line and scale of human creation, within which the birds dwell. The corridors they travel are curved around some other universe. When the birds passed over them, moving across the grain of sunlight, the soldiers must have stopped occasionally to watch, as we do. It is the birds' independence from predictable patterns of human design that draws us to them. In the birds' separate but related universe we are able to sense hope for ourselves. Against a background of the familiar, we recognize with astonishment a new pattern.

In such a moment, pausing to take in the flight of a flock of birds passing through sunshine and banking gracefully into a grove of trees, it is possible to move beyond a moment in the Valley of Mexico when we behaved as though we were insane.

45

Folklore from
Contemporary Jamaicans

DARYL C. DANCE
(circa 1985)

In these folk-stories from Daryl Dance's (no dates available)
Folklore from Contemporary Jamaicans (Knoxville: The
University of Tennessee Press, 1985), the reader is introduced
to a perspective of nature that derives from both West African and European
traditions, and that is further enriched by the Caribbean experience. In the two
"Bird Cherry Island" stories in "The Tar Banana Tree" we see a level of
familiarity and interaction between man and animals that is grounded in non-
western culture; these are also morality tales with stern lessons vis-à-vis greed,
betrayal, and stealing. "Town Mouse and Country Mouse" figuratively weighs
the relative virtues of living close to nature in the country as opposed to living in the
city, and comes down in favor of the former:"You a eediot, man, look how country
stay well green, well fertilize, well vegetable-up and ting, and you come tawk bout
town betta dan country." Dance describes "Tiger Work on Rolling Calf" as a
"duppy" tale, a "duppy" being a mischievious spirit common in West African
folklore. One is reminded of Ariel, the "airy spirit" of Shakespeare's "The
Tempest," which helps Prospero work his magic on the island; these tales similarly
speak to the universals of the human condition.

1. Daryl Dance. *Folklore from Contemporary Jamaicans* (Knoxville: The University of Tennessee Press, 1985), 35.

From *Folklore from Contemporary Jamaicans,* by Daryl C. Dance (Knoxville: The University of Tennessee Press, 1985).

Bird Cherry Island (A)

This is a story about Brother Anancy on Cherry Island and some birds. Once upon a time long, long ago Bredda Anancy and some birds decide to go to Cherry Island. Bredda Anancy wanted to go, but he didn't have any feather nor no wings, so he made a deal with the birds. If the birds will lend him their feathers, he will go to Cherry Island with them and pick all the cherry he could pick and share it even. Bredda Anancy got together with the birds and each bird took out some feathers and give Bredda Anancy. Bredda Anancy fix up himself and they both went to Cherry Island now. They all pick cherries, picking cherry, picking cherry, so, till the bag got fill. Bredda Anancy decide to move away with the bag of cherries.

When the birds saw that, they decided to take back their feathers, so Bredda Anancy decide to keep the feathers, and the birds they took away their feathers and leave him under the cherry tree at Cherry Island.

Bredda Anancy didn't know to reach home back, so he got near to the seaside, he saw a boat, but he didn't have any row stick, so he went nearby. He looked in. He saw Bredda Alligator. Bredda Alligator came up and say, "Well, Bredda Anancy, what happen?" He say, "Well, I want to reach home, but I went to Cherry Island and the birds, they took away their feathers, so I don't know how I going reach home." He say, "Well, then Bredda Anancy, I believe I can tek you across, but you have to do something for me. Right? I have some eggs down the bottom; I want you bring them up for me and put them in the hut." Bredda Anancy go down dere and start to bring it up, but Bredda Alligator say to him, "Won't you count all of dem before you bring dem?" Bredda Anancy go down and he count one egg two time, one egg two time, so he had six egg. Right? Count one egg twice. Anyway Bredda Anancy come up and Bredda Anancy burst the eggs and suck them out. Each time him go down him tell Bredda Alligator is one egg him see. When him go back, him see one. When him suppose fi have six eggs down deh. Anyway Anancy eat off all the eggs, so Bredda Alligator start to chase him and Bredda Anancy head for the sea, man. Alligator jump in and start to swim behind Bredda Anancy. Bredda Anancy couldn't swim good as Alligator. So Bredda Anancy saw two fish, one was deaf and one was dumb; one deaf, one caan'hear, one could hear, one caan'hear, and one could talk, but him caan't hear. Anyway Bredda Anancy went in the boat and told the fish them say to row, and Anancy say, "Row fast, row fast. Storm deh pon sea. Row fast." Fish said, the one weh deaf say, "What you say?" Bredda Anancy say, "Mi say fi row fast. Storm deh pon sea." The one weh cann'hear, him deh pon all the while, "Wha you say?" And the other one say, "Row fast. Storm deh pon sea." Alligator behind the boat, man, and the fish a row. Anancy say, "Row fast, storm deh pon sea, man." That is, this alligator deh behind me, you know. "Row fast. Storm deh pon sea. Row fast. Storm deh pon sea, man." And alligator ah cut water, man, and fish a row, you know! Anancy say, "Row fast. Storm deh pon sea, man. Row fast. Storm deh pon sea!"

Bird Cherry Island (B)

One bright mawning, a whole heap of birds fly go a Brer Anancy yawd. And Brer Anancy was sleeping. He said, "Birds, why you waking mi?" Deh seh, We are goin' to Bird Cherry land. Brer Anancy say, "Let's come with you." Dem say, "You caan' come for you cann' fly." And dem tek out some of dem fedder and dem fit inna Brer Anancy, and everybody fly go a Bird Cherry Island.

And when dem go a Bird Cherry Island to eat and when dem a come way now, 'im no wan' come way. Say, "Brer Anancy, we ready." Him sey, "Very nice to stay here. I am not coming wid you." And dem tak out dem fedder now, take out dem fedder now and dem gawn wid i'. And when evenin' a come now, him fi go home, den him mus' haffi go home, and 'im cutlis is in a river. And him sink himself wid bamboo stick . . . him wi' sink and him cutlis, 'im dash it in a di river, and him float way. Him say, "Me a go pon dat." And 'im go pon i', and when 'im go in a di river now, him buck Brer Alligator. And Brer Anancy say to Brer Alligator, say, "Evenin', Godfader," Brer Alligator say, "Who tell you sey you a mi godson?" "A mi ole parent, sah." And him tell him say him ole parents tell him.

And 'im say, "I goin' to pull you as you is mi godson." And Brer Alligator now draw one pot a porridge and give Brer Anancy, say, since 'im a him godfader. Anancy mek one sup and drink it out. And Brer Anancy say, "Godfader, it no hot now; put i' a sun fi hot more." Dat time a cool him want it fi cool, you know. And when Anancy feel i', and when 'im mek one bit drink and 'im done it, Brer Alligator say, "You is my godson, you is my godson." Dat time him no reach a yawd yet. And when 'im go a yawd now, Brer Alligator have nine nephew, nine pickney, and him left 'im wid Brer Anancy. And when him gone, Brer Anancy eat off eight, left one. And when Brer Alligator come now, Brer Anancy say, "Godfather, I get letter sey mi moder dead and mi fader dying and I ben wel waan go." "Awright." And Brer Alligator say now, "Bring di children dem come." And 'im tek di egg and 'im go, and 'im wash it off and 'im say, "One, Godfader"; so tell 'im reach nine. And dem put in a one ship and when di two fish start 'old, when di two fish start 'old one . . . and dem say, "Boatman, oh-h, bring back Brer Anancy." Dat time 'im eat off egg and only lef one. And dem say, "Boatman, bring back Brer Anancy." Him sey, "Whe you say, heavy wind deh pon sea. Sail fast." And dem sail and dem sail and dem sail and dem sail and dem sail till dem land di two fish. . . .

'Im get one pot and 'im put in Brer Anancy in deh. Him put in Brer

Anancy in a di big pot and when di water warm, him say, "Brer Alligator, water warm. Tek mi out." Brer Alligator tek 'im out. And when Brer Anancy now put Brer Alligator in a di pot now, and when di water hot now, him say, "Brer Anancy, water hot." Him say, "Tan in deh you too bad. You ben keep mi miles down a bottom." Dat a fish you know. And Brer Alligator mek di water hot till di fish cook and 'im eat 'im. East off di whole fish. And that's the end of the story.

The Tar Banana Tree

One time there was a landowner; he have a property wid some bananas. So every night a tief go in di field and tief out di bananas, and in the mawning him wake up him find some a him banana missin'. So him say, bwoy, him haf fi ketch da man deh wah a tief him bananas. So Anancy went to him and said, "Well, Boss, gi mi di job as a watchman, nuh, we mus' ketch di banana tief."

So Anancy him now—he was di tief. But he do it so, you know. Steal the banana and carry it, you know. The nex' mawning him reports to him Boss: "Boss, banana still a go, but mi caan' ketch di tief." So the Boss plan pon him and say, "Well, I goin ketch di tief." So the Boss him went ahead and put some tar, or pitch, or what you call it, on the banana tree.

The night Anancy went and work so, him saw this pretty hand of banana, so decide to steal it. So him hole on di bunch a banana and try to pull it, but instead of pulling it his hand stuck. So him kick the tree . . . with his right foot, and it stuck. So him kick the left foot now and it both stuck. Him thump the tree wid him right hand and the right hand stuck, and him thump it with di lef, but di both stuck. So on the way him saw Brer Nanny Goat coming. So him bawl out to Brer Nanny Goat and said: "Well, Brer Nanny Goat, you waan' see, bwoy, mi a try pick a banana and mi hand stuck on. So try to help me nuh!" Brer Nanny Goat him go ahead now and try to pull him off. Brer Nanny goat him now, instead of pull off Anancy him both stuck too. So Anancy manage to get off, and tie up Brer Nanny Goat and go to the Boss and show the Boss, say right now him ketch di tief. The Boss come now and say, "Yes, so you did a tief my banana all this good while!" Anancy hit him wid di whip now. So him say, "Brer-bre-bre . . . !" "Anancy," him trying to say. So from that day deh until now them say ram goat say, "Brer-bre-bre!" you know, that kind of sound deh.

Town Mouse and Country Mouse

Town Mouse and Country Mouse. Once upon a time Country Mouse com to town a look work, but Town Mouse say to Country Mouse, "You can a look word and a chuck badness dem from a way deh, man, and even waan' come steal up all I and I nuts and I family food and ting. Dat bad, you know. You caan' come a town do tem ting deh."

Country Mouse say to Town Mouse, "If you come a country, eat food till you belly *bus'!*"

Town Mouse say, "A lie you a tell, man, for mi can stay up yah and more time mi hungry, but my family half fi eat food."

Country Mouse say to Town Mouse, "You a eediot, man, look how country stay well green, well fertilize, well vegetable-up and ting, and you a come tawk bout town betta dan country."

Tiger Work on Rolling Calf

Going to mi yard—we did live round below the church there. A shower of rain comin' and wet up mi guitar, but di guitar, di guitar start to pull me on mi shoulder, same time di rain stop, and a rolling calf, Mam, believe you me, follows me! I have to go wake up a man out a his bed, him name Toach, bring me home. He woulda kill me pon the way! He woulda *kill* me pon the way! Anyway, when I go home, I had a dog, big black dog, name of Tiger. Tiger work pon him di whole night, work pon him di whole next day clean, eh-heh, tek him out a di yard completely.

46

Antigua

JAMAICA KINCAID
(circa 1988)

The effects of colonialism are still very much in evidence on Antigua, and Jamaica Kincaid (no dates available), a native of St. John's, writes authoritatively of the people and the island in her memoir A Small Place *(New York: Farrar, Straus, and Giroux, 1988). Kincaid's perspective is essential to achieving an understanding not only of the British West Indies, but also of the Caribbean as a whole. In Antigua, for example, where the population is over 80,000, approximately 35% of that population is unemployed. Centuries of sugar-cane monoculture have depleted the richness of the soil and altered the original vegetative patterns. Jamaica Kincaid reminds us that while it is true that "Antigua is beautiful," it is also true that the beauty is "a prison" insofar as a large segment of the population is still impoverished. In the Caribbean as elsewhere the environment and economics are inextricably intertwined, and we can not talk about improving nature without discussing how to solve the social problems of the human beings who live there.*

From *A Small Place,* by Jamaica Kincaid (New York: Farrar, Straus, & Giroux, 1988).

Antigua is beautiful. Antigua is too beautiful. Sometimes the beauty of it seems unreal. Sometimes the beauty of it seems as if it were stage sets for a play, for no real sunset could look like that; no real seawater could strike that many shades of blue at once; no real sky could be that shade of blue—another shade of blue, completely different from the shades of blue seen in the sea—and no real cloud could be that white and float just that way in that blue sky; no real day could be that sort of sunny and bright, making everything seem transparent and shallow; and no real night could be that sort of black, making everything seem thick and deep and bottomless. No real day and no real night could be that evenly divided—twelve hours of one and twelve hours of the other; no real day would begin that dramatically or end that dramatically (there is no dawn in Antigua: one minute, you are in the complete darkness of night; the next minute, the sun is overhead and it stays there until it sets with an explosion of reds on the horizon, and then the darkness of night comes again, and it is as if the open lid of a box you are inside suddenly snaps into place). No real sand on any real shore is that fine or that white (in some places) or that pink (in other places); no real flowers could be these shades of red, purple, yellow, orange, blue, white; no real lily would bloom only at night and perfume the air with a sweetness so thick it makes you slightly sick; no real earth is that colour brown; no real grass is that particular shade of dilapidated, rundown green (not enough rain); no real cows look that poorly as they feed on the unreal-looking grass in the unreal-looking pasture, and no real cows look quite that miserable as some unreal-looking white egrets sit on their backs eating insects; no real rain would fall with that much force, so that it tears up the parched earth. No real village in any real countryside would be named Table Hill Gordon, and no real village with such a name would be so beautiful in its pauperedness, its simpleness, its one-room houses painted in unreal shades of pink and yellow and green, a dog asleep in the shade, some flies asleep on the corner of the dog's mouth. Or the market on a Saturday morning, where the colours of the fruits and vegetables and the colours of the clothes people are wearing and the colour of the day itself, and the colour of the nearby sea, and the colour of the sky, which is just overhead and seems so close you might reach up and touch it, the way the people there speak English (they break it up) and the way they might be angry with each other and the sound they make when they laugh, all of this is so beautiful, all of this is not real like any other real thing that there is. It is as if, then, the beauty—the beauty of the sea, the land, the air, the trees, the market, the people, the sounds they make—were a prison, and as if everything and everybody inside it were locked in and everything and everybody that is not inside it were locked out. And what might it do to ordinary people to live in this way every day? What might it do to them to live in such heightened, intense surroundings day after day? They have nothing to compare this incredible constant with, no big historical moment to compare the way they are now to the way they used to be. No Industrial Revolution, no revolution of any kind, no Age of Anything, no world wars, no decades of turbulence balanced by decades of calm. Nothing, then, natural or unnatural, to leave a mark on their character. It is just a little island. The unreal way in which it is beautiful now is the unreal way in which it was always beautiful. The unreal way in which it is beautiful now that they are a free people is the unreal way in which it was beautiful when they were slaves.

Again, Antigua is a small place, a small island. It is nine miles wide by twelve miles long. It was discovered by Christopher Columbus in 1493. Not too long after, it was settled by human rubbish from Europe, who used enslaved but noble and exalted human beings from Africa (all masters of every stripe are rubbish, and all slaves of every stripe are noble and exalted; there can be no question about this) to satisfy their desire for wealth and power, to feel better about their own miserable existence, so that they could be less lonely and empty—a European disease. Eventually, the masters left, in a kind of way; eventually, the slaves were freed, in a kind of way. The people in Antigua now, the people who really think of themselves as Antiguans (and the people who would immediately come to your mind when you think about what Antiguans might be like; I mean, supposing you were to think about it), are the descendants of those noble and exalted people, the slaves. Of course, the whole thing is, once you cease to be a master, once you throw off your master's yoke, you are no longer human rubbish, you are just a human being, and all the things that adds up to. So, too, with the slaves. Once they are no longer slaves, once they are free, they are no longer noble and exalted; they are just human beings.

47

Of Buccaneers and
Biodiversity

DAVID RAINS WALLACE
(circa 1989)

David Rains Wallace (1945–   ), a graduate of Wesleyan
University and Mills College, has published nine books of
nature writing, including The Klamath Knot (San Francisco:
Sierra Club, 1983) and Bulow Hammock (San Francisco: Sierra Club, 1988).
He was awarded the John Burroughs Medal for Nature Writing in 1984 and has
twice received the Commonwealth Club of California's Silver Medal for Literature. Wallace lives in Berkeley, California, with his wife Betsy, who is an artist. In
this essay, which originally appeared in Wilderness (Winter, 1989), the author
provides a comprehensive overview of the state of wild nature in the Virgin
Islands, Puerto Rico, and the Florida Keys. While there is some basis for guarded
optimism, there is also some alarming information here: the Puerto Rican parrots
cling perilously to their inadequate mountain habitat, the cruise ships destroy coral
reefs in Virgin Islands National Park with their large anchors, and uncontrolled
development threatens wildlife refuges in the Florida Keys. Never have the wild
places in the Caribbean been as endangered, but never have we had the knowledge
that science now provides in order to control and mitigate those dangers. "No
island is an island," Wallace concludes.

From "Of Buccaneers and Biodiversity," Wilderness (Winter, 1989).

Caribbean National Forest (CNF) gets so much rain—240 inches a year—that trails have to be paved. Otherwise, the leached soil simply washes away. Even stepping off the pavement can reduce soil to mud, since there's little humus, little holding the clay together except roots. The Trade Winds Trail in the forest's El Toro wilderness study area reminded me of the 500-year-old Inca Trail to Machu Pichu: both are carefully paved with small native stones. (Although the CCC built the Trade Winds Trail in the 1930s, the Inca Trail is in somewhat better repair.)

Rain fell hard at intervals as I walked the trail along the roughly 3,000-foot ridgetops at the center of the national forest. When it wasn't raining, overhanging tangles of gnarled *Clusia* trees, Sierra palms, bamboos, and bromeliads kept dripping. The tangles (called elfin forest in Puerto Rico) might have been gloomy if they hadn't been so noisy with life. Cicadas and tiny frogs called "coquis" sang happily. A brown bird scolded me, attracting a green, long-billed bird that looked like a cross between a hummingbird and a kingfisher. Black, red-breasted finches whistled on the slopes below, and I heard woodpecker-like rattles and parrot-like squawks in the distance.

None of these birds was familiar, and I realized why when I looked them up. They were all endemic species. The brown bird was a Puerto Rican tanager, the green one a Puerto Rican tody, the black ones Puerto Rican bullfinches, the rattling one a Puerto Rican woodpecker, the squawking one a Puerto Rican parrot. A first-time visitor to the island, I was encountering a forest virtually full of birds that live nowhere else.

The experience was striking, but not unusual for the Caribbean. With a cumulative land area the size of Oregon, the Caribbean islands support more vertebrate species per square mile than any other part of the Western Hemisphere. In sheer numbers, they support almost as many species as the United States and Canada combined. Within its 28,000 acres, Caribbean National Forest contains thirty-two known reptile and amphibian species and sixty-eight bird species. One bird, the elfin woods warbler, wasn't discovered until 1972. CNF contains 263 native tree species, twenty-three of which grow nowhere else. With biodiversity emerging as one of *the* global environmental issues, little islands like Puerto Rico are looking bigger.

Caribbean National Forest is also typical of the Caribbean in that it contains most of the one percent of original forest left on the island. Throughout the region, native and endemic species are reduced to remnant wilderness pockets. The Puerto Rican parrot is an extreme, but probably prophetic, example. Once common throughout the island, it survives only in CNF's Luqillo Mountains, and not very securely even there. Too much rain falls in the forest for optimum parrot reproduction: the species originally bred mainly in drier lowlands. CNF's parrot population fell from seventy in the 1960s to fourteen in 1975 and has only been brought back to thirty-five or so wild birds through the efforts of three full-time biologists, two full-time technicians, three aviary workers (to maintain a captive flock), and ten volunteers.

At least twenty-six species of macaws, parrots, and parakeets inhabited the West Indies when Columbus landed. Fourteen are extinct, including all the native macaws, which disappeared so quickly that not even a stuffed speciment remains except for the Cuban macaw, which lingered into the nineteenth century. All surviving species have undergone "massive declines in population," according to U.S. Fish and Wildlife researcher James W. Wiley.

Parrots are only the colorful, noisy canopy of Caribbean extinctions. As much as 40 percent of historical vertebrate extinctions has occurred in the region, according to Swedish naturalist Kai Curry-Lindahl. Puerto Rico presently has six endangered bird species beside the parrot. Ground sloths and large rodents called hutias once lived on the island, but all native mammals are extinct except bats (eleven of which inhabit CNF alone). Large reptiles have suffered similar fates: the Puerto Rican rock iguana is now confined to a few offshore islands, and the Puerto Rican boa is listed as endangered. Human activities, or human-introduced plants and animals, caused most of these extinctions, although natural predation contributed.

Caribbean biodiversity isn't confined to the islands. The mosaic of mangrove swamps, shallow seagrass beds, and coral reefs that surrounds them is among the most diverse of marine environments, although the evolutionary isolation that produces island endemics is less prevalent in the sea. To my inexpert eye, at least, the reef off Key Largo, Florida, resembled the reef off St. Croix, Virgin Islands. Stoplight parrotfish, blue tang, yellowhead wrasse, and sergeant majors swam over tall elkhorn corals and squat brain corals. There were so many other kinds of fish and corals, however, that big differences could have slipped by me. The Florida reef tract alone supports over 300 fish species.

Marine diversity also is fast disappearing from the Caribbean. The manatees, monk seals, and crocodiles that once swam throughout the region are largely gone, and the green, hawksbill, and leatherback turtles are all endangered. Civilization continues to batter reefs, seagrass, and mangroves, overfishing them and flooding them silt from hardscrabble farming, burying them under resorts, ports, and oil refineries.

As a giant market for sugar, tourism, and other amenities, the United States has assisted significantly in the dismantling of Caribbean biodiversity. Historically, we've had the excuse of not being a ruling power in a region colonized by Spain and other European empires. The excuse has worn thin the past century as American military adventurism has skipped southward from Cuba to Grenada. It doesn't apply at all to the Caribbean islands we've acquired over the years—the Florida Keys, bought from Spain in 1819; Puerto Rico, grabbed from Spain in 1898; the U.S. Virgin Islands, bought from Denmark in 1917. We have done something for biodiversity in the largely random assortment of conversation units that began with designation of Key West and Culebra national wildlife refuges in 1908 and 1909, but we haven't done enough. . . .

Arriving in Puerto Rico, I had vague notions of hundreds of machete-wielding peasants hacking at Caribbean National Forest's boundaries. Instead, I found a Puerto Rican equivalent of Yosemite—a heavily visited (one million a year) but beautiful and cherished place that serves more as a national park than a national forest. It is usually called "El Yunque," an Indian name referring to a Peak in the middle of the forest. The Spanish crown first established El Yunque as a forest reserve in 1876.

Forest acreage is increasing in Puerto Rico because of rural emigration. The Commonwealth's Department of Natural Resources maintains a number of forest reserves throughout the island. At least one of these produces some commercial timber, but like El Yunque, the reserves serve more as parks than commercial forests. Largely deforested Puerto Rico lacks the infrastructure for a significant timber industry. This lack did not discourage the Forest Service a few years ago, when it put together its ten-year management plan under the National Forest Management Act (NFMA). Although CNF has been managed for research and recreation for fifty years, the new plan proposed putting over 5,000 acres of El Yunque's lowland rainforest (called "tabonuco" forest after its dominant tree species) under commercial management. The largest of El Yunque's four forest types, with 13,335 acres, tabonuco is also the most diverse, although the elfin forest has more endemics. The plan also included a wilderness study area of 5,254 acres comprised mainly of the three higher elevation forest types, palo colorado forest, Sierra palm forest, and elfin forest. Logging these steep, sodden forests would have been impractical, so the Wilderness Study Area (WSA) was the rainforest equivalent of wilderness on the rocks. Wilderness on the laterite.

If the Forest Service assumed that Puerto Ricans didn't care about forest wilderness, it got a rude awakening. Thousands marched on forest headquarters to protest the plan after it was issued in 1986. Local and National conservation groups also opposed it. Protestors objected to the plan's being printed only in English, to the lack of wilderness protection for the tabonuco forest, to the lack of management provisions for rare species other than parrots, and to the proposal for timber harvests in a country that doesn't have a large timber industry. Because of the protests, the Forest Service lost credibility with the Puerto Rican government. There was talk of the land reverting to the Commonwealth.

The regional forester directed CNF to lose the timber harvests and revise the plan. When I visited in April, 1989, acting Forest Supervisor Dan Nolan told me that revisions included another roadless area evaluation using the criteria for eastern wilderness instead of RARE II criteria (which had identified only about 10,000 acres of study area). The new evaluation identified 23,600 acres of potential wilderness and proposed four alternatives: the entire 23,600 acres; two separate wilderness areas adding up to 13,000 acres; a single

8,000-acre area; and a 10,000-acre area. Nolan anticipated that the 10,000-acre area would be the preferred alternative when the plan came out in late 1989.

The forest was between biologists when I visited, so I got a less clear idea of its response to complaints about neglect of biodiversity and rare species. A biological technician and a wildlife biology trainee were on duty, but I didn't get any sense of a directed, coordinated program. Workers felt their efforts lacked continuity: someone would do a study or project, then move on.

I had to go downstairs to the U.S. Fish and Wildlife Service office to get a clear sense of what was happening even with the glamor bird, the Puerto Rican parrot. Biologist Gerald Lindsay told me that the wild parrot population is increasing, but only by about two birds a year, which is not encouraging considering the amount of work being done. Lindsay said heavy rains keep flooding parrots out of their treehole nests, although the recovery team has reduced another cause of reproductive failure, nest predation by the pearly-eyed thrasher. Thrashers compete with parrots for treeholes, but biologists have found that if they provide a nest box for a thrasher pair near a parrot-occupied treehole, the pair will drive away other thrashers. Lindsay still feels that they're a long way from the recovery goal of two separate 250-bird parrot populations, and said there's "no way" the present level of expenditure on parrots can continue indefinitely. He hopes natural reproduction will improve once the population expands to lower, drier areas.

The Forest Service's most publicized response to the management plan upheaval is a proposed "Tropical Forest Visitor Center" near present head-quarters. "Now the good news," begins the handout describing the center, "Benefits are far-reaching!" Planned for construction in 1991, with a 12 million dollar projected budget, the center will include an "interpretive visitor center," an "environmental education program," "tropical forest management training" ("sustained multiple use of tropical forest is the core of the center's demonstration and training programs"), an "endangered species recovery program" (centered on parrots but also promoting "public awareness about other endangered species"), and "recreation and research planning."

"The international learning center will spread understanding and improve the management of tropical forests far beyond the boundaries of the Forest," the handout concludes. "Managers of tropical forests will be better trained and educated. Tropical forests will be better managed, better protected, and more productive in a sustainable manner . . . the Forest will be a more enjoyable place for visits, without the congestion that now exists. The Center will attract more visitors from around the world and contribute millions of dollars annually to Puerto Rico's economy." Opening is planned for the Columbus cinque-centennial in 1993, which should please the media, if not any Carib Indian ghosts that might be lurking around El Yunque.

Despite the far-reaching benefits, some Puerto Ricans expressed skepticism about the center. Plans include "demonstration logging" but are vague about how much will be cut, although Dan Nolan told me it wouldn't be more than 200 acres. There is also doubt about the center's international role. There are those who wonder if El Yunque's local conditions would have significant applications to forestry in other places. They may also have wondered just what kind of international learning the U.S. government might fund. According to the Spring 1989 issue of *Earth Island Journal,* Caribbean National Forest was used to test the herbicide Agent Orange in the 1960s. Some saw the center as well-meaning but ambiguous and unrealistic at best, and as an attempt to manipulate the public into accepting scaled-down commercial logging at worst.

El Yunque has other needs for federal funds. Wilderness trails and shelters are deteriorating: I couldn't even find the El Toro trailhead at the forest's western edge. Dan Nolan told me the forest badly needs to acquire a land parcel along the Mameyes River at the north boundary because it is one of the main recreation sites and is in danger of private development. (Picknicking and socializing around the many gorgeous cascades and waterfalls are the favored recreation in the forest.) Nolan said that as many as 700 people a day use the Mameyes site, now without facilities. Even developed recreation sites at waterfalls along the west boundary are not being maintained. Parking lots are littered, and the guard station at the western forest entrance is abandoned.

Puerto Rico has three national wildlife refuges and two national estuarine sanctuaries, but I was only able to glimpse part of Culebra NWR from the air. It looked refreshingly deserted. The five units are islands or coastal areas important for nesting birds, sea turtles, and manatees. The Inventory of Caribbean Marine and Coastal Protected Areas published by the Organization of American States and the U.S. Department of the Interior says that landfills, littering, use of acquifers for agriculture and industry and pesticide pollution threaten the sanctuaries, while poaching is a problem in Culebra and Desecho NWRS. According to the inventory, Cabo Rojo NWR has no problems or disturbances. It sounds like paradise.

Virgin Islands National Park on St. John *looks* like paradise, its forests as green, beaches as white, and covers as azure as the glossiest of resort ads. An hour's talk with Chief Ranger Richard Jones dispelled any notions of bliss, however. Although the 9,500-acre park covers over half the island (Laurance Rockefeller donated most of the land in the 1950s), Jones sees relentlessly building environmental pressures.

"Every square foot of developable land on the island will be developed, mostly sooner than later," he said. "There are 261 inholdings, from 100 acres to quarter acre slivers, and it's unlikely the park will acquire many of them." (The park actually owns only 6,955 acres within its authorized boundaries.)

Jones reeled off problems with the familiarity of eight years on the island. Visitation is increasing by 10 to 15 percent annually and is now about a million. Autumn used to be a quiet season, but cruise ships, resorts, and local population growth have brought year-round crowds. Jones expects growth to accelerate once a large airport is finished on neighboring St. Thomas, and more South American and European tourists can reach the island. "That, to me, is the future," he said. Meanwhile, park staff has remained static since the

1970s, and eleven authorized positions are vacant because of budget shortfalls. Island housing is so expensive that the park has trouble holding personnel.

Jones expressed the greatest concern about the 5,600 offshore acres that Congress added to the park in 1962 to protect coral reefs. He said siltation from development is a threat to corals, but expects that to subside once "everything is developed." Fish populations are declining, as indicated by the average size of legal catches, and some species like the red hind and Nassau grouper may be endangered. Garbage and spilled oil from the open sea are a problem. Even more worrisome to Jones is the effect boat traffic is having on the seabed, not only reefs, but seagrass and what he called "algal plain" as well.

About sixty percent of visitors arrive by cruise ship (many of them unaware they're visiting a national park), and when the huge ships drop anchor, they can sweep the sea floor bare of life. In fall, 1988, a 2,300-ton ship dragged its anchor 400 feet across Francis Bay on St. John's north side, destroying an estimated 283 square meters of coral reef. The park is developing a system of mooring buoys that will reduce the amount of anchoring in its waters and also limit access somewhat. Because of the dramatic increase in cruise ship and chartered boat activity, such measures seem justified.

Another change Jones would like to see in the cruise ship-park relationship is increased financial support for the park. Ron DeLugo, the Virgin Islands' elected delegate to Congress, has complained that none of the two dozen or so ships that visit St. John contribute directly to the park. Jones said one cruise line donated $10,000 when asked to contribute to park programs. He sees "a lot of future in private donations."

Virgin Island National Park's welter of financially up-scale problems shouldn't obscure its fundamental ecological values. Although the second smallest national park, it contains a substantial portion of the protected lowland and coastal habitat in the Caribbean. It is the only UNESCO biosphere reserve in the Lesser Antilles, and thus is "a benchmark against which the status of surrounding unprotected areas can be evaluated," according to the Virgin Islands National Park "Briefing Statement." The park will become more valuable, Jones said, "because other islands don't have the desire or the ability to protect resources."

St. John's resilience in light of the years of colonial deforestation and exploitation impressed me. A cross-island walk led through a vigorous forest of ceiba, fig, gumbo limbo, guapinol (West Indian locust), and *Clusia* growing on abandoned plantation terraces. I saw a lot of mongoose (the introduced predator that has extirpated some native species) and no native iguanas or boas, but the forest was full of small native anole lizards and cuckoos, bridled quail doves, hummingbirds, and warblers. One large anole escaped a mongoose by running up a cliff. A native bird, the bananaquit, seemed to have solved the mongoose problem by nesting in the cactuses that stud the island's dry south slope. Richard Jones mentioned the possibility of restoring extirpated species to the park, although nobody is sure of all the species that lived on St. John originally.

The reefs bordering the white beaches may have suffered from siltation and overuse, and they didn't have the swarms of fish I'd seen at Key Largo, but they impressed me, too. I'd had to ride a boat eight miles to the Key Largo reef; at St. John, I could virtually walk to it, and there was something magical, if vulnerable, about that. It wasn't paradise—the glum faces of concession service workers attested to that—but it might be as close as the public sector can come to it in 1990.

One has only to visit the other "virgins" to see what St. John would look like if it wasn't protected. From the air, St. Thomas looked like Santa Monica. Development hasn't gone as far on St. Croix, but it's getting there, with the giant Hess refinery and container port on the south shore filling in the background. A drive around the island with Phyllis Slayden of the St. Croix Environmental Association was a tour of missed conservation opportunities and new or impending luxury developments that made the remaining natural landscape seem ghostly. Laurance Rockefeller offered to sell thousands of acres of the island's hilly northwest to the Virgin Islands government in the 1960s, but the government didn't buy. Now Carambola, one of the biggest resorts, sprawls in the same hills, its wide expanses of lawn and tile-roof mansions a paradise privatized.

Conservation has a toehold on St. Croix. The Park Service administers Buck Island National Monument off the northeast, and the Fish and Wildlife Service has Green Cay and Sand Point NWRS. From talking to Park Service Superintendent Robert L. Greer, I got the impression his problems were like St. John's—too little budget and staff, too many visitors and exploiters. "I've got three commissioned law enforcement rangers for Buck Island and Christiansted National Historic Site," Greer said, "and one of those is Chief Ranger, so he's covered in paperwork. We can't be out there all the time, and when we come in, the scavengers and poachers go out."

We almost didn't get to Buck Island when I visited it with Ranger Irv Brock. We shipped so much water trying to right a capsized sailboat that we were in danger of sinking ourselves, a situation that would have been more bearable if the sailboat had seemed grateful for the help. When we did get there, I saw what Greer meant. A flotilla of private and concessionaire boats lay off the island: seven concessioners with twenty-two boats are licensed to take people there. "We've got three large files stuffed with letters from the past four months just about permit renewals, and three applications for new permits," Greer told me. "We don't grant new permits because we don't have enough of a data base to tell what the impact of the present use level is."

As well as recreation, Buck Island provides nesting habitat for sea turtles, brown pelicans, and magnificent frigatebirds, but the main attraction is the surrounding reef, which is probably in better shape than parts of the St. John reef because it gets less use. The St. John reef I saw adjacent to resort beaches, had a scuffed, dusty look; the Buck Island reef looked brighter and sharper, with more horny corals—sea whips, sea fans, and gorgonians. Buck Island was like St. John in that the reef didn't exactly teem with fish. Fishing is legal for local people around much of the island (although not within protected "marine garden" areas), and Irv Brock told me that just about every kind of fish is eaten.

The other ranger, Joel Tutein, said a sea bottom study in the past few years showed a significant decline from 1972 numbers of fish, conch, and spiny lobster. "We could hardly find any lobsters."

I glimpsed scrubby Green Cay NWR on the way to Buck Island. The cay is the last resort of a native ground lizard elsewhere exterminated by the mongoose. Ironically, island planters had introduced the mongoose in the early 1900s to control rats. The tactic failed, however, because rats are nocturnal and mongooses hunt (mostly birds and reptiles) during the day. Mongooses destroyed 23 percent of endangered sea turtle nests according to a 1980–81 St. John study. Trapping reduced nest predation to six percent. The Park Service then tried to trap the mongoose off Buck Island, apparently with success. I saw no mongooses during ten minutes on Buck Island. I did see a rat.

There is still a good chance for a major new conservation unit on St. Croix. According to the Park Service, the Salt River watershed and estuary a few miles west of Christiansted "contains the only intact natural ecosystem remaining in the entire Virgin Islands. The continuum of freshwater stream, wetlands, and floodplain, a salt pond, mangrove forests, shallow estuary with relatively expansive seagrass beds, coral reefs and coral gardens, and a biologically rich submarine canyon is unique anywhere in the Caribbean today." Green, hawksbill, and leatherback turtles nest and feed in the area, and twenty-one threatened or endangered bird species occur there, as well as several endangered plants.

The Carib Indians had a village at Salt River in 1493, when Columbus anchored his second expedition off the bay and sent troops ashore for food and water. An exchange of arrows and gunfire marked the first recorded hostilities between Europeans and Native Americans. This is another compelling, if ironic, reason for a park at Salt River, which also contains the remains of an Indian ballcourt and European fort, and has been called "the most important historic site on the Virgin Islands." There are other compelling reasons. Salt River is a National Natural Landmark and a National Historic Landmark. It is the site of the Nature Conservancy's Triton Bay Sanctuary, and of a major project of the National Underwater Research Program.

Salt River has so many compelling reasons for protection that it's surprising there isn't a park there already. In 1958, the Virgin Islands legislature authorized purchase of 50 acres, but no funds were appropriated until 1961, when they bought the five-acre Columbus landing site. Ensuing years saw development of a twenty-boat marina and restaurant, unsuccessful development of a large hotel (the gray shell of which squats on the estuary like something left from plantation days), dredging and filling of the salt pond, and building of many homes on surrounding slopes. The Virgin Islands Coastal Zone Management Act designated Salt River an Area of Particular Concern, a Significant Natural Area, and an Area of Protection and Restoration, but this didn't stop the Coastal Zone Management Committee from issuing permits for a 288-room hotel, 300 condominium units, and a 125-slip marina there. In 1987, the Virgin Islands Conservation Society and other environmental groups went to court to stop this development, called the Virgin Grand complex. The case is still in court.

Since 1987, the Park Service has been studying the feasibility of a Salt River Park in response to a dialogue with the Virgin Islands government. It has developed three alternatives, ranging from a 20-acre national historic landmark at the landing site, to a "Comprehensive Salt River Unit" that would encompass "the entire Salt River Bay shoreline, floodplains, and adjacent landscape to make it an ecologically viable unit." Virgin Island Congressman Ron De Lugo supports nomination of Salt River as a World Heritage Site, which would place it in a class with the Great Barrier Reef as having "universal value to mankind." The National Park Service Associate Director for Cultural Resources, Jerry Rodgers, expressed approval of the idea at hearings in February 1989, but added: "If we cannot arrive at an accommodation with the Virgin Islands government that causes the local community to be as concerned about it as we are, then we don't have a viable situation. . . . We need a guarantee that the property will be preserved, or it will not be available for World Heritage classification."

It's a property worth preserving, as I saw during my brief auto tour. With big, open headlands sloping sharply to wetlands and gallery forest, Salt River has a grandeur and opulence that some believe dwarfs St. John's paradise coves. It's true that deforestation, houses, roads, and landfill dim that grandeur somewhat, but it could be restored, although not cheaply. Phyllis Slayden told me that a large chunk of the area could have been bought for $300,000 in the late sixties—what a single lot in a new development would cost now. Robert Greer said his present budget would allow him to "put up a gate at a Salt River National Park, and drive by once in awhile to see if it was still there." . . .

Whatever the islanders decide to do or not do about the extraordinary biodiversity they've inherited, it will be felt on the mainland as well. On my last day at El Yunque, I climbed Los Picachos, misty rocks among the central peaks. Puerto Rican tanagers and bullfinches again surrounded me as dusk fell. I glimpsed a flash of black and white in the bamboo—an elfin woods warbler? A small, calico-colored bird darted about a clearing, and I eagerly looked it up, anticipating yet another endemic species. It was a female American redstart, presumably taking a break from her spring journey to nest in Michigan or Massachusetts—one of the millions of mainland songbirds that use the Caribbean for wintering or migration. No Island is an island.

48

The Coral Reef at Akumal

JOHN A. MURRAY
(circa 1991)

Many years ago I visited Akumal, then a remote and little-known fishing village on Mexico's Caribbean coast about seventy miles south of Cancun City. Today Akumal has four luxury hotels, providing everything from tennis courts to Cable TV, and is one of the more popular resorts in the state of Quintana Roo. In this selection, gleaned from my old journals and published here for the first time, I describe how it was before "The Discovery."

The first day. I awaken early, just as the last red rays of dawn crackle from the throat of the village rooster. Behind the hut, an expansive coconut plantation extends far back into the coastal jungle. The younger palms are for the most part erect, a plaza of colonnades like the Mayan Court of a Thousand Columns at Chichen-Itza. Some of the older trees, bent by the autumn furies, grow almost parallel to the ground. Not one trunk, however, touches the sand, and so, despite being forced to bow before the storm, they have not lost their dignity. Atop each one is a crown of green fronds that bends gracefully to accommodate the slightest breeze. The ripening nuts fall steadily day and night, an incessant but irregular thumping, the perfect rhythm for the antiphonal sounds of the winter birds: resident parrots and toucans, migratory warblers and vireos, itinerant gulls and terns. Before me, a translucent green lagoon glistens like a fire. Out further, a thin crooked line of coral thunders even in the calm of early morning. In the center of the reef an intriguing water geyser erupts with each crashing wave. Beyond that, the washed blue darkness of the Caribbean—Wallace Steven's "ever-hooded, tragic-gestured sea"— forever beckons to all that is restless in the human spirit. At the furthest distance, balanced perfectly on the horizon, a mountainous island of storm clouds grows even as I watch it, with plunging black canyons and cool white peaks trailing banners in the high winds.

There are sharks and barracudas in these waters. Yesterday evening, just as I arrived, a local fisherman shot and killed an eight-foot Scalloped Hammerhead (*Sphyrna lewini*) in the lagoon. The fisherman—a short muscular man with a broad face and thick black hair—paddled alongside the dorsal fin, knelt down in the wooden canoe, and fired a burst of lead pellets into the brain. The leviathan erupted from the surface of the lagoon, rose up on its smooth lovely tail thrashing in a luminous shroud of sea spray, and then plunged back heavily on its side. A red nebula of blood spiraled outward as the animal convulsed in the clear green water, the pale underbelly facing the sky. Barracuda began to flash back and forth in the water as another, bigger boat with several older men was launched. Once the behometh was hauled to shore, the flattened head extensions and scarred pectoral fins still fighting with the strange new freedom of death, the children of the village attacked the body with fishing knives, not wantonly, but with a precocious knowledge of where to find the best steaks. The span of the hammers—all that was left by nightfall—measured just under thirty inches.

The sand fleas and mosquitoes congregate around me in the still air of early morning. I pick up the snorkeling gear and walk bare-foot down the beach into the warm shallows. Small pompano dart here and there, brushing against my legs. I put on the flippers, mask, and snorkel and dive in. The scene is somewhat surreal, for everything outside the face plate is magnified about one-quarter larger than true size. Also, underwater the primary colors are gradually shifted, as depth increases, toward the blue end of the spectrum. I swim out several dozen yards—long stretching strokes that loosen a body stiff from sleep—and surface to get my bearings. The rolling combers of the open sea—the surf is running high before the storm—thunder resonately against the coral heads of the outer reef. All life is drawn to that sound, which is amplified underwater like a mother's heartbeat in the womb. Of greatest interest to me is the off-shore blow-hole, and I chart a route over the open water and through the reef. The submarine city of hard and soft corals, herbivores and carnivores, specialists and mutualists is still a long way off, though. Getting there will take some time. I let my arms hang loose and kick slowly, not wishing to miss a thing.

This is the lagoon, the tranquil lake of saltwater that forms between the edge of the dry land and the barrier reef. The water is slightly turbid in the distance—the storm has roiled up the bottom sand—but still possesses near optical clarity. I glide alternately over patches of open sand and lush beds of Manatee and Turtle grass. Both of these sea grasses possess flowers that scatter pollen and seeds in the tides much as terrestrial grasses fertilize and propogate via the winds. Unfortunately, both the manatees and the sea turtles—once ubiquitous—are increasingly rare around Akumal and elsewhere in the Caribbean. On virtually every patch of sand there are a dozen or so Long-Spined Black Urchins (*Diadema antillarum*). These heavily-armored echinoderms (spiny-skinned animals) feed on detritus, algae, and turtle grass at night and gather in crevices and aggregates during the day. Interestingly, they often form fairly symmetric equilateral triangles in these group formations. Finding one large urchin with spines as long as sewing needles, I swim down so that my face mask is only a few inches from its defensive array. Even without an organ of sight, the urchin instantly responds by tightening a cluster of barbed poisonous spines in my direction. Some specialized fish, such as the Queen Triggerfish (*Balistes vetula*), have discovered how to successfully prey upon spiny sea urchins, turning them over carefully in much the same manner that mountain lions kill porcupines.

Nearly as prevalent as the urchins are the Queen Conchs (*Strombus gigas*), whose grey humped shells rise like the buried helmets of conquistadors from the bottom sand of the lagoon. This edible mollusc with the brightly enameled pink lip has all but disappeared from many parts of the Caribbean, but, because of the lack of souvenir-collecting, is still fairly common in the waters off Mexico and Belize. About fifty yards out—the water is now as deep as the lanes of a lap pool—I find a Spotted Eagle Ray (*Aetobatus narinari*) hidden in the sand, its presence betrayed by the two alert eyes protruding from the sand. I hover over this beautiful cartilaginous fish in captive fascination. The dorsal surface of the ray's widely flattened body is as green as a philodendron leaf, with small cream spots scattered here and there as camouflage. This ray would be a terrifying predator to a flounder, a crab, or a small lobster—the span of the wings is about four feet. Even a man must respect the fish, for its huge stinging tail can produce an incapacitating wound. The most disarming aspect of the Spotted Eagle Ray, however, are its eyes—as attentive but impassive as the inscrutable eyes on the jade Mayan death masks. I swim on.

Soon after this I encounter the first coral—a chandelier-sized chunk of dead Mountainous Star Coral that was blasted off the reef and hurtled here by a hurricane at some time in the recent past. Looking ahead, I can see that assorted pieces of storm-broken coral form a sizeable rubble yard on this side of the reef. Some new living coral—primarily Fire Coral and Flower Coral—have colonized the debris field, and the fish are plentiful—thickly-packed schools of Silver Damselfish and Blue Chromis and the more solitary, coral-eating Stoplight Parrotfish. Most fish in and around coral reefs have suprisingly small habitats and, like people living in large urban areas, spend their life-times in local neighborhoods they know intimately well. Many of these fish conceivably never leave this circumscribed precinct of the lagoon. Twenty yards further on, I find a purple anemone growing on a small boulder coral about the size of a child's school box. The anemone, which looks like an exotic flower from another planet with far less gravity than earth, moves its delicate deadly tentacles at the slightest current, reaching with a hundred paralyzing arms for passing fish. In some cases, certain fish develop an immunity to the sting of the anemone and can actually live within the writhing mass of Hydra-like arms. Just below the anemone a brown reticulated starfish is trying to pry a bi-valve mollusc from a crevice with two of its powerful five arms. Fortunately, the Caribbean does not have the Crown-of-Thorns Starfish (*Acanthaster planci*). As the name suggests, this starfish—indigenous to the Great Barrier Reef of Australia—has a formidable protective shield of sharp spines. Because its primary predator—a mollusc known as the Great Triton (*Charonia tritonia*)— has been virtually extirpated through excessive souvenir-collecting, the Crown-Of-Thorns Starfish, which feeds voraciously upon coral, has devastated vast portions of the one-million year old Great Barrier Reef. This catastrophic starfish plague illustrates the fragility of complex tropical systems—whether coral reefs or rain forests—and the unpredictable results of removing even one species from a highly specialized community. Even more disturbing for the Caribbean—should a similar situation ever arise—is the fact that the Indo-Pacific coral reef systems are much older and more diverse—with up to 700 coral species—whereas the more vulnerable Caribbean coral reefs are physically smaller and based on only around 40 coral species.

The floor of the lagoon drops suddenly away. Here is where the water deepens to three or four fathoms in a broad moat-like trench before the reef. To my right and well within striking range four Great Barracudas (*Sphyraena barracuda*) hover like attack submarines on the edge of the blue darkness, waiting for a school of fish or a single fish to foolishly attempt a daylight crossing from the open meadows of the lagoon to the safe forests of the coral reef. With a stab of adrenalin, I realize that I am wearing my old Marine Corps dogtag chain, on which hangs (ironically) a St. Francis medallion. Glittering metal objects attract barracudas. It is too late to turn back, and so I just look straight ahead and proceed on my route, trying to ignore the four hungry mouths full of hideous teeth. They show little interest in me, thankfully, and are soon far behind. About half-way across the trench, I pass over the wreck of the *Mantanceros,* a Spanish galleon that sank on the Akumal reef in 1741. All that remains of the vessel are its cannons, pitched this way and that on the floor of the lagoon and thickly encrusted with Deadman's Fingers and Candelabrum, both soft corals. I recall Ariel's haunting song in Shakespeare's *The Tempest*:

> Full fathom five thy father lies;
> Of his bones are coral made;
> Those are pearls that are his eyes;
> Nothing of him doth fade
> But doth suffer a sea-change
> Into something rich and strange.
> Sea nymphs hourly ring his knell: Ding-dong.
> Hark! Now I hear them:
> Ding-dong bell.

Feeling adventuresome, I take in a lungful of air and dive down, kicking as hard as I can. Despite all efforts, I can not reach the cannons. Perhaps the trench is deeper than I thought. After two failed attempts, I surface and resume my course for the reef. The cannons, tempting as they are, will have to wait for another day.

The bottom pitches up gradually and in a short time I am face to face with the living reef. I swim through the portals, past the towering spires of cathedral coral and the gently waving purple sea fans, and pause for a moment, in wonder. There are few places in the world where the human senses are so overwhelmed by the creative exuberance of nature as in a coral reef. Channels open invitingly in every direction. An iridescent green and blue Queen Angelfish (*Holacanthus cilaris*) drifts down one enticing passageway, bordered on either side by mounds of cavernous star coral and smooth brain coral, and, like Dante led by Beatrice into the radiance of Paradise, I follow. After several turns to look back at me, the Angelfish hovers in place and begins to nibble delicately on a toxic Touch-Me-Not Sponge (*Neofibularia nolitangere*). These sponges, which like all sponges help to clean and filter the water, are a favored food of the Queen Angelfish. The fish stops as I near, looks directly at me, and opens its blue lips, as if emitting some strange sweet music to the surge, made more beautiful from its never being heard. Actually, of course, the Angelfish is not singing, but is actively defending its home—Angelfish are very territorial fish. The freshwater angelfish I kept in a twenty-gallon aquarium as a boy fiercely defended the tank from all interlopers—from Yucatan mollies to my index finger—and I soon gave up on trying to find any compatible species. They wished to have the aquarium solely to themselves. I leave the Queen Angelfish to its daily routine, which consists of a minute inspection and patrol of its home waters.

A short distance later—the reef is as complex in its ramifications as a Mycenian labyrinth—I swim from a long narrow canal into a deep, tranquil basin. The reef is full of these quiet galleries, each its own cozy world, soaked in sunlight, busy with a profusion of fish, and bright with dozens of coral species. The colors are extravagant and sometimes outrageous, patterns such as children would create if given ceramic fish and coral and an entire studio of glazes from which to choose. At the bottom of the sandy basin a tiny Star-Eyed Hermit Crab (*Dardanus venosus*) scurries purposefully toward a miniature Tricolor Anemone (*Calliactis tricolor*). Hermit Crabs, which live inside the discarded shells of sea snails, are resourceful scavengers and will eat just about anything, living or dead. Their most distinguishing characteristic are their starlike, sapphire blue eyes. I watch closely as the crab squeezes the pedestal of the anemone with its over-sized claw. Just when I expect the crab to crush the anemone to death something remarkable happens. The anemone releases its grip on the limestone and the crab gently picks the animal up by its trunk and places it on top of the shell. The two then go off together over the sandy floor of the amphitheater. I follow them for several yards and it appears that the marriage is, for the moment, happy. From this arrangement it would seem that the anemone secures a free ride and food leftovers and the crab acquires a formidable set of poisonous tentacles atop its house to discourage the un-welcome attentions of predators like the octopus. This is an impressive feat of intelligence for an animal with less cortex than a poppy seed, but is one of the numerous examples of mutualism on the reef.

The incoming waves, rolling massively before the rain storm, are surging and cascading over the exposed coral now, as I approach the sea, and I must be careful to avoid both the stinging fire corals—which produce slow-healing welts—and the many inconspicuous openings where dangerous animals like Scorpionfish (*Scorpaena plumieri*) and Moray Eels (*Gymnothorax moringa*) retreat during the day. The waves throw both me and the corals—even the thick stands of Staghorn coral—around with ease, and a single miscalculation on my part could have serious consequences. I regret not having a snorkeling partner; swimming alone this far from shore is never advisable, even if it is sometimes unavoidable. While the Akumal coral reef is a paradise to a North American naturalist, it is also a realm in which—like any well-designed utopia—perils necessarily abound. Probably most amazing is the fact that, despite the abundance of animals present during the day, the coral reef is *most* active during the night. It is at night, for example, that the individual corals—each hard polyp is a predatory animal—expose their soft feeding surfaces to the water and absorb the plankton that migrate upward after dark. The plankton bloom, however, is not enough to explain what was for a very long time the central mystery of the coral reef: How is it that so many animals can exist with so little apparent plant life? Modern science has shown that every coral polyp actually contains several microscopic plants within it, and that these zoo-anthellae, as they are called, produce oxygen for the coral and also absorb carbon dioxide through photosynthesis. In turn, the zooanthellae receive a comfortable residence and plentiful waste nutrients. The coral reproduce themselves by dispersing larvae into the water. These ciliated organisms swim around until they locate a suitable surface on which to build their own calcium carbonate colonies. The planktonic larvae can survive in the current flow for up to three weeks. That is why Bermuda—about two weeks drift time on the Gulf Stream north of the Bahamas—has a flourishing assemblage of coral reefs, even though it is at the latitude of North Carolina; and that is why isolated coral "gardens" (not true reefs) can be found as far south as Brazil, where the water finally becomes too cloudy from jungle river siltation for corals to exist.

With some trepidation I swim out past the last coral into the open sea. The full force of the waves is on me now and I am reminded of climbing mountains in the Rockies on days when the wind blew so hard I had to hold on to the heavy talus with all my strength in order to keep from being blown into Kansas. There is the same pure exhilaration here in the raw power of nature. Below, the water sinks rapidly away from light blue through cobalt blue into utter blackness, those lowest regions where luminous fish play with the lanterns about their heads and storm-wrecked ships sink into incomprehensible solitudes. Along the outerside of the reef, I notice that the coral fauna pass through several distinct life zones—each with less diversity than the one above—as the water depth increases, much as mountain vegetation changes relative to altitude. It is here, finally, beyond the outer edge of the reef, where the branching elkhorn coral flourish defiantly in the midst of the ever-pounding breakers, that I warily approach the water geyser I had observed an hour earlier from the shore. The going is difficult, for there are two equally powerful and wholly opposed forces at work. First, the incoming swells discharge a violent amount of energy as they crash against the living rock barrier. Second, the backwash of the receding waves draws everything into the next comber with the irresistible pull of a collapsing universe. I find I must swim up the side of the approaching wave at an angle, then dive headfirst into the trough, and, while submerged, peak down through the turbulent, bubble-filled water toward the source of the geyser. After several exhausting dives, my survey is complete, and this is what it reveals: Over the years the waves have carved out a substantial cavern in the basement rock. In rhythm with the advancing waves, the seawater surges into the cave and then explodes out through a sharp aperture in the roof, shooting up in the air like a static rocket test in the desert. In time the ceiling will collapse, but for now it seems to be holding firmly. It would be a fearsome thing to be sucked into the chamber—to be ripped apart and unceremoniously drowned—and yet, despite the vigorous wave action, there is a stable community of corals, starfish, and anemones living on the inner walls. It was in this sort of secret chamber that Poseidon, the Greek god of the sea, heard the cries of his one-eyed son Cyclops after Cyclops had been blinded by Odysseus:

> O hear me, Poseidon, blue girdler of islands!
> If I am yours, indeed, and you are my father,
> grant that Odysseus, raider of cities, long be

kept from his home. . . . Let him lose all companions and
return under a tattered sail to bitter days at home.

Tired from the long swim, I turn back from the geyser and slip through a
narrow, winding corridor to a pool beyond the breakers where, finding a half-
dead brain coral above the water line, I climb up and rest. I carefully avoid
sitting on the living coral, because coral, like alpine tundra, can be easily
destroyed. Like a human brain, the brain coral has extensive convolutions that
greatly increase surface area and suggest—if only in the cerebral patterns—the
presence of an awareness. Soon I am joined on the exposed coral by a redlip
blenny (*Ophioblennius atlanticus*), a funny-looking fish about the size of a
child's pocket knife. Blennies live in the shallows around coral reefs and
maintain cleaning stations where they remove parasites from larger fish. This
blenny has a blunt, human face with a high forehead and pensive eyes and
reminds me of my 10th grade World Literature teacher Mr. Downey. The
blenny crawls half out of the water on its outstretched red pectoral fins, shifts
its weight impatiently from side to side, and considers me appraisingly. I lean
closer and although the blenny's tiny fierce eyes widen, they do not blink, nor
does the brave lilliputian retreat. No life is possible without such simple acts of
courage. This is the blenny's home, and it wants me gone. Looking over my
shoulder, I see a solid wall of black clouds advancing toward the mainland. I
shake the water from my ears just in time to hear the thunder crack as a skeletal
finger of lightning touches the sea.

The rains come soon after I reach *terra firma*—the driving relentless
downpour of the tropics—and I retire to my hut to spend the day with a
tattered copy of Virgil's *Aeneid*, a schoolteacher's gift from long ago. Reading
once again of Aeneas' travels in Book III—he, too, encounters the Cyclops and
rescues a seaman accidentally left behind by Odysseus—I am struck by the
many geographic similarities between the Mediterranean and the Caribbean:
the Darien Gap and the Barbary Coast, the Orinoco and the Nile, the lesser
Antilles and the Cyclades and Sporades, Puerto Rico and Crete, Hispaniola
and Greece, Jamaica and Sicily, Florida and Italy. Perhaps one day a Caribbean poet will write a literary epic of the Americas, with the Mayan *chacs* and
the Arawakan forest spirits playing the supernatural role of the Graeco-Roman
gods in the poems of antiquity. As beautiful and inspiring as the Mediterranean is, however, it does not have the coral reefs of the Caribbean. Coral reefs
grow only in certain discrete locations—the South Pacific, Australia, the
Indian Ocean, the Red Sea, the Caribbean—where the conditions are wholly
favorable to this unique variety of life. Great poetry—Augustan Rome,
Elizabethan England, T'ang China—requires just as fertile a cultural environment in order to flourish.

Toward evening the rains blow off and after the sun goes down—the
sunsets near the equator are as brief as old Lennon-McCartney songs—the
stars appear with a brilliance I am accustomed to seeing only in the high valleys
during the cross-country skiing season. The Milky Way hangs above the wild

Caribbean coast like a giant luminous coral reef, its ancient bulk glowing with a dozen grottoes and dark gulfs. The galaxy seems no further from my fingertips than the silhouettes of the dripping palm leaves overhead. To some extent it is, for both the palm and I are *in* the Milky Way, albeit in the vast curve of one of its spiral arms. At this latitude—about 20° north of the equator—the Southern Cross is visible, four bright stars in the middle of the Milky Way, as well as Alpha Centauri, the closest star to our solar system. The moon is not out tonight, but Mars is visible, rising through Orion's chest, a steady beacon of reflected red light that beckons warmly against the scintillating cold radiance of deep space. In a way, the living earth is like an enormous coral polyp which has been four billion years in the maturing. Only now, with the rise of the human species, has the mother world begun to disperse her progeny, like planktonic larvae, across the cosmos. Although posterity may travel widely—from the Sea of Tranquility to the rugged uplands of Mars, and beyond—nowhere in this universe will they find a beauty to surpass the coral reefs of home.

Bibliography

Adams, Alexander. *Eternal Quest: The Story of the Great Naturalists*. New York: Putnam, 1969.

Adams, Frederick Upham. *Conquest of the Tropics: The Story of the Creative Enterprises Conducted by the United Fruit Company*. New York: Doubleday, Page and Company, 1914.

Acosta, Joseph. "Historia Natural Y Moral De Las Indies (1588)," *Purchas His Pilgrimes* (vol. XV), by Samuel Purchas. London: Hakluyt, 1906.

d'Anghiera, Pietro Martire. *The Decades of the New Worlde or West India*. Translated by Richard Eden. London, 1555.

Audubon, John James. *Ornithological Biography, or an Account of the Habits of the Birds of the United States of America*. 5 volumes. Philadelphia: J. Dobson, 1831 (vol. 1); Boston: Hilliard, Gray & Co., 1835 (vol. 2); Edinburgh: A. & C. Black, 1835–1838 (vols. 3–5).

Audubon, Maria R. *Audubon and His Journals*. 2 vols. New York: Scribner's 1897; Dover, 1960, 1986.

Bartram, William. *Travels Through North and South Carolina, Georgia, East and West Florida, The Cherokee Country, The Extensive Territories of the Muscogulges, or Creek Confederacy, and the Country of the Choctaws*. Philadelphia: James & Johnson, 1791; New York: Macy-Masius, 1928; New York: Dover Publications, 1955.

Beebe, William. *The Book of Naturalists: An Anthology of the Best Natural History*. New York: Knopf, 1944; Princeton: Princeton University Press, 1971.

Beebe, William. *Edge of the Jungle*. New York: Holt, 1921; Duell, Sloan and Pearce, 1950.

Beebe, William. *High Jungle*. New York: Duell, Sloan and Pearce, 1949.

Beebe, William. *Jungle Days*. New York: Putnam's, 1925.

Beebe, William. *Jungle Peace*. New York: Holt, 1918.

Bent, Arthur Cleveland. *Life Histories of North American Gulls and Terns*. Washington, D.C.: U.S. Government, 1921 (Smithsonian Institution Bulletin 113); New York: Dover, 1963.

Bergon, Frank, ed. *The Wilderness Reader*. New York: New American Library, 1980.

Bermuda Assembly, An Act of. From Archie Carr. *So Excellente a Fishe: A Natural History of Sea Turtles*. New York: Charles Scribner's Sons, 1967.

Brathwaite, Edward Kamau. *Mother Poem*. New York: Oxford University Press, 1977.

Brooks, Paul. *Roadless Area*. New York: Knopf, 1964.

Brooks, Paul. *The House of Life: Rachel Carson at Work*. Boston: Houghton Mifflin, 1972.

Brooks, Paul. *The Pursuit of Wilderness*. Boston: Houghton Mifflin, 1971.

Brooks, Paul. *Speaking for Nature*. Boston: Houghton Mifflin, 1980; San Francisco: Sierra Club, 1983.

Burnett, Paula, ed. *The Penguin Book of Caribbean Verse in English*. New York: Penguin, 1986.

Caras, Roger. *The Endless Migrations*. New York: E. P. Dutton, 1985.

Caras, Roger. *Animals in Their Places: Tales from the Natural World*. San Francisco: Sierra Club, 1987.

Carr, Archie. *So Excellente a Fishe: A Natural History of Sea Turtles*. New York: Charles Scribner's Sons, 1967.

Carson, Rachel. *The Edge of the Sea*. Boston: Houghton Mifflin, 1955.

Carson, Rachel. *The Sea Around Us*. New York: Oxford University Press, 1950; Simon & Schuster, 1958; rev. ed., Oxford University Press, 1961.

Carson, Rachel. *Under the Sea-Wind: A Naturalist's Picture of Ocean Life*. New York: Oxford University Press, 1941, 1962.

Carson, Rachel. *Silent Spring*. Boston: Houghton Mifflin, 1962, 1988; New York: Fawcett Crest, 1964; Ballantine, 1982.

Casas, Bartholomew de la. "A brief Narration of the destruction of the Indies by the Spaniards (1542), *"Purchas His Pilgrimes* (vol. XVIII), by Samuel Purchas. Glasgow: Maclehose, 1906.

Catesby, Mark. *The Natural History of Carolina, Florida and the Bahama Islands*. 2 vols. London, 1731–1743.

Cesaire, Aime. *The Collected Poetry*. Berkeley: University of California Press, 1983.

Clough, Wilson O. *The Necessary Earth: Nature and Solitude in American Literature*. Austin: University of Texas Press, 1964.

Columbus, Christopher. *Selected Letters of Columbus,* by R. H. Major London: Hakluyt Society, 1870.

Cousteau, Jacques-Yves. *The Silent World*. New York: Dutton, 1950.

Cox, Edward Godfrey, ed. *A Reference Guide to the Literature of Travel*. Seattle: University of Washington Press, 1938.

Crassweller, Robert D. *The Caribbean Community*. New York: Praeger, 1972.

Crosby, Alfred W. *Ecological Imperialism: The Biological Expansion of Europe, 900–1900*. Cambridge: Cambridge University Press, 1986.

Cudhoe, Selwyn R. *V. S. Naipaul: A Materialist Reading*. Amherst: The University of Massachusetts Press, 1988.

Cutright, Paul Russell. *The Great Naturalists Explore South America*. New York: Macmillan, 1940.

Dampier, William. *Voyage Round the World*. London, 1697.

Dance, Daryl C. *Folklore from Contemporary Jamaicans*. Knoxville: The University of Tennessee Press, 1985.

Darwin, Charles. *The Structure and Distribution of Coral Reefs*. London, 1842.

Diaz, Bernal. *The Conquest of New Spain*. London: Hakluyt, 1908.

Defoe, Daniel. *Robinson Crusoe*. London, 1719.

Douglas, Marjory Stoneman. *The Everglades*. St. Simon's Island: Mockingbird, 1947.

Douglas, William O. *My Wilderness: East to Katahdin*. Garden City, N.Y.: Doubleday, 1961.

Drake, Francis. "A summarie and true discourse of sir Francis Drakes West Indian

Voyage," *Hakluyt's Voyages* (vol. x), Richard Hakluyt. Glasgow: Maclehose, 1904.

Eiseley, Loren. *Darwin's Century: Evolution and the Men Who Discovered It.* Garden City, N.Y.: Doubleday, 1958, 1961.

Elder, John and Robert Finch. *The Norton Book of Nature Writing.* New York: Norton, 1990.

Endean, R. and O. A. Jones. *Biology and Geology of Coral Reefs* (vols. one and two). New York: Academic Press, 1973.

Gill, Thomas. *Tropical Forests of the Caribbean.* Baltimore: Read-Taylor, 1931.

Glacken, Clarence J. *Traces on the Rhodian Shore: Nature and Culture in Western Thought from Ancient Times to the End of the Eighteenth Century.* Berkeley: University of California Press, 1967.

Gosse, Philip. *A Naturalist's Sojourn in Jamaica.* London, 1851.

Graham, Frank, Jr. *Since Silent Spring.* Boston: Houghton Mifflin, 1970; New York: Fawcett Crest, 1970.

Gurney, Joseph John. *A Winter in the West Indies.* London: John Murray, 1840.

Hakluyt, Richard. *The Principal Navigations, Voyages, Traffiques, and Discoveries of the English Nation.* 12 vols.: Glasgow: Maclehose, 1903–1905.

Halpern, Daniel. *On Nature: Nature, Landscape, and Natural History.* San Francisco: North Point Press, 1987.

Hannaway, Patti. *Winslow Homer in the Tropics.* Richmond: Westover, 1980.

Harcourt, Robert. *A Relation of a Voyage to Guiana.* London: Hakluyt, 1926.

Harvey, Thomas and Joseph Sturge. *The West Indies in 1837.* London, 1838.

Hawkins, John. "The second voyage made by Sir John Hawkins knight." *The Principal Navigations* (vol. x), by Richard Hakluyt. Glasgow: Maclehose, 1904.

Head, Suzanne and Robert Heinzman. *Lessons of the Rainforest.* San Francisco: Sierra Club, 1990.

Hearn, Lafcadio. *Two Years in the French West Indies.* New York: Harper and Brothers, 1890.

Hemingway, Ernest. "Letter to Maxwell Perkins." *Ernest Hemingway: Selected Letters 1917–1961,* by Carlos Baker. New York: Charles Scribner's Sons, 1981.

Hemingway, Ernest. *To Have and To Have Not.* New York: Charles Scribner's Sons, 1937.

Hemingway, Ernest. *The Old Man and the Sea.* New York: Charles Scribner's Sons, 1952.

Hemingway, Ernest. *Islands in the Stream.* New York: Charles Scribner's Sons, 1970.

Horowitz, Mike. *Peoples and Cultures of the Caribbean.* New York: Natural History Press, 1971.

Hughes, Griffith. *The Natural History of Barbados in Ten Books.* London, 1750.

Humboldt, Alexander von. *The Island of Cuba.* New York, 1856.

Huth, Hans. *Nature and the American: Three Centuries of Changing Attitudes.* Berkeley: University of California Press, 1957.

Kennan, George. *The Tragedy of Pelée.* New York: The Outlook Company, 1902.

Kincaid, Jamaica. *A Small Place.* New York: Farrar Straus Giroux, 1988.

Kolodny, Annette. *The Land Before Her: Fantasy and Experience of the American Frontiers, 1630–1860.* Chapel Hill: University of North Carolina Press, 1975.

Krutch, Joseph Wood. *Great American Nature Writing.* New York: William Sloane, 1950.

Labat, Pere. *Nouveau Voyage aux Iles de l'Amerique.* Paris, 1722.

Laudonniere, René, "The voiage of captaine Rene Laudonniere to Florida in 1564."

The Principal Navigatigations (vol. ix), by Richard Hakluyt. Glasgow: Maclehose, 1904.

Ledru, Andre Pierre, *Voyage aux Iles*. Paris, 1810.

Levine, George, editor. *One Culture: Essays in Science and Literature*. Madison: University of Wisconsin Press, 1987.

Lewis, Gordon K. *Main Currents in Caribbean Thought: The Historical Evolution of Caribbean Society in its Ideological Aspects, 1492–1900*. Baltimore: The Johns Hopkins University Press, 1983.

Ligon, Richard. *A True and Exact History of the Island of Barbados*. London, 1657.

Long, Edward. *The History of Jamaica*. London, 1774.

Lopez, Barry Holstun. *Crossing Open Ground*. New York: Charles Scribner's Sons, 1988.

Marquez, Gabriel Garcia. *The Story of a Shipwrecked Sailor*. New York: Knopf, 1986.

Marsh, George Perkins. *Man and Nature*. New York: Scribner's, 1864; Cambridge: Harvard University Press, 1965.

Matthiessen, Peter. *Wildlife in America*. New York: Viking, 1959. Rev. and updated ed., New York: Viking, 1987.

Matthiessen, Peter. *Far Tortuga*. New York: Random House, 1975.

Mitchell, Lee Clark. *Witnesses to a Vanishing America: The Nineteenth-Century Response*. Princeton: Princeton University Press, 1981.

Morison, Samuel Eliot. *The European Discovery of America: The Southern Voyages, A.D. 1492–1616*. New York: Oxford University Press, 1972.

Morison, Samuel Eliot, ed. and trans. *Journals and Other Documents on the Life and Voyages of Christopher Columbus*. New York: Heritage Press, 1963.

Murray, John. *Report on the Scientific Results of the Voyage of H.M.S. Challenger, 1873–1876*. 50 vols. Edinburgh, 1880–1895.

Murray, John. *A Republic of Rivers: Three Centuries of Nature Writing from Alaska and the Yukon*. New York: Oxford University Press, 1990.

Naipaul, V. S. *The Loss of Eldorado*. New York: Knopf, 1970.

Naipaul, V. S. *The Middle Passage*. London: Andre Deutsch, 1962.

Naipaul, V. S. "Introduction." *East Indians in the Caribbean: Colonialism and the Struggle for Identity*. New York: Kraus International Publishers, 1982.

Naipaul, V. S. "An Island Betrayed." *Harper's* 268 (March 1984): 62–72.

Naipaul, V. S. "V.S. Naipaul: 'It is Out of this Violence I've Always Written.'" *New York Review of Books,* September 16, 1984, pp. 45–46.

Nash, Roderick. *Wilderness and the American Mind*. New Haven: Yale University Press, 1967; rev. ed., 1973; 3rd ed., 1982.

Nash, Roderick. *The Rights of Nature: A History of Environmental Ethics*. Madison: University of Wisconsin Press, 1989.

Norwood, Richard. "Relations of Summer Ilands," *Purchas His Pilgrimes* (vol. xix), by Samuel Purchas. London: Hakluyt, 1906.

Oviedo, Gonzalo de. "General and Natural History of the Indies." *Purchas His Pilgrimes* (vol. xv), by Samuel Purchas. Glasgow: Maclehose, 1906.

Parks, George. *Richard Hakluyt and the English Voyages*. New York: Hakluyt, 1928.

Parsons, Elsie Clews. *Folk-Tales of Andros Island, Bahamas*. New York: American Folklore Society, 1918.

Parsons, Elsie Crews. *Folklore of the Antilles, French and English*. New York: American Folklore Society, 1943.

Patterson, B. D. and L. R. Heaney, eds. *Island Biogeography of Mammals*. New York: Academic Press, 1986.

Peattie, Donald Culross. *Green Laurels: The Lives and Achievements of the Great Naturalists*. New York: Simon & Schuster, 1936.

Peattie, Donald Culross. *Singing in the Wilderness: A Salute to John James Audubon*. New York: Putnam's, 1935.

Pinkard, George. *Notes on the West Indies Written During the Expedition Under the Command of the Late General Sir Ralph Abercromby, Including Observations on the Island of Barbadoes, and the Settlements Captured by the British Troops, upon the Coast of Guiana*. 3 vols. London: Longman, Hurst, Rees, and Orme, 1806.

Porter, Charlotte M. *The Eagle's Nest: Natural History and American Ideas, 1812–1842*. Tuscaloosa: University of Alabama Press, 1986.

Prescott, William H. *The Conquest of Mexico*. New York, 1843.

Prescott, William H. *The Conquest of Peru*. New York, 1843.

Purchas, Samuel. *Hakluytus Posthumus or Purchas His Pilgrimes*. 4 vols. London, 1625. Reprinted in 20 vols., Glasgow: 1905–1907.

Raleigh, Walter. "The Discoverie of the large, rich, and beautiful Empire of Guiana." *The Principal Navigations* (vol. x), by Richard Hakluyt. Glasgow: Maclehose, 1904.

Rice, Prudence M. and Arlen F. Chase, eds. *The Lowland Maya Postclassic*. Austin: The University of Texas Press, 1985.

Roberts, W. Adolphe. *The Caribbean*. New York: 1944; Reprinted ed. by Negro Universities Press, 1969.

Rousseau, Jean Jacques. *A Discourse on Inequality*. Geneva, Switzerland, 1755.

Rushdie, Salman. *The Jaguar Smile: A Nicaraguan Journey*. New York: Penguin, 1987.

Sabloff, Jeremy A. and David A. Freidel. *Cozumel: Late Maya Settlement Patterns*. New York: Academic Press, 1984.

Schaw, Janet. *Journal of a Lady of Quality, 1774–1776*. Reprinted ed. by New Haven: Yale University Press, 1936.

Sherzer, Joel. *Kuna Ways of Speaking: An Ethnographic Perspective*. Austin: The University of Texas Press, 1983.

Sloane, Hans. *A Voyage to the Islands Madera, Barbados, Nieves, S. Christophers, and Jamaica*. 2 vols. London, 1707, 1725.

Smallwood, William, and Mabel Smallwood. *Natural History and the American Mind*. New York: Columbia University Press, 1941.

Smith, William. *A Natural History of Nevis*. Cambridge, 1745.

Stephens, John L. *Incidents of Travel in Yucatan*. 2 vols. New York: Harper & Brothers, 1843.

Stowe, Harriet Beecher. *Palmetto-Leaves*. Boston: James R. Osgood and Company, 1873.

Strachey, William. "A true reportorie of the wrack, and redemption of Sir Thomas Gates, Knight; upon, and from the Ilands of the Bermudas: his coming to Virginia, and the estate of that Colonie then, and after, under the Govern-Ment of the Lord La Warre, July 15. 1610." *Purchas His Pilgrimes* (vol. xix), by Samuel Purchas. Glasgow: Maclehose, 1906.

Taylor, E. G. R. *Late Tudor and Early Stuart Geography 1583–1650*. London: Hakluyt, 1934.

Tedlock, Dennis, ed. *Popol Vuh: The Definitive Edition of the Mayan Book of the Dawn of Life and the Glories of Gods and Kings*. New York: Simon & Schuster, 1985.

Terres, John K., ed. *Discovery: Great Moments in the Lives of Outstanding Naturalists*. Philadelphia: Lippincott, 1961.

Wafer, Lionel. *A New Voyage and Description of the Isthmus of America*. London, 1699.

Walcott, Derek. *Sea Grapes*. New York: Farrar Straus and Giroux, 1976.

Wallace, David Rains. *The Untamed Garden and Other Personal Essays*. Columbus: Ohio State University Press, 1985.

Wallace, David Rains. *Bulow Hammock*. San Francisco: Sierra Club, 1989.

Wallace, David Rains. *Life in the Balance*. New York: Audubon, 1987.

Williams, Eric. *From Columbus to Castro: The History of the Caribbean 1492–1969*. London: Andre Deutsch, 1970.

Wilson, Edward O. *Biophilia*. Cambridge: Harvard University Press, 1984.

Wilson, Edward O. *Sociobiology: The New Synthesis*. Cambridge: Harvard University Press, 1975.

Wilson, Edward O. *On Human Nature*. Cambridge: Harvard University Press, 1979.

Wilson, Edward O. and Bert Holldobler. *The Ants*. Cambridge: Harvard University Press, 1990.

Wood, Peter. *The Caribbean*. New York: Time-Life, 1975.

Wyckoff, Jerome, *Rocks, Time and Landforms*. New York: Harper and Row, 1966.

Zans, V. A., L. J. Chubb, H. R. Versey, J. B Williams, E. Robinson and D. L. Cooke. *Synopsis of the Geology of Jamaica, 1962*. Bulletin No. 4, Geological Survey Department, Jamaica.

Index